303/6409.

30/3/12.

Viva La Revolution!

The Story of People Power in 30 Revolutions

Derry Nairn

For Richard and Wendy

First published 2012 by
Elliott and Thompson Limited
27 John Street, London WC1N 2BX
www.eandtbooks.com

ISBN: 978-1-907642-40-1

Text © Derry Nairn 2012

The Author has asserted his right under the Copyright, Designs and Patents
Act, 1988, to be identified as Author of this Work.

9 8 7 6 5 4 3 2 1

A CIP catalogue record for this book is available from the British Library.

Printed and bound by CPI Group (UK) Ltd, Coydon, CR0 4YY

Typeset by Marie Doherty

Contents

Introduction
History Repeating?

A Year of People Power

In their May/June 2011 issue, the Vancouver-based anti-corporate magazine *Adbusters* made 'a sincere call for an American Revolution against the decadent, vile plutocrats driving our nation into the ground...'.[1] Most readers, presumably, scoffed. At the time, popular protest showed no signs of spreading from the squares of North Africa to the plazas of Manhattan. Within six months, however, the writers of the *Adbusters* manifesto could claim at least partial responsibility for kick-starting the Occupy movement – already one of the more remarkable grassroots political reform efforts of recent American history.

The Occupy movement is still just that; a movement. But it is also the latest in a series of extraordinary events in 2011 – a year of popular uprising around the world. It has followed on from the downfall, earlier in the year, of the Ben Ali and Mubarak regimes by popular will; and the Gaddafi dictatorship by force of arms. Real revolutionary fever swept Tunisia, Egypt and Libya; three Arab states to reject the rule of despots during 2011. At times, Bahrain, Syria and Yemen have seemed set to follow them. Events in Azerbaijan, Iran, Iraq, Israel, Bahrain, Kuwait and Morocco, to name but a handful, suggest the Middle Eastern rim has not been left unaffected by clamour for change.

The loudly hailed 'Arab Spring' represents an epochal shift. For generations, dictators had governed in the Middle East. So long had even a hint of democracy been absent from the region, its societies seemed almost inherently unsuited to popular government. Revolution surprised analysts of the region as much as its inhabitants. In the wake of the Arab Spring, this book examines the revolutionary traditions and forms that have gone before it. It tells the story, through 30 examples from around the globe, of people power in action over the centuries.

Waves of Change

Every modern nation state boasts some event which its citizens commemorate together. For many, that 'founding myth' is a popular uprising; something as simple as the story behind a flag design or a national hero who fought against the odds to secure their country's liberty. So many currents of contemporary life meet at the subject of people power – politics, culture, geography, religion, technology – that a glance at popular revolution through world history also yields a rich portrait of the world as it stands today.

Across the world, through history, revolutions have shown a tendency to occur in groups. Collections of major revolutions occurred across South America in 1817–21 and across Europe in 1847–49. The late 1950s and 1960s bore witness to near continuous anti-colonial revolutions, often in the form of bloody and exhausting civil wars. The Eastern Bloc came down in 1989, followed by the downfall of the Soviet Union in 1991. The 'Colour Revolutions' decorated the ex-Soviet rim in the first decade of the 21st century. During 2011, true to form, revolution did not confine itself to national borders. The sustained appetite for change displayed by those marching in Tunis and Cairo had direct influence over protests elsewhere. In the shadow of the Eurozone debt crisis, Spain and Greece saw sustained unrest, its forms and symbols derived in part from the images of Tahrir Square. Beyond the Arab world, outside the EU, major protests or demonstrations seemed to be announced in some new location every day. In August, Britain witnessed its worst urban rioting in 30 years. Chile's students clashed repeatedly with police and the army.

Tunisia, Egypt and Libya – where the Arab Spring began – have passed the first litmus test of a revolution: tyrannies felled. Whether or not the dozens of other major popular uprisings which broke out across the globe that year do the same is another matter. Real revolution, the epoch-altering type, takes years to pan out. Strong leaders tend to guide revolutions, but those leaders can turn despotic themselves when the battle is won. Elections provide new reasons to diverge. United fronts against a dictator often descend into anarchy. As such, analysing recent political events with accuracy is a thankless task. By comparing some of the experiences of yesterday's rebels, both eulogised and forgotten, however, this effect can be lessened. There may be lessons on offer for the young democrats born of the Arab Spring, as well as budding revolutionaries elsewhere.

Not that the amount of media coverage dedicated to upheaval during 2011 would suggest any shortfall in information. Newspapers and satellite channels lapped up the epic drama in Tahrir Square. The cream of the world's reporters dashed to experience a potentially era-defining moment. Social media updates and streaming video were broadcast live to the world from the protests and assemblies. Twenty-four-hour rolling news channels boast breadth of coverage. Twitter hooks its users on the thrilling immediacy of information. One of the goals of this book is to provide some historical context to the sometimes breathless reporting that resulted.

History Leads the Way

One of the most common themes of media coverage of unrest across the world in 2011 was that of mystification. At first, as at any news of dramatic political upheaval, there was shock. But after came the confused query: what is it we are witnessing? Simply alluding to the remarkable global spread of popular unrest during 2011 goes some way towards answering the question. What the world witnessed – a world more populous, more interconnected than ever – was unprecedented. No one continent was left untouched by political upheaval. A new generation, born after the collapse of the Berlin Wall, was introduced to direct political action. It is wise, however, when analysing events as yet incomplete, to be cautious. The hallmark of most revolutions is failure. Lack of resources, weather patterns, or, more simply, boredom, can stymie an assault on power. But the reassuring news is that this particular question is not a new one. At each juncture in the past when a batch of international revolutions has broken out, most observers are left bewildered.

As well as the fact that, in many cases, events are still progressing, what makes the range of protests in 2011 so unreceptive to analysis is their diversity. Though chains of interaction and inspiration between countries are to be found in some places, there are marked differences too. Youth rioters in Britain, for example, showed little, if any, awareness that their disturbances were part of a larger pattern; either geographically or historically. The rioters elected no leaders and made no demands. Can their brief criminal crusade through British city centres be credibly considered alongside the more structured movements happening at the same time around the world?

This is the sort of query to which history can provide an answer. In 1848, for example, more than a dozen European countries witnessed outbreaks of protest and violent reprisals from authorities. The links between them were many. Radicals travelled from Parisian suburb to German city-state to partake. A common, broadly democratic, proto-nationalist theme emerged. And yet the socialists of the 'Paris Spring' and the industrial workers of Flanders had quite different designs on the world than, from a modern perspective at least, the quite moderate and polite requests of German *burghers* for lightened taxation and the right to assemble. Some marched to win rights. Others looted for short-term gain. Understanding the motivations of rioters in 2011 may be less important than appreciating the fact that a number of young British people, who while a minority nevertheless made themselves loudly heard, came together to shatter public order *en masse*.

The events of 1848 amount to just one of the historical processes whose inclusion here will, hopefully, help interpretation of recent events. That said, there is no reason to expect that the marches, protests and revolutions of 2011 will produce similar results. They represent entirely new processes in their own right. Novel methods of organisation, of communication and of action, have emerged, just as they have done throughout history. Will authorities and despots, too, find imaginative new methods of suppression? Only time can tell.

A Wide Scope, a Long View

The uprisings collected here are designed to offer as wide a scope as possible on the phenomenon that is revolution. Humanity has struggled with orderly political change since records began. The selection reflects this, with the earliest revolution here taking place over 2,000 years ago, against the Roman

Republic. The most famous, the bloodiest and the most topical are all included. Peasant rebellions rub shoulders with failed attempts chosen for their later legacies. There are so-called 'Great Revolutions', difficult to ignore because of their wide influence. The list is not meant to be exhaustive. But each event, even the most distant in time or seemingly obscure in motive, is designed to reflect back on the course of events in 2011. Each should point the reader towards a different characteristic in the evolving story of revolution and its immediate future.

Argentina in 2002, for example, is included primarily because the major causal factors – economic mismanagement and IMF debt default – are highly topical. But it is also here because of the positive reaction of ordinary Argentines to a comprehensive meltdown of normal society. Yes, chaos reigned. But the country quickly learned that money and politicians do not, contrary to popular assumption, make the world go round. They picked themselves up, formed assemblies on street corners to deal with crime, empty shelves and overflowing bins. Then they got on with it. Today, in the midst of a global recession, Argentina boasts one of the fastest-growing economies on the planet. Positivity and togetherness shine brightest from the Argentine *cacerolazo* of 2002.

Unsuccessful efforts to overcome power can be equally relevant. Has there ever been, for instance, a more influential political and military failure than Shimon Bar Kozeba? The Jewish rebel raised a guerrilla army in 2nd-century Judea to challenge the mighty Roman Empire. Unsurprisingly, he failed. After defeat, Emperor Hadrian installed harsh penalties on the province. A diaspora was created, rabbis came to prominence in the religion and a minor sect calling themselves 'Christians' broke off from the main branch of Judaism. But most directly relevant, Bar Kozeba was resurrected by Zionists in the early 20th century as an exemplar of 'muscular Judaism' – the willingness of Jews to use aggression to create a homeland for themselves. Today Bar Kozeba's story holds meaning for both sides of the protracted Israeli-Palestinian struggle.

Certain events are simply too important to ignore. The late 18th-century French Revolution first became the model for other revolutionaries: jettisoning an aristocratic system, guillotining a king and even erasing God. But gradually, its events have become the model by which the world understands *all* revolution. Journalists wait to report the revolutionary 'moment', a Bastille-storming equivalent that shows an uprising has overturned rulers and become a revolution. Just like the National Assembly waited before judging the Paris mob, foreign politicians and international bodies hold back during revolutions. When the balance shifts decisively in one direction, their legitimising blessing is conferred.

A Classic Form

Another lasting effect of France's 1790s was to prescribe *the* revolutionary routine to be followed. It goes something like this: reacting against the tyranny of a despotic ruler, an iconic leader emerges to lead the people. Storming the heart of power, a new regime is established, only to itself descend into vengeful bloodletting. The book's chapters follow loosely this 'classic' procession from despotism, to liberty, and back again. This thematic basis is designed to examine whether all revolutions really follow such a set course. Although as many theories and definitions of revolution exist as successful revolutions themselves, this is not a book about historical or political theory, but about events. Yet despite their individuality, many revolutions do share common themes.

Despotism and Persecution – Merciless persecution is the clearest cause of uprising. Once a revolution is complete, and despotic rulers have been ejected, the newly empowered can sometimes themselves become abusive. The concept of persecution itself can change. As time has gone on, different forms have manifested themselves. The physical bondage of 18th-century plantations has been joined by 21st-century economic enslavement. The definition of who deserves freedom, and of what type, will continue to evolve. This chapter covers the American, Haitian, Iranian, Argentine (2001–02) and Bolshevik/October (Russian) Revolutions.

Martyrs and Icons – Many revolutions can be referenced solely through the biography of prominent individuals. During unrest, these transformative personalities give voice to previously subdued grievance. Frequently martyred, revolutionary icons embody the greater cause around which later institutions are built, their actions often shaped to fit contemporary political circumstance. The rebellions of Babak, Taiping and Pugachev are examined here, as are the Cuban Revolution and Simon Bolívar's various revolutionary campaigns for Latin American independence.

Just Violence, Radical Peace – During a revolution, violence by the forces of authority to quell dissent is frequently justified in the name of law and order. Given that government forces are usually better equipped, and that the use of force by rebels is easily portrayed as illegitimate, guileful subversion of the established rules, rather than full-frontal assault, tends to define successful revolutions. The pan-European revolutions of both 1848 and 1989 are discussed here, as are the Mau Mau and Huang Chao rebellions and India's 20th-century struggle for independence.

The Hidden Hand – Allegations of revolutionary actors at work beyond the simple rebel/ruler facade are commonplace, but often groundless. Revolutions are complex combinations of events. The number of active participants sometimes encompasses hundreds of thousands. But more often than malicious agents, non-human actors – such as rapid technological advance or strange ecological patterns – can play a decisive role. Under the microscope here are the Zapatista movement, the 1970 Shield Society coup attempt in Japan, the revolts of Spartacus, of 1381 in England and of 1916–18 in the Hijaz (Arabia).

The Revolution Eats Itself – Drunk on power, former comrades in the rebel movement commonly turn on each other once victory has been won. The normal results are savage reprisals, diverting the revolution disastrously from its former intended course. The rollcall of revolutions whose early, idealistic dramas were hijacked by ulterior agendas makes long and sad reading. This chapter covers the English, Mexican, Spanish, Indonesian and Orange (Ukrainian) Revolutions.

Remembering the Future – The extent to which modern states choose to either remember or forget the individuals who died to achieve their establishment is usually based on contemporary political concerns rather than facts. But remembering revolution is an act performed not only through formal means on assigned days of the year. So pervasive has the influence of particular events become, that they may often be commemorated unknowingly. The French Revolution joins the revolt of Bar Kokhba and the Bagaudae, under discussion with the Irish Rebellion of 1798 and China's revolutionary 20th century.

The chapter titles and themes are based on a purposefully impressionistic view of the stages in which a classic revolution is commonly theorised to proceed.* The term impressionistic is used because, it's safe to say, the chance that any revolution has stuck rigidly within the boundaries of such theory is close to nil.

The View from Space

The story of popular revolution can be told two ways: by the practitioners; and by those who analysed the events. Sometimes these individuals are one and the same; T.E. Lawrence and 'Che' Guevara are two examples. Mostly they are not. Having been proactive on the ground, rebel accounts relate first-hand all the colour and gore of bloody dedication to a cause.

Those who analyse, on the other hand, produce bird's-eye views. Such observation can offer detail and perspective that the outspoken, and often eccentric, rebels lack. However, theoretical accounts can also feel like a view from outer space. It is rare that accuracy, incisiveness and readability fully combine in abstract analyses. The language of political detail can be as dry as Lawrence of Arabia's memoirs are bombastic. Such a divisive subject as revolution, too, produces bitter ideological gulfs, particularly in the realm of theory.

The main strands of revolutionary theory fence different types of events off from one another. The mid-20th-century anti-colonial struggles of Algeria, Kenya and Malaysia sit in one spot. In another section are the 'Classic', 'Atlantic', or 'Grand' revolutions of the late 18th century: America and France as main events; England and the Netherlands as precursors; Ireland and Haiti as sideshows. There is no such attempt here.

---

* A more thorough setting for each theme is given at the start of each chapter.

Instead, centuries are wilfully mixed with continents on the basis of striking or topical features.

Neither are all of the revolutions included here considered successes. Even the most famous eruptions – America, France – left questionable gaps in the completion of their stated programme. Many failed outright. Still others fall short of the requirement of full-blown popular revolution. Not enough people participated; or power was won, but society's core principles were not altered. Adhering to the strictest precepts, a coup could not be included. Neither could a revolutionary war for independence; nor a slave uprising. Topicality, rather than theoretical purity, has informed this collection. Consequently there are efforts to reverse change, as in the Japanese section and localised indigenous movements, as with the Zapatistas. Standing at a crossroads in history, this book takes in as wide a swathe of radical, popular political events as possible.

The objective is not just to offer a fuller evaluation of where 2011's momentous events are taking the world, but to hazard a guess at how those events are changing conceptions of the world itself. Rebels of the past have successively pushed back the boundaries to popular participation in politics, not merely through their own actions, but through the memories and consequent philosophies of others. Will the rebels of 2011, as in 1789 or 1917, become the foundation of a new model for implementing change and running government? Will they fail? A thought, perhaps, for those protesters who have faced overwhelming opposition, of for those left out of global media coverage: history shows that ideas born through revolutionary struggle do not necessarily tally with the importance of that particular struggle's success. To act is sometimes enough.

Understanding the Past

Whether those who acted to bring about revolution in past times saw their revolutionary ideas spread, or not, their internal motivations are much less evident than those of the rebels of today. If they existed, access to these people's email archives would be wonderful. What were the stormers of the Bastille thinking? How did Chinese rebel bandits of the 9th century *feel*? A seemingly endless stream of headcounts, official reports, public death tolls, personal reflections and journalistic opinions, have already been published on the Arab Spring. Our information-soaked century will offer future historians almost *too* large a sampling.

Just as the relevant available data has grown in line with mass society, so too has the definition of what actually constitutes 'popular' changed. Popular musicians in Victorian London could be defined by the size of music hall they played at; 20th-century popularity was described by a million records sold and a stadium tour. Nowadays, a fleeting viral surge means a song is a hit. Similar processes affect the analysis of past revolutions. There do not need to have been thousands of proactive participants for a revolution to be considered 'popular'. Fidel Castro and 'Che' Guevara started their Cuban Revolution with only a dozen men. Three years later, less than 500 guerrillas entered Havana in triumph. But between the two points, new recruits, supply networks and cheering crowds demonstrated the undoubted support of a majority of the Cuban population.

This book embraces the general concept of people power, without dwelling on comparisons of exact percentages, or party numbers. For an event to have been included, it needs to have convincingly professed the desire for popular change. Yukio Mishima, for example, was probably one of the most unpopular revolutionary leaders in history. He had only a handful of supporters with him when attempting a coup in Tokyo in 1970. Live news coverage, however, beamed his dramatic last speech into millions of homes, bringing with it traditionalist sentiments that arguably still run deep in Japanese society today. For an event to have touched the lives of a significant portion of people, however latent their support, is enough to warrant inclusion here.

Shifting definitions influence our understanding of people power as time goes on. Can the meaning of revolution itself change? The evidence suggests so. What, for example, is represented by the label 'conservative'? During street battles in Paris in 1848 such a person might have put his life on the line to protect king and established church. In our time, French conservatives defend diametrically opposed institutions: the 'tradition' of secularity; the republic. A successful revolution, for the socialists manning the barricades in the same time and place, would have instituted social legislation such as state welfare and bans on child labour, both of which are now firmly entrenched in law in most countries.

* * *

Nobody seems certain whether it was Winston Churchill or George Santayana who first said, 'Those who fail to learn from history are doomed to repeat it'. Either way, the principle endures: those fighting tyranny today, or dreaming of toppling future kings, must learn from events past – the glories and the failures alike. But they should also pay attention to how those events have been translated, twisted and reinvented over time. There are lessons here for Occupy; for the Tahrir heroes; for those still in the dark, waiting to emerge into light.

Despotism and Persecution

For more than 23 years before they rose up in anger Tunisians had endured the presidency of Zine al-Abidine Ben Ali. Egyptians had laboured under Hosni Mubarak for almost 30 years; Muammar Gaddafi had ruled for nearly 42 years. Why, Western journalists pondered, had North Africans taken so long to end their persecution?

In hard times, people find novel ways to tolerate oppressive circumstances. Haitian slaves danced. People living under authoritarian Communism sought escapism in humour. Extreme circumstances can be endured. At an indefinable point, however, acceptance of the status quo is not enough any more. Exploring five diverse revolutions, this chapter seeks to investigate how that point is reached. At length, each society discovered that without some of life's essentials – food, faith, dignity – formerly contented and conservative civilians can be transformed into desperate revolutionaries.

The end times of Imperial Russia suggest the depths to which a proud people can be reduced to before such a point is reached. While the Tsar floated in opulence, the masses laboured in factory and field. Antiquated military strategies and incompetent leadership led to the sacrifice of millions of lives in the First World War. Harvests were requisitioned. Transport lines became bottlenecked. Strikes paralysed the country. Food and fuel shortages became *de rigueur* for civilians; a lack of food and ammunition was just as familiar to the army. This cocktail of lethal social ingredients finally exploded in February 1917. Having watched friends and family freeze in starvation at home, be ripped apart by jagged white-hot shrapnel on the front lines, or fall to disease everywhere, many felt revolution offered an escape other than death. Active resistance to the oppressive structures of state which held this system in place became an element of survival.

America's revolution had come much earlier, in response to the mercantile tyranny of colonial overlords. The USA emerged to become the 18th-century world's most democratic state, and certainly its most radical. But because women, slaves and Native Americans were left unserved by the country's founding documents, internal conflict would plague the nation in its infancy. In the long term, however, the very same issues as at independence – the democratic deficit, over-taxation, the power of global capital – still beset the former Thirteen Colonies in the 21st century.

The economic interests of an elite had spurred America to revolution. In Argentina, at the beginning of this century, the effects of financial ruin on the middle classes plunged society into chaos. A population well-accustomed to a high quality of life was forced into revolutionary action by unilateral decrees from national government and international banks. The results included spontaneously established barter systems and mass marches; the cost, apart from several presidents and a few hundred billion dollars, was a lasting distrust of government's ability to provide for daily needs.

In Iran, in the late 1970s, the economic ruination of the country by a despotic Shah combined with a powerful Islamic radicalism to lethal effect. The Muslim Shia cleric Ruhollah Khomeini led the overthrow of the Pahlavi regime, shaped the Iranian state in its aftermath, and so, even in death, affirms the great historian of the Roman Empire, Edward Gibbon, in his portrayal of persecuted religious believers as 'the most furious and desperate of rebels'.[1]

But what if government goes further than religious, economic and political enslavement of its population? The bonded plantation labourers of Haiti were restricted the rights to have a family, to movement and to virtually all free will. Perhaps more than any revolutionaries in history, they deserved their liberty, rising up against their slave masters and successfully casting off invading armies. In doing so, they revealed the hypocrisy at work at the heart of revolutionary France, from whose slogans they took their cue and whose leaders they outmanoeuvred.

It seems that the Arab leaders who fell from power in 2011 were outmanoeuvred by the coming together of two great urges: the need for work and for liberty. The most iconic image of the Tunisian Revolution was the unidentified figure, caught in an AFP photo, wielding a baguette at ranks of riot police as if it were a deadly weapon. 'Bread and circuses' was the simple formula for maintaining order and contentment among the citizenry of the late Roman Republic. While the circuses have proved easy to maintain, an absence in the basics of life – bread, religion, freedom, money – explains much about how revolutions have arisen and will continue to arise.

American Fall
USA 1776

That the proclamation of political perfection is a dangerous business has not deterred people from investing in it. No less a mind than Plato described the form an ideal democracy should take. His ancient Athenian city-state was of limited size. Because of conditions on citizenship and the practice of slavery, the actual numbers eligible to vote were even smaller. Eighty-five million people participated in the 2010 US congressional elections. Not for America the possibility of meeting on a hillside like the Athenians to decide important matters by a show of hands.

Nevertheless, the vision of small-scale local democracy still permeates to the very top of American mass politics. In what other empire have all-powerful leaders visited town halls to put across their case for election? Where else on earth are citizens offered the chance to elect every government official, from president down to police chief?

Visit during a public holiday and the other permanent fixture in American political culture is revealed: a deep and expressive love of one's country. Throughout the year, citizens celebrate together the country's flag, its living veterans, its war dead and independence. The focus on the local, the fierce nationalism and that searing independence of spirit can all be traced to one point: the victorious result of a late-18th-century revolution.

The American Revolution played out against a geography unrecognisable today. Across only thirteen Atlantic coast colonies, Old World religious exiles eked out a living under the direct control of Britain. West of the Appalachians, the lands of the upper Mississippi were patrolled by the Sioux; the great river's mouth guarded by French Louisiana. To the north, British and French fur trappers encroached on the Great Lakes. Texas and California were wild outposts of Spanish Mexico; Alaska, of tsarist Russia. The waves in Pearl Harbour were split only by the dipping paddles of native islanders' outrigger canoes.

America, in short, was small and weak; far from the global colossus it would become. Perhaps more importantly, it was disunited. Tension between the thirteen colonial assemblies often became fractious, with rivalry particularly evident between the influential commercial elites in Virginia (where crops were cultivated) and Massachusetts (where ports shipped goods abroad). Unrest among slaves occurred with increasing frequency in the decade before revolution. Tenant riots occurred in New Jersey in the 1740s and in New York in both the 1750s and 1760s.[1]

Britain provoked America into revolution through measures originally aimed at India – another, then much more important, imperial dependent. The East India Company was a powerful multinational trading corporation (the world's first). Its fluctuating ability to withdraw cash profits from the subcontinent affected both private and public finances in Westminster. So broad were the levels of mutual dependency that panic arose in London at even the smallest setback.

In 1770, a famine in Company-controlled Bengal caused over a million deaths and ruined the profitability of India's main cash crop: tea. Scrambling for a bail-out, the British government slashed duties on East India Company tea imports to the USA. This effectively undercut the revenues of American growers and merchants, uniting in one stroke the formerly argumentative Massachusetts and Virginia factions. The intention of the measure had been to help the Company in a difficult trading environment. The actual result changed the world forever.

In December 1773, a group of disgruntled merchants disguised as Mohawk Indians boarded a ship in Boston Harbour and tossed 342 chests of East India Company tea into the rising tide. America had its first mythological revolutionary event. But the Boston Tea Party was not an isolated action. Rather it represented the melodramatic finale of successive punitive laws. Americans had been banned from settling in Indian lands in 1763. The 1765 Stamp Act had levied direct taxation on the increasingly militant and resentful colonists. Boycotts and riots had accompanied the higher taxes on staple goods brought about by the Townshend Acts in 1767. All injustices were conceived of in distant London and imposed by the muskets of British troops.

Revolutionary propagandists had little difficulty depicting the chief and willing signatory to these injust acts, King George III, as a tyrant to be overthrown. One such, Thomas Paine, insisted in his pamphlet *Common Sense* that:

> A new era for politics is struck; a new method of thinking hath arisen. All plans, proposals... are like the almanacks of the last year, which though proper then, are superseded and useless now.[2]

Paine, like very many of the colonists, was a native son of Britain. He mixed suggestions of sedition and the prevailing rationalism of the Enlightenment with strong echoes of a 17th-century England which had beheaded its own king and instituted republican government. Paine's writings sold in their thousands in the early 1770s, on both sides of the Atlantic. Americans identified with the need for new political structures.

As relations with Britain worsened, a series of Continental Congresses gathered leading representatives of the Thirteen Colonies to formally express American grievances.

Despite the colonies' brewing anger, however, mass events in the mould of the storming of the Bastille are surprisingly thin on the ground in revolutionary America. The Boston Tea Party, from which the mass neo-conservative reform movement takes its name (if not its numbers), amounted to the involvement of a dozen irate merchants. The War of Independence's famed 'first shots', fired by British troops on Lexington Green in Massachusetts in 1775, were aimed not at an imposing rebel army, but the backs of thirty-eight local 'minutemen', leaping walls in disordered retreat.

Open hostilities followed. Britain declared the rebels traitors and, in response, on July 4th 1776, the Second Continental Congress declared outright independence for the USA, with the famous opening:

> We hold these truths to be self-evident, that all men are created equal, that they are endowed by their Creator with certain unalienable Rights, that among these are Life, Liberty and the pursuit of Happiness.
>
> That to secure these rights, Governments are instituted among Men, deriving their just powers from the consent of the governed.
>
> That whenever any Form of Government becomes destructive of these ends, it is the Right of the People to alter or to abolish it, and to institute new Government...

Never before had the rights of humanity been stated with such blatancy, nor such eloquence. Drafter of the declaration, Thomas Jefferson, had brilliantly fused John Locke's 17th-century assertion of economic rights to the popular political dissention of Paine. Here lies the radical genus of America's forthcoming strength and the source of its immediate conflict. The resulting war sucked half the world into its orbit.

Conscripted soldiers from all thirteen colonies were involved. So too were British brigades, North American loyalists and Native American allied nations. The Dutch Republic and the Spanish intervened for the rebels. Crucially the French did too, General Lafayette and the Comte de Rochambeau blockading the Royal Navy and reinforcing General George Washington at strategically decisive moments. After six years and tens of thousands of casualties, the British Commander-in-Chief finally surrendered at Yorktown in 1781.

Out of the war emerged a new ruling elite. Washington, the winning general, became the first US president. Jefferson, the third president, helped establish the new country's diplomatic and commercial ties overseas. James Madison, the fourth president, conceived much of the new country's political structures. Benjamin Franklin had been, until the mid-1760s, a committed monarchist. John Adams, the second president, and Alexander Hamilton, founder of the Federalists, arguably remained so. All of these 'Founding Fathers' were rich men before and after the event. They were both architects and benefactors of revolution.

'That all men are created equal' may have been self-evident, but the statement had hidden clauses. Most prominent southerners, Washington included, were also slave owners. The liberty at stake during the revolution did not stoop to include freedom for the forced labourers and servants on his, or any other, plantation. Neither was the US Constitution (1787) or the Bill of Rights (1791) an invitation for American women to partake in democracy.

Independence, moreover, did not end anti-authority feeling among newly baptised US citizens. New protests occurred for the same reasons the revolution had ostensibly occurred: overtaxation and non-issuance of paper currency. Shays' Rebellion in Massachusetts in 1786 was followed in the same year by unrest in New Hampshire and Rhode Island. In 1790 Alexander Hamilton supervised the imposition of duties on whiskey. The extended Whiskey Rebellion in Western Pennsylvania (1794) was the result.

Violent events aside, the most important products of America's founding were ideas. The American Revolution gifted the world a prototype of modern democracy. It encased universal Enlightenment values in law for the first time. It offered the conception, if not the realisation, of a perfect, democratic republic. These philosophies were, for the most part, realised to their fullest elsewhere. Inspired by the USA, France guillotined its Washingtons. Unlike America, Haiti's slaves freed themselves in the 1790s. Women voted and ran for office for the first time elsewhere too.

The story of the USA since 1787 is of a country catching up with its own constitution. Slavery was outlawed outright only after a bloody civil war tore north from south. The long-term status of Native Americans was decided not through compromise, as Thanksgiving suggests, but as a result of their wholesale eviction and elimination as settlers shifted westward.

This geographic expansion was *at least* as important as the revolution itself in ensuring the existence of the American project beyond its brilliant first generation. Intrepid early explorers, such as Meriwether Lewis and William Clark, changed the young country's self-image from a collection of small colonies, to a continental power in itself. The Louisiana Purchase (which doubled American territory in size) and the wars with Mexico in the 1830s and 1840s, moved things along: 'Tejas' became Texas; 'Alta California' lost its Spanish prefix and Mexican overlords; the fertile land on either side of the Rockies phalanx began to welcome the grateful wagon trails.

The rhetoric of 1776 has carried even less meaning in foreign affairs. America, a country founded on the principle of combatting the tyranny of kings and the excesses of empire, entered the 20th century tub-thumping into expansionist colonial war against Spain and the Philippines. US corporations, backed by gunboat diplomacy, annexed Cuban coffee plantations, strong-armed fields of Puerto Rican sugar and appropriated silver mines and oil wells in Mexico. Twice saving Europe from all-consuming wars earned American planners the design and leadership of the post-1945 world. Though the founding documents don't allow it to be admitted, the 20th century had transformed the former colonial weakling into an empire itself.

Since its inception, the USA has experienced exponential growth and a near continuous state of internal flux. Thomas Jefferson's Declaration of Independence expresses the simple but momentous right of early American settlers to decide their own rulers. Simply put, governments should expect to be removed whenever their actions appear at odds with the ideal of their citizens. Today, for the simple reason that this founding idea has not lost one iota of its relevancy, radical grassroots movements again sweep the political landscape. Recent events suggest the revolutionary process still has some distance left to travel. This is the case not only in the USA, but across a globe which has, for better or worse, taken American values to heart.

Dancing About History
HAITI 1791

Those passing through the increasingly gentrified London district of Dalston can be forgiven for failing to notice its connection with the Haitian Revolution. That connection is C.L.R. James, the brilliant writer and activist who spent much of his life in London and whose name now adorns Dalston's new library building. James' account of the rampaging violence that established the Caribbean's first modern republic in Haiti between 1791 and 1804 has achieved classic status. James chose his subject well. As an African Caribbean native of Trinidad, he identified with the details of Haiti's pre-modern slave society. As a Marxist, James' interest in the revolution redoubled.

What is known today as Haiti, was in the late 18th century the French colony of St. Domingue. The island of Hispaniola, of which St. Domingue made up the western half, had been one of the earliest landing sites of Columbus. It boasted rich growing conditions for sugar, coffee and other valuable commodities. Throughout the 18th century, Haiti's slave-based, agricultural export economy boomed. Sales of the main cash crops to Nantes and Bordeaux – for France was the only country with which St. Domingue could legally trade – hit unprecedented levels.

C.L.R. James chose as the focus of his study the pre-eminent figure of the revolutionary period: François-Dominique Toussaint L'Ouverture. L'Ouverture was born into an enslaved family in 1743. Millions of black Africans, his Benin-born father included, had been extracted from their homes and encaged on the long sea journey to St. Domingue. If lucky enough to disembark these ships alive – if lucky is the word – they were then welcomed to a life where control of their own labour, freedom, education and general well-being was set beyond their reach.

The absolute best possible lifestyle a St. Domingue slave could hope for, as experienced by Toussaint L'Ouverture in his first 40 years, was still very low. Slave life, such as it was, was subject to separation from family, aborted births, rampant and deadly disease, primeval or non-existent healthcare and the ever-present terror of cruel and injust capital punishment.

In spite of the harsh conditions of life, all slaves were not defeated in spirit. The memories of Africa survived through tribal dances and animist religious practices. For the dancers, these actions held deep meaning, inspiring the belief that 'bullets could bounce off their chests'.[1]

Contemporary *Creole** traveller M.L.É. Moreau de Saint-Méry observed that slaves danced 'to escape the vigilance of the authorities and even more to ensure the success of the secret meetings'.[2]

L'Ouverture, as a trusted plantation headman, by all accounts did not partake. He led a partially Europeanised life, holding limited command over other slaves and learning to write. Some of his African kin managed to buy, win or trick their way into the divided society outside the plantation. Escaped slaves were known as *Maroons*. Roaming the mountains and scraping an existence, they needed little excuse to hope for a revolution. At least before L'Ouverture came to prominence, however, they were not strong enough in either numbers or leadership to pursue it seriously.

---

* Creole – of European ethnicity but born in the Americas.

While rich whites controlled local governance and policing, commodity prices and duties for the colony were set by officials in France. Two distant revolutions changed this relationship. After 1781, plantation owners viewed with envy the independent United States, cut free from constrictive British overlordship, just as they desired to be liberated from the dictates of traders in Nantes and Bordeaux; as well as from the ordinances of the colonial authorities in Paris. Toussaint L'Ouverture's owner and his peers must have noted how American 'planters' had won their own liberty from British control, while retaining mastery over slaves.

In the motherland itself, the French Revolution's events influenced every step of the unfolding drama in St. Domingue. No one sentence emphasises this better than the first article of the 'Declaration of the Rights of Man and of the Citizen', issued by the National Assembly in Versailles in 1789: 'All people shall have equal rights upon birth and ever after.' *Mulattos* were the mixed-race portion of the island's population, free to own slaves and become rich themselves, but barred from civil rights or administrative roles. Groups of poor whites resented both growing *mulatto* prosperity and their own lowly status. In late 1789, the *Declaration*'s momentous words reached St. Domingue. Both the poorer whites and the *mulatto* gentlemen of leisure took the Assembly's phrasing quite literally. Just like their *sans-culottes* brethren at the Bastille, *liberté*, *égalité* and *fraternité* were not merely expected, but demanded.

These wishes were disappointed in 1790 when a *mulatto* uprising was crushed. Armed bands of *mulattos* and whites then attacked each other, with inconclusive battles and stand-offs between these two groups continuing for some twelve months. However, until 1791 the large slave population remained quiescent, L'Ouverture among them. In that year, *maroons* descended from the hills and rallied slaves in the north-west to a revolt. The town of Cap François (modern day Cap Haïtien) and the surrounding plantation region was the scene for vengeant attacks on the white population by a slave army. Amid the chaos, L'Ouverture left his post to become a medical officer.

In a desperate effort to becalm the chaos, France extended the previous offer of political rights to *mulattos*. The government dispatched troops and representatives to the island. Their mission was to enforce *mulatto* liberty, restrict the plantation owners' aspirations to independence and quell the slave uprising. But discord among the mission members had been sown by social splits at home in France, where the common people of Paris had united with the National Assembly against the interests of the landed gentry, bishops and king.

Amid the wrangle of contending factions, meaningful action became impossible. As C.L.R. James put it:

> The Commissioners were revolutionaries, the commanding officers were officers of the King… The National Guard were civilians of the revolution. The troops were soldiers of the King. As soon as Desparbes [*sic*] [the military commander] landed, instead of mobilising all his forces for an attack against the slaves, he conspired with the local royalists.[3]

All the while, a conflict of savage reprisals continued between the warring corners of St. Domingue. The black slave armies had entered into coalition with the Spanish crown (its colony, Santo Domingo, occupied the eastern half of the island of Hispaniola). L'Ouverture and his fellow fighters launched attacks from the mountainous frontier. During this period, the former slave proved himself an effective organiser, a workaholic, and an astute judge of character. He was moved with haste from a lower position of command, to become a general.

Once the revolution in France radicalised, during early 1793, mainland control of St. Domingue was effectively lost. First, Louis XVI was executed. Then, in March, France declared war on Britain. The Royal Navy shuttered Atlantic shipping lanes, blocking French reinforcement and resupply.

Sonthonax, the French government representative, was left facing multiple enemies: the armed *mulattos*; the plantation owners; the slaves, including L'Ouverture, allied with the Spanish; the Spanish themselves, opportunistically threatening invasion from Santo Domingo; the British, looming from their neighbouring island colony of Jamaica; not to mention the French royalist soldiers he had arrived with. Realising the weight of the situation, and with a month's delay on updates and directives from Paris, Sonthonax took a radical step: he liberated the island's slaves. This perceptive strike gained him an alliance with L'Ouverture, who he was able to tempt back from the clutches of the Spanish.

From there, what had been a multi-faceted civil war was transformed into a true revolution. The keystone was L'Ouverture. Working alongside the French general Laveaux, his helming of the slave armies overcame, firstly, the combination of his old comrade generals and the Spanish. He then outmanoeuvred Sonthonax and *mulatto* forces in the south and west of the island, both politically and militarily. A large British invasion force was defeated in 1798, partly through its own susceptibility to yellow fever. Finally, Santo Domingo, the Spanish half of the island, fell to L'Ouverture. By 1801, though nominally still under French command, the former plantation worker reigned supreme over the entire island of Hispaniola. All slaves were liberated. Their former masters were defeated. A new consitution had been declared. But Haiti's economy, society and landscapes stood devastated by a decade of continual war.

The closing twist of the French Revolution wrought a final tragedy on L'Ouverture. Napoleon Bonaparte, perhaps resentful of L'Ouverture's position as 'governor-for-life', sent an army to recapture France's trade monopolies and reimpose slavery. Having initially repelled French forces, L'Ouverture was deceived and removed to a prison cell, high amid the rocky crags of Franche-Comté in south-eastern France. It was here that the great leader died, gracelessly, in 1803. Thankfully that was not where the story of Haiti ended. Jean-Jacques Dessalines, L'Ouverture's former ally, established himself as successor. He completed the revolution, inflicting a last defeat on Napoleonic forces in 1803. The following year Dessalines proclaimed himself emperor. The colony of St. Domingue had become independent Haiti.

L'Ouverture's revolution stands unique in history. It is the only instance of a slave rebellion translating itself into revolution proper, and right through to the successful achievement of a fully-fledged state. It serves as a fascinating counterpoint to the limits of the ideals expressed by the classic Atlantic revolutions. The French, for example, were far less enthusiastic about their expression of universal fraternity once it became clear to them that the population of their prosperous slave-operated sugar colony might take them at their word.

The contrast with America is similarly instructive. There, a larger, more complex slave-owning society, similarly underwent a revolution through which it first realised independence. There were few *Maroon* equivalents, however, and the plantation slaves in the newborn USA failed to rise up on the same scale as in Haiti. It was slave-owners who, instead, emerged to frame the meaning of American liberty. For the 'Founding

Fathers', slaves were technically property, a status which negated their inclusion in the famed clause, 'all men are created equal' (see *American Fall*, p 5).

There is, of course, a sad contemporary epilogue for Haiti. An earthquake in January 2010 ruined what little development had occurred in the country in recent times. Its effects killed over a quarter of a million people and left a million Haitians homeless. Their misery was only an adjunct to years of social neglect and political mismanagement. Most notorious in the 20th century were the gruesome exploits of father-and-son dictatorial team, François and Jean-Claude Duvalier. More recently, in 2011, former entertainer Michel Martelly won the presidency in the first free elections for a generation. Despite recent horrors, hope exists.

Unlike L'Ouverture, and Haiti itself, C.L.R. James gets a moderately happy ending. A threat by the local council in Dalston to remove his name from the new library building in the autumn of 2010, met with scandalised outcry from the local community. The planners finally saw sense and relented. Although the Trinidadian Trotskyite never saw the global revolution of the oppressed that he wrote and dreamed of, James is now guaranteed a place in the minds of future readers in a small corner of London.

Twin Peaks
RUSSIA 1917

This is no jesting matter; revolution is a serious business. None of us is scared of firing squads… But the thing is to know whom to shoot…[1]

Leon Trotsky

Editing his speeches from Mexican exile at the height of the Stalinist purges, Leon Trotsky had every reason to feel bitter. Having helped direct and defend the Bolshevik Russian Revolution in its infancy, he was forced to watch as secret police forces spread terror, rewarding his former party comrades who remained in Moscow only with show trials and execution.

Progressive practices established in the warm afterglow after the revolutions of 1917 had been steadily absolved into a centralised authoritarian project. In its leaders' paranoia the empire stretching from the Baltic to the Sea of Japan differed little from that of the deposed tsars. How did the situation slip so quickly from one form of despotism to another?

The manner in which power was originally seized explains a lot. Two revolutions happened in 1917. Only the second event, in October, involved Trotsky, his nemesis Stalin and their overseer, Lenin. By the time their small group's plan came to fruition, however, Tsar Nicholas II had already vacated his Winter Palace six months previously. Revolution had long since happened. Lenin's group, the Bolsheviks, took the next logical step: they grabbed power from the people instead.

The February edition of Russia's two 1917 revolutions not only pre-dated its more famous October cousin, it was more spontaneous and genuinely popular. Mutinying sailors, deserting soldiers and hungry *babushkas* performed much of the bloody work of rebellion which the Bolsheviks, at that time, were still in the stages of planning. Not only was the autocracy of the tsar ended in February, but the resulting Provisional Government promised elections before the year was out. More fundamentally, in the aftermath of the tsar's fall, the concept of village councils planted itself across society. New deliberative unions were formed. Factories were taken over by committees of workers, or *soviets*. Even the army and navy saw a dissolution of hierarchical command and the development of new, inclusive decision-making structures.

Between February and October 1917, then, domestic Russia existed in a democratic but rather anarchic vacuum. The *soviet* councils held control on a hyper-local level while, at the top, Georgy Lvov and Alexander Kerensky, hapless leaders of the Provisional Government, lurched from one counter-coup to another. Neither the leftist sympathies of the armed forces' rank-and-file, nor the regularity of catastrophic defeat on the battlefields of the eastern front, helped matters. Lenin's Bolsheviks, by now armed and multiplying their membership with each passing day, were called upon to help crush a monarchist coup in July. This helped strengthen the grip they had already begun to establish over the *soviets* in the administrative and economic capitals, Petrograd (St. Petersburg) and Moscow respectively.

The Provisional Government's decision to continue fighting under such duress brought matters to a head. Wartime conditions for the average Russian, having been less than acceptable under the command of the tsars, worsened. Conscription was maintained for all able-bodied adult males. Extreme shortages occurred in everything from food, to fuel, to cigarettes. While limited food stocks bypassed towns and cities for deployment along the front lines, not nearly enough ammunition and artillery followed suit.

Unsurprisingly, once they had the vote, soldiers chose not to fight. Coerced or convinced to stay, they often shuffled into the sights of German mausers carrying little more than bayonets. Military command was led by Kerensky himself. The resultant defeats led to mass desertions and further mutinies in both the army and navy. Shortages reached crisis point in the autumn. Lenin, astute student of rebellion, intent on the need for a revolutionary 'moment', ordered the warship *Aurora* up the river Neva in Petrograd to fire blank shells at an empty Winter Palace. The token act did little more than confirm what was already obvious. Devoid of armed defence and popular support, the Russian Provisional Government simply imploded.

The fate of two popular revolutionary slogans hints at the nature of the Bolshevik victory. 'Bread, Peace, Land!' describes the disappointment felt by many Russians after February. The tsar was gone, but the urban working classes were still hungry; the soldiers still battle-weary; the village peasants still downtrodden and landless. Not yet in power and often out of the country after February, the Bolshevik leadership supported the credo. They also invented a new one: 'All power to the soviets!'

Once safely ensconced in the Kremlin, however, Lenin subverted the power settled in the *soviet* councils, levering Bolsheviks into key positions and erecting an all-powerful centralised control mechanism above them, with himself at its head. Nothing illustrates this antipathy to popular decision-making better than the Bolshevik reaction to the promised November 1917 election. When Lenin realised his party had gained barely a quarter of the popular vote, he simply annulled the results. And so revolutionary Russia's very brief fling with electoral democracy shuddered to an abrupt halt.

A brutal civil war followed. From 1918 until roundabout 1922, a motley coalition of monarchists, moderates and foreign militias haphazardly attacked the new Communist government.* Their improbable failure did much to enshrine the Bolsheviks' despotically centralised system in power for the next three-quarters of a century. Victory for Lenin brought territory previously lost to submissive wartime treaties back under Kremlin control. Bolshevik Russia met with Bolshevik Ukraine, Belarus, Armenia, Georgia and Azerbaijan. The Union of Soviet Socialist Republics (USSR) was the result.

These republics, equitable nations under the Soviet hammer and sickle in its early years, witnessed the gradual imposition of preferment for Russian culture and language, as the open-mindedness of the early 1920s gave way to a darker era. Nothing better emphasises the failure of centralisation than the inhuman famine suffered in the early 1930s on the once-rich Ukrainian plains. Women's rights, genuinely progressive during the 1920s, were rolled back once Lenin died and Joseph Stalin had elbowed his way to maniacal stewardship of the original one-party state.

There *were* some economic success stories. The New Economic Policies and first Five-Year Plans of the late 1920s delivered improvements in both general well-being and industrial output. Freedoms, however, continued to be restricted. Classical forms and traditional 'Great Russian' themes became a necessity for any artist wishing to make headway. A new set of '-isms' – formalism, structuralism, constructivism, modernism – were banned outright. After Stalin's rise to power, their public use, or even promotion, was a guarantee of the Siberian Gulag, or worse. To take a sample of the late-1930s: poet Boris Pasternak died in suspicious circumstances; novelist Mikhail Bulgakov survived,

---

* In truth, hostilities continued in some isolated and far-flung corners of the newborn USSR into 1923.

but kept his masterpieces in hiding; architect Alexander Vesnin conveniently reverted to classicism; poet Osip Mandelstam was deported to a life of Siberian forced labour; author Boris Pilnyak was executed. A few years after writing *The Stalin School of Falsification*, the sharp end of an ice pick ended Trotsky's life.

Middle-aged or older Soviet citizens of the 1930s would not have been unaccustomed to such despotism. Life in pre-revolutionary Russia had been just as hard. The highly developed tsarist secret police, the *Okhrana*, had transferred a repressive tradition to Stalin's dreaded *Cheka*. Political debate had been banned under the last tsar, with no free press and explicit criticism of his person punishable by exile or death (until Mikhail Gorbachev's *glasnost* policy in the late 1980s, much the same statement could be made about Soviet Russia). An oligarchic class loyal to the tsar had held the keys to industry, had staffed officer positions in the Imperial Army and had controlled the hundreds of millions of acres of land on which the vast majority of Russians laboured. Pogroms against Jews and other minorities had been commonplace.

When the tsar had led his countrymen to humiliating defeat by Japan in 1904–05, Russia's revolutionary warm-up had been sparked. A combination of striking workers and constitutional politicians had forced Nicholas's assent to demands for bread, civil rights and a *duma* (parliament). Almost as soon as these modest improvements had taken effect, however, a crackdown began. The Emperor of All the Russias had had no intention whatsoever of ceding power to parliamentarians, as both his relations King George V of Britain and Kaiser Wilhelm II of Germany had done. In any case, as Lenin and, much later, Vladimir Putin would go on to prove, the forces of democracy have always been weak in Russia, at least when compared to its European neighbours. The tsar and his family had greeted the patriotic rally accompanying the outbreak of war in 1914 as a welcome breather from a tiresome decade, little knowing it would prove their nadir.

Of all the historical controversies to emerge from the Russian revolutionary era – and there are many – perhaps the most unresolved is the question of foreign involvement. On the one hand, the depth to which an alliance of western, capitalist governments committed themselves during the civil war is clear and well-documented. On the other, question marks hang over just how much Imperial Germany helped the Bolshevik staging of Red October. The first part of the puzzle is known: Lenin, then a minor political player at best, managed to secure passage from Swiss exile, across wartime German territory, in a sealed train with special diplomatic status.

The question of how far Imperial German silver aided subsequent Communist recruitment and purchase of arms is, and will most probably always remain, unsettled. Proponents see the motive for such a move as obvious. German generals, their First World War forces bled between two fronts, were correct to presume that one of the Bolshevik government's first acts would be to sue for peace, allowing Central Powers to break through the allied trenches stretched from Flanders to Alsace. In the immediate context of the First World War, a Communist Russia was good for Imperial Germany.

Sceptics note, however, that if General Hindenburg and Comrade Lenin were in cahoots, their act of pretending otherwise appears extremely well rehearsed. December 1917 peace negotiations between the two forces were not a foregone conclusion. On more than one occasion, Bolshevik negotiators walked out of the hall at Brest, ordering the hastily assembled Red Army back onto the battlefield (with disastrous results).[2] The contrasting ideologies at work in such a conspiracy are also hard to reconcile. Communists were among the most persecuted political dissidents in Imperial Germany. Indeed, leftist-inspired revolts both in the capital Berlin and among naval stations in the Baltic, signalled the death knell for the German war effort. The Kaiser and his princes were finally toppled in November 1918.

The pattern continues into our time. A much-favoured tactic among despots under pressure is to dub protest leaders subversive foreigners. Overt, alleged, conspiratorial or otherwise, involvement from abroad was a constant theme during the 'Arab Spring' of 2011. In March President Assad of Syria was quick to identify Israeli agents among his rebellious subjects. In the same month Bahraini authorities were blatant in their use of Saudi Arabian and UAE commandoes to storm and kill the camps of pro-democracy marchers, all the while accusing Iran of secretly orchestrating the rebel actions.

During the civil war in Libya, allegations of malevolent foreign agency emanated from both the Gaddafi loyalist and rebel sides. Sub-Saharan militia members were regularly paraded by rebels, either as POWs or corpses, as proof of their opponent's treachery. A UN resolution was the justification for NATO to intervene directly on the rebel side, with Gaddafi not alone in questioning how the bombing of civilian areas helped protect Libyan citizens.[3]

Whatever the truth of foreign involvement, the twin Russian eruptions of 1917 can teach one sure lesson to the 2011 vintage: systems of deliberation and government, erected and adhered to in the early days of revolution, will define the political make-up of the country in the future. Those Egyptians, Syrians, Tunisians and Libyans intent on living in a democracy must insist that the early, mostly positive moves towards elections and uncorrupted local governance continue. The world has already seen enough Arab tsars. It cannot afford another Stalin.

Rightly-guided
IRAN 1979

Even though the most widely accepted definitions of modern democracy outline a total separation between church and state, they are rarely followed to the letter. American presidents are inaugurated with a hand on a Bible. The British monarch is also the head of its state-endorsed church. Many of his subjects assume the Japanese emperor has superhuman heavenly ancestors.

God and humanity come together most completely in the state of Iran. Its institutions enmesh the traditions of both modern secular democracy *and* religious practice. Its Supreme Leader is an Islamic cleric. Yet Iranians, unlike most of their Middle Eastern neighbours, can elect the public face of the government; the president and parliament.

Just as secular political theory in most developed democracies can be traced back to the 'Atlantic' revolutions of England, France and the USA in the 17th and 18th centuries, so too can Iran's current system be explained by reference to the prelude, drama and aftermath of its epic 1979 popular uprising. A single figure helpfully embodies all three stages. Ruhollah Khomeini was first and foremost a dissonant cleric. From 1964 until 1979, he remained influential in exile. After the revolution that he had done so much to provoke, Khomeini became the first ruler of the Islamic republic of which he had been the architect.

On June 3rd 1963, as Khomeini addressed followers outside the capital city of Tehran, the listening crowd could have guessed little at coming events, nor how central a role the cleric was to play in them. The timing of the event dripped with symbolism.

It was Ashura; the day when Shia Muslims remember Husayn, Muhammad's grandson, martyred in rebellion against an unjust ruler. The speech that Khomeini delivered held little back in connecting religious myth with his own, ongoing battle against Iran's absolute Shah, Mohammad Reza Pahlavi:

> You wretched, miserable man, forty-five years of your life have passed. Isn't it time for you to think and reflect a little, to ponder about where all this is leading you, to learn a lesson from the experience of your father?[1]

That father was Reza Khan. A military strongman, he had come to power in a 1925 British-supported *coup d'état*. After first assembling a large army through conscription, Reza attempted to modernise society. Western dress codes were enforced for women. Nomadic tribes of Iran's massive deserts and steppes were forcefully resettled. Tehran University was founded, civil courts were instituted and non-clerical teachers appointed. This insistence on secular public institutions impinged on the traditional influence of the clerics, among whom he became a figure of hate.

Khan, however, stayed faithful to his most important constituents. The British had operated an oil monopoly in Iran since a successful 1908 strike in the south of the country. The strongman's Nazi affections became too pronounced, however. In 1941, Reza Shah abruptly departed power via the same route he had assumed it. The British and Soviets installed his son.

Mohammad Reza Shah was initially more hesitant than his father in imposing Western-oriented reform on the reluctant, rural Iran. For the early years of his rule, nationalist politicians in the *Majles* parliament made the bolder political moves. The role of the Shah was overshadowed when Prime Minister

Ahmad Qavam managed to shunt invading Soviet troops from northern Iran. Qavam's successor, the democratically elected Mohammad Mossadegh, went one step further. In 1951, he nationalised the oil industry; one step too far for MI6 and the CIA. In August 1953 American and British agents instigated a coup, handing supreme power back to Mohammad Reza.

The second Pahlavi Shah endured. Billions of dollars in oil revenues bought the latest American military technology and a highly developed internal secret police network. Expatriate oil workers and English language teachers swamped Tehran. Isolated progressive reforms sat incongruously amidst an increasingly authoritarian society, in which political parties were outlawed.

With private sources of funding and international links to foreign Shia communities, Iran's Muslim clerics represented a dangerously independent threat. In the decade preceding Khomeini's 1963 speech, Mohammad Reza Shah set about diminishing their power. Tracts of rural land were ripped from clerical control. Women sporting the traditional Islamic chador were forcibly disrobed. Seminaries suspected of harbouring anti-regime politics were shut down. Khomeini himself was finally exiled in 1964.

State controls on the media and courts stamped out political debate. The Shah's will was imposed through exile, imprisonment and torture. Even as tales of abuse seeped out of Tehran's notorious Evin prison, cold war US governments treated the Shah's regime as a valued friend; a bulwark against Soviet expansion. Reciprocal trade in arms and oil rocketed in the 1970s.

However, price fluctuations after the Oil Shock of 1973 meant lower wages and declining standards of life for those in Iran's packed and polluted cities. Underground communist activity increased, with consequent secret police crackdowns.

As inflation jumped, austerity measures kicked in and the Shah opened the economy to international competition, Tehran's merchants – the *bazaari* – turned their powerful weight of opinion against the Shah. They began to actively engage with opposition groups, supporting strikes and compensating victims of secret police violence. A campaign of civil resistance was begun by senior Shia. Dissent spread outward from the mosques and markets.

The leading voice of resistance, often smuggled into the country via audio cassette, was that of Ruhollah Khomeini. He did not merely critique the excesses of the Shah's system, but proposed the establishment of an Islamic Republic in its stead. Khomeini's unique vision of theocratic statehood offered a powerful leader who combined both religious and political 'guardianship'. In all matters, this infallible Supreme Leader would stand over the civilian president, the judiciary and the parliament.

More crucially, and as was the case with his 1963 Ashura speech, Khomeini's visions tapped into deeply held religious tradition. The Twelfth Imam is a mystical Shia leader, hidden from the sight of believers, but promised to return at the end of the world to resist tyranny and end suffering. For most Iranians, the suffering and tyranny of 1970s Iran were tangible; and Khomeini's stern image represented perfectly how the Twelfth Iman *should* look and act.

Throughout 1978, with Khomeini still blocked from entering the country, public strikes paralysed industry. Public meetings of all types were banned, but happened anyway. Protesting crowds were swelled by students, members of outlawed left-wing or democratic organisations and unemployed rural migrant workers. The demonstrators' variety of political creeds sat under one overarching demand: an end to the Shah's rule.

When the marchers met with violent suppression, victims' traditional Islamic memorial gatherings, delayed by forty days according to custom, created renewed and enlarged protests. Again, these memorials met with secret police and army bullets, and the cycle continued. John Simpson, reporting in Iran for the BBC at the time, describes the bloody cycle as 'doing the forty-forty'.[2]

The overt brutality employed by the authorities did much to move moderate domestic public opinion against the regime. Yet the USA seemed shocked by the speed of events. It offered nothing of the outside help requested by the Shah and so familiar to students of Persian history. With the level of protest overwhelming – millions of Iranians poured onto city streets in December 1978 – the loyalty of the lower ranks of the police and military disintegrated. Offered no protection and little choice, the Shah fled the country in January 1979. Two weeks later, Khomeini returned from exile to popular adulation.

In the aftermath of the Pahlavi regime's downfall, an intense struggle for power ensued between previously united protest groups. Khomeini held the backing of the *bazaari* merchants. The Islamic cause was supported too by the might of the newly formed Revolutionary Guard militia. They imposed terror on suspected communists and liberals in the *komiteh* 'street courts'. A radical, Islam-centred constitution was drawn up, enshrining Khomeini's theories of 'guardianship'. This was, in turn, approved by an obliquely worded referendum. Khomeini, the overriding icon of the revolution, was accepted as the newborn Islamic Republic's first Supreme Leader.

The Shah, seemingly impregnable only months before, had met a swift end. The watching world, though stunned, had no reason to be. Events had followed precisely the 'classic' form historians had expected of all revolutions: despotic rule; horrible persecution; popular protest; post-revolutionary infighting; despotism by another name. Only the winning cause did not fit expectations. The theocratic Islamic system was alien to both prevailing cold war worldviews: the capitalist ideas of liberty and multiparty democracy; and the Marxist deterministic course of history. Radical political Islam had leapt to the forefront of 20th-century world affairs for the first time.

The USA, accustomed to playing the puppet-master behind the Pahlavis, was dismayed at the revolution's outcome. It had profited from cheap Iranian oil, a strategic beachhead on the Persian Gulf and the Shah's bottomless military and nuclear technology shopping list. All of these were now gone.

Relations with Khomeini's new regime were further troubled when the Shah was granted political refuge by Washington in late 1979. When radical students in Tehran detained US diplomatic staff in retaliation, all foreign-held Iranian assets were frozen. The 'Hostage Crisis', as it became known, resulted in the first demonisation of Khomeini by the international press. It was certainly not the last. The domestic reputation of the Supreme Leader soared.

In September 1980, Iraq took advantage of its neighbour's chaos by invading. The US attempted to make up for its former indecision by backing a certain Saddam Hussein. The ensuing eight-year conflict was marked by all the worst aspects of 20th-century warfare: human shields; vicious treatment of prisoners; chemical bombardment; little physical or diplomatic progress towards any discernible goal.

Behind Iranian lines, the revolutionary regime's new secret police force matched merciless antecedents by torturing and eliminating political opponents. Liberals, secularists and communists who could get out of the country, did so. Many emigrated to the 'Great Satan' (as the USA now became universally known within Iran). A common method of escape was to subvert the closely watched airports and road borders by walking eastwards to the Afghan and Pakistani frontiers, a ten-day desert hike, often made carrying children and possessions.

The dark tales of the exiles and the ferocity of the hostage crisis did much in the 1980s to isolate the Iranian regime diplomatically. Its belligerent response set a lasting tone. The patriotism drummed up by the Iran-Iraq War ended virtually all domestic opposition, at least until the death of Khomeini in 1989. Since then, anti-regime protests have occurred (and been put down) in 1999, 2003, 2006, 2009 and 2011.

A global media storm has followed Iran's every move in recent years. Current international news coverage does not venture far beyond Iran's rigged elections, its ranting leaders, the presumed nuclear threat and alleged interventions in neighbouring states. But search engines and news snippets rarely underline the link between contemporary, revolutionary Iran and the persistence of the Persian rebel tradition. Between 1890 and Khomeini's Ashura speech in 1963, political unrest occurred repeatedly. Major protests, riots or coups happened in 1906, 1911, 1921, 1925, 1935, 1945, 1951–53 and 1963.

Likewise, foreign meddling has not ceased. Mainstream American policymakers regularly call for invasion. John McCain was applauded during his failed Republican US Presidential candidature in 2008 when he paraphrased the Beach Boys' song 'Barbara Ann' with 'Bomb-bomb-bomb / Bomb-bomb-Iran'. Meanwhile, the lessons of the 1970s have been ill-learned. The domestic economy in Iran, still massively dependent on oil revenues, appears fragile. It is safe to assume that the dusty streets of Tehran, Tabriz and Qom have not seen the last of revolution.

Human Capital

ARGENTINA 2001–02

What happens when a society suddenly has its supplies of cash, credit, food, work and essential utilities shut off? The initial and disheartening evidence from Argentina's popular revolution of 2001–02 is violence and political disorder. But sifting amid the rubble of what is probably the most complete social and political breakdown of a modern peacetime state, reveals novel interpretations of democracy, spontaneous economic systems and hope for a similarly afflicted world. How did such a naturally well-endowed land arrive at so low a point? Suitably enough for a country whose name means 'land of silver', Argentina's revolutionary fable can be told almost entirely through the fate of its many and various currencies.

Up until independence was won in 1825, Spanish colonists traded the cattle of Río de la Plata for silver *reales*. In the first decades of the 20th century, foreign investment brought *peso papel* (paper money) and a wave of European immigrants. Then came the Depression. International demand for Argentine exports fell away. A military coup – the first of many in the period – deposed a democratically-elected president in 1930. An army man named Juan Domingo Perón courted union support and, flanked by his iconic actress wife Evita, won the presidential election of 1946. He was forced into exile in 1955. But Perón's economic sleight-of-hand had been learned well by the Argentine political class: printing enough money buys jobs for key union supporters, winning power regardless of the inflationary effects. 'Perónism' became a political trick to be repeated *ad nauseam* for the rest of the century.

His own death, followed by a time-honoured military coup to oust his third wife from power, curtailed the Peróns' 1970s reoccupation of the Casa Rosada presidential palace. But even the generals couldn't force good behaviour on a chaotic new currency: the *peso ley*. After invasion of the Falkland Islands failed in 1981, Argentina went bankrupt, drowning in international debt. Perón lived on in the form of a labour-friendly, kickback-addicted Perónist party, and yet another new currency accompanied the 1983 arrival of democracy: the *peso argentino*. Corrupt habits, however, were hard to give up. After only two years, the treasury replaced the *peso* with the *austral*. But by its nadir in 1989, the new currency's value was dividing by the minute. Urban myths emerged of taxi drivers changing rates of fares several times during a journey.

Unaffordable food, urban rioting and the presidency of Carlos Menem were the immediate results. Another crisis; another currency: the *peso convertible* was tied to the value of the US dollar in 1991. Convertibility, as this policy was known, essentially barred the government from printing its own funds. This policy – enacted on April Fools' Day – had the short-term effect of stabilising previously rampant inflation. Incomes began to rise and, with the traditional union connection curtailed, Menem's finance ministry was free to open the Argentine economy to international competition and investment. Wall Street dived in. Buenos Aires in the 1990s became a boomtown, flush with speculators in the domestic stock market and bidders in the frequent auctions of state-owned assets. Financial analysts held Argentina up as an ideal case of developing market liberalisation. Lenders were more than happy to loan Menem's government all the cash it wanted.

As the 1990s progressed, however, convertibility revealed a cutting edge. The USA revalued the dollar against European and Brazilian currencies – Argentina's main trading partners – and the fixed 1:1 ratio of exchange meant Menem could do nothing to control the value of the *peso* rising with it. Suddenly, Argentine exports became expensive and uncompetitive abroad. To make matters worse, most foreign-manufactured goods imported to Argentina fell dramatically in price. For want of demand, domestic manufacturing caved in and unemployment suddenly shot up.

In line with the terms that accompanied loans, state holdings had been sold off. State control of airlines, power companies, telephone providers and even pension funds were turned over to foreign corporate control for short-term profit. The first act of most international investors was to slash their Argentine workforces, bloated by 50 years of Perónist job-buying. 'Rationalisation' – as sacking people *en masse* is often referred to by businessmen – led to violent protests. Arriving unannounced at major roads and industrial sites, masked men and women chanted slogans and burned rubber tyres until they were dispersed by police or the army. But however direct and confrontational they got, *piquetes* didn't gain much attention internationally until Argentina's crisis turned into a middle-class cataclysm at the turn of the century.

Enter the International Monetary Fund (IMF). Established at the close of the Second World War in an attempt to 'correct imbalances' in world trade and currency values, the IMF was backed by the seemingly bottomless credit of the US government. It had already bailed out Argentina in 1976 and 1982. It lent money to the government twice in 2001. So it was with hope that Argentina's finance officials lodged loan applications for the third time the same year.

The IMF turned down the request: a resounding expression of no-confidence in Argentina's economy. But because convertibility still allowed *pesos* to be withdrawn as the more trustworthy dollars on a 1:1 basis, Argentines queued in their thousands to do so. Dollars were then sent abroad or stashed for safekeeping. The drastic government response was to freeze all cash withdrawals and foreign cash transfers. The crisis froze action at all levels of society. With no way to meet its schedule of repayments to international creditors, Argentina defaulted on its dollar debt; a very public admittance of the government's incompetence. With state salaries frozen, and with no cash to pay for imports, essential government services such as healthcare and rubbish collection simply stopped.

The middle classes, unaccustomed to having no food to buy or money to buy it with, revolted. Large-scale demonstrations led by housewives occurred both in the capital and across the country. A general strike was called. President De La Rua, Menem's successor, resigned. But the refusal of protestors to accept his successors resulted in the farcical sight of five presidential regimes being sworn in over a matter of weeks. A general antipathy towards the depth of corruption in Argentina's political culture emerged. '*Que se vayan todos*' ('Out with them all') became the marchers' war cry.

The final straw came in January 2002. With private bank accounts still inaccessible by government decree, convertibility was ended. The *peso*, unhooked from the trusted dollar, was suddenly prone to the realities of the Argentine economy's weakness. Its value plummeted. On the ground, this meant that those whose salaries were paid in *pesos*, but who held personal loans or mortgages in dollars, now faced insurmountable debts. Worse still, in desperate need of foreign reserves to rectify its own situation, the government converted all private dollar savings accounts to *pesos* at a unilateral (and highly unrealistic) rate. In one stroke middle-class savings and pensions were wiped out.

The mass scale of demonstrations which followed was dramatic. The *cacerolazo* protests earned the revolution its lasting image; housewives drummed on kitchen pots, leading rowdy processions to occupy banks, government offices, courts and foreign corporation headquarters. The crisis had affected virtually every facet of society and the *cacerolazo* marches were composed of students, farmers, union members, journalists, nurses, unemployed labourers, salsa bands and beeping mopeds.

Not only did foreign currency traders flee Argentina, many recent investors simply locked their new factories and caught a one-way flight back to North America, Europe and Japan. Cases emerged of groups of unemployed workers taking over the running of abandoned or closed businesses. They were backed up in these endeavours by the re-emboldened union networks, many of them radicalised by the turn of events. Requisitioned businesses were commonly run by democratic committee, with their goods bartered against those of similar enterprises.

Novel political forms also emerged on a local, civic level. Urban neighbourhoods responded to the anarchy by initiating local assemblies unburdened by officialdom. Participants spoke, deliberated and voted together. They executed mundane tasks normally carried out by the missing municipal services. These 'horizontal' *asambleas* – so-called because they lacked permanent leaders or hierarchical political parties – also decided on lists of demands, communicated with other neighbourhood assemblies and organised further protest.

Through all of this, the *piquete* movement had grown larger and bolder. Exponents of *cacerolazo* and *piquete* demonstrations often joined forces at traditional sites of protest. A favourite was the central *Plaza de Mayo* square, where families of the victims of the 1976–83 military dictatorship had met and marched for years. When food shortages reached dangerous levels, peaceful protest sometimes descended into looting and riots. The inevitable response from the police and military came in the form of tear gas and bullets. A combined crackdown resulted in dozens of deaths.

The national power vacuum lasted a year. President Néstor Kirchner was elected in 2003. He won immediate popularity by sacking military leaders associated with the repressive pre-1983 regime. Kirchner also won praise for restructuring the unpopular Supreme Court. Gradually, the value of the *peso* stabilised and Argentina began to recover from its crisis. The *cacerolazos* ceased and the *piquetes* lost momentum. In 2005, Kirchner cemented his support by confronting the IMF and other international creditors with an ultimatum: Argentina would repay only 35¢ in each dollar which it owed; or nothing. It was accepted. Kirchner's most high-profile concession to classical Perónist ways, was to be succeeded by his wife, Cristina Fernández de Kirchner. He died in 2010.

The wider fallout from the crisis has landed at the door of the IMF. It cannot be blamed for the corrupt aspects of Argentine politics – that dubious honour lies with Perón. But IMF analysts repeatedly delivered positive reports on Argentina as an investment opportunity even as national debt grew to unmanageable levels. The IMF fomented the wholesale privatisation of the Argentine economy as part of its insistence on free trade, liberalised stock markets and the mobility of global capital. Former *Washington Post* journalist Paul Blustein refers to the IMF's mismanagement of Argentina in 2001–02 as 'exhibit A for critics of global free markets'.[1]

To cap it all, the IMF received little censure for its actions. It continues to impose financial straitjackets on sovereign states with little regard for their social effects. Nobel prize-winning economist Joseph Stiglitz commented on the organisation's lack of accountability:

> [The IMF is] making rules and policies that affect workers, that affect small businesses, that affect everybody in our society. And yet these other people have absolutely no voice.[2]

Ireland, Portugal and Greece were loaned large funds by the IMF in 2010–11. The loans allowed the governments and central banking systems of each country to continue to operate, even with disproportionately swollen public debt.

In each country, just as in Argentina, auctions of public resources, cuts to services and the raiding of pension funds, will all be carried out so that the interest-accumulating IMF loans can be serviced. Athens has seen mass *cacerolazo*-type protests against these measures. Dublin and Lisbon witnessed demonstrations, though not yet on the scale of anything in Argentina. Perhaps this disparity is attributable to the fact, made clear during the Argentine crisis, that revolutions tend to only be recognised as such when a bulk of the middle classes are affected. Greek austerity measures have been more drastic than in Portugal or Ireland, provoking normally moderate middle class groups to get actively involved. It is intriguing, too, to note the parallels between the neighbourhood assemblies of Buenos Aires and the direct democratic formations that have occurred in Greece as protests gathered pace, their form later replicated by the 15-M movement in Spain and by 'Occupy' protests across the world.

Argentina's collapse caused hardship and misery on a massive scale. But the forms of governance developed locally to deal with the outcome offers hope for the future of other indebted states. So too does the country's subsequent recovery. It re-elected Cristina Fernández de Kirchner in 2011 and continues to outstrip global growth averages. If nothing else, this displays the certainty that there are alternatives to saddling the public with the debts of bad politics, be their origins at an electoral national level, or that of the more usual, unaccountable supranational. Another way exists.

Martyrs and Icons

Washington crossing the Potomac; Bismarck uniting the Germans in conquered Versailles; Churchill urging compatriots to stand tall against the Nazi threat: great historical events have great personalities indelibly attached. Revolutions are no different. Some of the world's most iconic figures have presided over the great revolts and uprisings of history: sometimes egotistical, occasionally megalomaniacal, but always charismatic. This chapter seeks to investigate the relationship between five particularly eminent examples and the revolutions that they led.

Operating under great stress, outside the law and on the fringes of society, rebel groups benefit from strong leadership. Leaders concentrate energies and bind formerly divided individuals in loyalty. They give impetus to formerly shapeless plans. In South America in the 1810s, however, the fate of something even greater than a rebellion hinged on one man. Gran Colombia was the country which Simon Bolívar built from the ashes of independence from Spain. But the unitary state relied too heavily on the iconic force of his personality, splintering only months after he died.

In China, less than 30 years later, another rebel leader arose whose revolution teetered precariously on the condition of his imbalanced personality. Not only did Hong Xiuqang believe he was destined to lead the Taiping Rebellion to victory, he asserted he was doing it on the direct instruction of both God and Jesus. Such claims tend to result in committal to an institution in the 21st century. In China in the late 1850s, they were enough to gain Hong rule over 30 million people. Just as in Gran Colombia, however, the Taiping Heavenly Kingdom was dependent on the fate of its founder. When Hong died, the godly rebellion was overrun, his vision of heaven on earth destroyed.

Hong and Bolívar defined their revolutions. Yemelian Pugachev, born a Don Cossack in imperial Russia in 1742, experienced the opposite process. By middle age he had risen in military rank. But when the southern Russian hinterlands rose in rebellion, Pugachev saw his true calling. He successfully impersonated Catherine the Great's dead husband, Peter I, promised redemption to the repressed Cossacks and led a huge peasant army against the state. The revolution had moulded its leader into an entirely different person.

Pugachev was an arch imposter in life. In death, 'Che' Guevara has gained a similarly augmented standing. Cast as the 20th century's revolutionary hero, his instantly recognisable image has come to be seen as an iconic representation of rebellion.

What drives Cubans and other supposedly secular people to worship at the altar of past heroes? The tendency of modern populations to seek out idols in all walks of life is nothing new. Leaders have sprung upon this, adapting iconography, the visual symbolism of religion, to political contexts as 'focal points where differences merge'.[1] In 1931,

Stalin dynamited the golden *ikons* of a cathedral in central Moscow to make space for a giant hall and towering statue of Lenin in its stead (monuments that, ultimately, remained unbuilt).

Babak Khorram-din, Azerbaijan's medieval revolutionary, is known to the present day largely as a result of the country's 20th-century Communist rulers. Babak was a fire-worshipper and had unified the southern Caucusus against Islamic encroachment. By the 1920s, Soviet atheists were engaged in just such a battle and on the very same spot. The proto-Communism of Babak was just the historical backdrop the egalitarian Azeri state required.

The trend for revolutions to produce martyrs continues. When street vendor Mohamed Bouazizi poured a can of petrol over himself and struck a match in Tunisia in late 2010, little could he have guessed how his actions and death would inspire a wave of uprisings across the Middle East. The outcome of the revolutions of 2011, just like those of the past, will hinge on the martyrs who rally them and the icons who lead them. Yet while martyrs proliferate, the lack of dominant leadership icons amidst the Arab Spring is notable. It is unclear yet if this libertarian tendency will prove a benefit, or the movement's Achilles Heel.

A Change in the Pipeline
MEDIEVAL AZERBAIJAN

> Drivers barreled through the city, leaning on their horns and fly-
> ing huge flags. Those not satisfied with leaning out car windows
> climbed onto the roofs — or, in some cases, into the trunks —
> and hung on for dear life.
>
> Hummers and Land Rovers and boxy Soviet-era Ladas got so
> snarled on Oilmen's Avenue, a palm-lined boulevard skirting the
> Caspian Sea, that everyone just got out and danced.[1]

These were the scenes as described by a *New York Times* correspondent on May 15th 2011 in the city of Baku. The capital
of Azerbaijan was not rejoicing, as might be expected, in fraternity with the wave of pro-democracy protests then sweeping
the Middle East. There had not been a rigged election, nor even
victory in a football match. Instead euphoria had been gener-
ated by two Azeris topping the polls at that night's Eurovision
Song Contest. People *had* marched for democracy in Baku
earlier in the year. But stiff policing and harsh reprisals had
greeted the small number of protestors in attendance.

As the gaze of the world fell on this small state, many
western Europeans looked on in bewilderment. Why did
Azerbaijanis prefer to celebrate pop schmaltz than demand
reform of their leaders? And what was a Muslim country with
an Iranian border and Caspian coastline doing in a European
competition anyway?

Yet Azerbaijan, sitting at the base of the traditional
Caucasus edge of Asia, posits strong claims for consideration

in European affairs. Baku itself has long served as a point from where occidental armies – Hellenistic, Roman, Tsarist and Soviet – have leapt into the orient. Azerbaijani representatives sit on the Council of Europe. Its boxers, athletes and soccer players battle for European championships. The country was even early off the mark with democracy; Azeri women were voting and running for office before their British, German and French sisters obtained the same rights.

This cultural portmanteau is explained in part by its iconic medieval rebels. The history of what is known today as Azerbaijan is closely bound to the numerous rulers and empires emanating from Persia, to the south. In the 9th century, Azerbaijan was a northern province in a vast Islamic empire centred on Persia. Its rulers were the Abbasid *caliphs*. Their territory stretched from the Atlantic coast of modern Morocco to the shores of the Indian Ocean. Upon the birth of Babak Khorram-din, in the northern section of the caliphate in the late 8th century, the Abbasids were merely beginning to build their future global primacy in science, medicine, engineering, the arts and warfare, a role that would extend, in different forms, into the 13th century. The Arab Islamic conquest of Persia was a recent phenomenon, its hold on the caliphate tentative. Only the upper tiers of the Abbasid leaders were Muslim. Persian Islam sat atop a stormy collection of contending ethnic, linguistic, tribal and religious groups: Nestorians; Jews; Diophysites; animists; Samaritans.

Abbasid rulers took pains to override such differences. They integrated certain groups while suppressing the most threatening. As the state religion of pre-Abbasid Persia, Zoroastrian fire-worship bore the brunt of their attention. Fire temples were demolished and restrictions were placed on its practitioners. For Babak, raised in a Zoroastrian family and trained in warfare from a young age, the persecution was a call to arms.

A rebel group known as the *Khurramiyya* fought the oppression of the Abbasid regime. Originating in the central region of Khurasan, they spread across Persia during Babak's childhood. Zoroastrians were pitched against Muslims, but the rebellion was also a battle between poor and rich, Persian and Arab. The *Khurramiyya* were drawn from the lower ranks of native Persians. They opposed both their new Arab rulers and, as they saw it, the treasonous Persian elites who had sided with the invaders. Fire-worship was still widely prevalent in Persia at the time. The rebels were able to draw into their ranks many non-Arab, non-Muslim Persians, unhappy with life under the Abbasids.

Assuming the lead of the *Khurramiyyah* in 816, Babak established a base of operations in remote territory, far north from the Abbasid capital in Baghdad and close to present-day Azerbaijan. Under Babak the rebels developed a strong military capability. Several Abbasid generals sent against the group in the early phase of its rebellion were defeated. The attention Babak is given by Abbasid chroniclers in subsequent years shows he must have commanded a significant force. The *Khurramiyyah* never won power outright, but Babak provoked and resisted the Abbasids over the span of three decades, before his capture and execution in 838.

Despite meeting with eventual defeat, Babak's martyrdom was carried into 20th-century Azerbaijan on the turrets of Soviet tanks. They chugged into Baku in 1920, dismantling in its infancy the democratic but weak Azeri republic. Once a Soviet Azerbaijan had been established, its historians found much to praise in Babak's tale of resistance. Sketchy as it was, it offered a valuable historical link between Azerbaijan's 'socialist paradise' and the wider, ongoing battle with the capitalist world. Babak's resistance to Islamic domination, too, gave Azeri Reds a precedent for suppressing the Muslim religion; by then the dominant faith in the country. The contemporary nickname for the *Khurramiyya* – '*surkh'jamigan*' or 'wearers of red' – was merely the icing on a historically convenient cake.[2]

Babak and his followers, however, were not the only revolutionary icons that were conjured from the past to fit Azerbaijan's 20th-century Communist present. A mysterious rebel group called the Mazdakites operated in pre-Muslim Sassanian Persia between the 5th and 6th centuries. Like the *Khurramiyya*, the Mazdakites were Zoroastrian. Their iconic priest leader, Mazdak, interpreted fire-worship in radical ways. Property was held in common. Meat was deemed unholy. Women were no longer beholden to enter polygamous marriages, as was otherwise standard Zoroastrian practice. The parallels, for Soviet historians at least, with Bolshevik visions of society are, once again, not difficult to trace.

Though short-lived when compared to that of the *Khurramiyyah*, the Mazdakite uprising differed in one important respect: the level of success. For a period, the Sassanid king Kavad forced Mazdak's egalitarian philosophies onto the Persian population at large. But people power, just as in the 21st century, made swift enemies at the top of society. Orthodox fire-worshipping priests opposed Mazdakism as a heretic contortion of Zoroastrianism. They conspired others to bring down Kavad and put his son on the throne. Pacifism and vegetarianism quickly lost their sheen. The egalitarian Mazdakites were violently suppressed.

In truth, both Azeri rebel patriot legends present jarring contradictions. In neither the 6th nor the 9th centuries, the periods when the Mazdakites and the *Khurramiyya* respectively operated, was Azerbaijan the entity it is today. As the stepping stone between several civilisations, a bewildering number of states and rulers have held sway over the Caucasus region. War has pushed migrants and invaders across shifting borders in the region. In the small space from the contested region of Nagorno-Karabakh, down through Georgia, Armenia and east to Baku and the Caspian Sea, hundreds of languages, tribal loyalties and religions overlap repeatedly.

Mazdak and Babak, moreover, were of Persian extraction. The dominant ethnicity in Azerbaijan today is Turkic, the direct result of Mongol invasions, which only swept south and west out of the Central Asian steppes from the 13th century onward. Azeris, therefore, are likely to share more common DNA with Anatolians and Seljuk Turkmen, than the old Sassanids of Persia from whom their rebel heroes are drawn.

Azeri Soviets historians, of course, are not solely responsible for bearing these rebels down to the present day. After all they were not the only claimants of the Mazdakite legacy. Ferdowsi, the Persian poet, wrote verses on the topic. Reza Shah, in pre-revolutionary Iran, used visions of the avenging *Khurramiyya* sword to strike fear into Shia clerics (unsuccessfully, it would turn out). Neither is this the first case of a historical figure's nationality or ethnic background jarring with the modern nation who chose him: Soviet leader Stalin was himself a product of the Caucasian ethnic melange. At the expense of outlying nationalities – his native Georgians included – he engaged in a chauvinistic promotion of all things Russian.

Back in the Baku of today, simplified portraits of Azeri nationalism clash with the complexity of history. Caspian pipelines deliver hefty chunks of European oil and gas. Ilham Aliyev, the mineral-enriched country's authoritarian ruler, would prefer not to mention either Babak's uprising, or

Mazdak's egalitarianism, *too* often. Not for him the Norwegian model of 90 per cent taxes on oil profits, social democracy and citizen choice. Here Azerbaijan shies away from Europe; the Middle Eastern model of perpetual dictatorship and wealth concentration will do just fine.

Neither do the recent Baku protests slot either side of the neat line drawn by media commentators in 2011 between the 'Arab Spring' on the one hand and, on the other, anti-austerity demonstrations in the USA, Greece, Spain and elsewhere. The former, it is said, demands democracy. The latter, we are told, are a result of the global recession and the debt crisis. But general economic woe and democratic deficiencies are not mutually exclusive. There are poverty-stricken ghettoes in Western countries just as there are greedy financial elites in the Middle East. The internal motivations of protestors should not always be presumed readable, nor immune to contradictions. Reporting that a protest has happened at all is more important than psychoanalysing its participants.

The few committed Azeri political activists who *do* brave the attentions of Aliyev's security forces by speaking out, might observe how even this minimal condition has not been met. There has been a focus by European media outlets, understandably enough, on the dramas of the Middle Eastern unrest. Yet that focus has obscured a wilful ignorance of simultaneous protests in countries with which the EU holds strategic arrangements, or, indeed, those taking place on European city squares. From politicians, the recent lack of criticism of unfree but mineral-rich Azerbaijan has been as deafening as it is understandable. Unrest there would be as painful for European energy consumers as it would be for the country's dictator.

Baku has always been an oil town, as it was in 1920 when it fell to the Soviet Union. Lenin did not conquer democratic

Azerbaijan in homage to Mazdak. The Bolshevik leadership recognised that securing oilfields would shore up their precipitous quest for survival against enemies both foreign and domestic. Hitler would have agreed. Between 1942 and 1943, at Stalingrad, one of the largest-scale battles ever fought represented Nazi Germany's attempt to gain access to Caucasian oilfields. Sixty-five years later, the EU is in a similar position. With the other sources of Europe's regular energy supply threatened by Middle Eastern unrest and Russian monopoly, not upsetting Azerbaijan's rulers has become a priority. Emphasising the country's European connections and downplaying pro-democratic revolutionary movements does no harm to mutual relations and energy contracts negotiations.

The Eurovision circus rolls into Baku in May 2012. The light entertainment extravaganza will be accompanied, no doubt, by a bandwagon of television crews and a slew of slickly produced films from the Azeri tourist board. It is doubtful whether appetites for real change or open minds will be included.

Another False Dmitri?
THE PUGACHEV REBELLION 1773-74

A riddle: identify the following two countries: both morphed from colony to intercontinental power within a few hundred years. Both expanded through hardy settlement of barren frontiers. Both have occupied the same piece of territory at different times. The answer, of course, is Russia and the USA. For longer than their leaders would like to admit, these giants have displayed a strange tendency to mirror each other's patterns of development. (The shared territory is, of course, Russian Alaska, whose bears and salmon 'turned yankee' for the bargain price of two cents an acre in 1868.)

The 1770s marks crucial revolutionary turning points for both. While thirteen colonies on the Atlantic seaboard made their bid for freedom, a large-scale peasant uprising convulsed Russia. Most of us know the outcome of the American Revolution. But the lesser-known Pugachev's Rebellion held similarly longstanding consequences for tsarist monarchs.

The community who headed the rebellion were Cossacks; a horse-riding, martial people who lived on Russia's hinterland. Russian princes had long been acquainted with the Cossacks. The 15th-century reign of Ivan III saw Muslim Mongol overlords cast off and the fate of nascent Russia, quite literally, married to that of Christianity itself.* Muscovy expanded from a small duchy to an early modern state. Settled on the riverbanks and steppes to the south, Christian Cossack communities

---

* Ivan III's second wife was the niece of the last emperor of fallen Constantinople. As a result, Russian patriots have envisioned, and continue to envision, Moscow as a 'Third Rome'; a bastion of the true faith.

acted as a natural bulwark against re-invasion by Mongols and other barbarian threats. To the west, Cossacks on the river Don in present-day Ukraine formed a similar barrier to hostile European kingdoms.

Cossacks could not always be controlled, however. Famine, invasion, disease and civil unrest beset Muscovy in the first half of the 17th century. The Razin Rebellion of 1649 broke out along Russia's southern and western Cossack frontiers. A driving force among rebels was 'usurpation': the conspiracy that the 'true tsar' had been replaced by an imposter. During the early-17th-century 'Time of Troubles', for example, no less than three claimants to the tsarist crown appeared in succession. All three were named Dmitri. All were supported by a different political faction.

The advent of usurpation is linked to the changing relationship between Cossacks and their religion. In the 1650s, the Eastern Orthodox Christian church had initiated wide-reaching reforms. Many Cossack communities rejected these changes, adhering instead to an unreformed version of prayer and procession. This branch of Orthodoxy called themselves the Old Believers. Their scripture, notably, reserved a special place for the concept of an Antichrist of flesh and blood, alive and abroad in the world. This tied in directly to the rumours of false tsars. From the mid-17th century onward, Old Believer Cossacks attached religious symbolism to unpopular leaders.

Tsar Alexis I became the first of those. It was during his reign that the status of unpaid peasants was set in law. Serfdom disproportionately affected the roaming Cossacks of southern Russia, tying them to a particular estate or lord. Alexis then placed reformed Orthodoxy – the antithesis of Old Believer belief – at the core of the imperial Russian state. From this point onward, Russian emperors could rely on a cult following among Orthodox Christians, as their political head and protector. Thus, during the reign of Alexis, Old Believer Cossacks became both political *and* religious dissidents.

This was the setting, in 1772, in which an illiterate army deserter landed among Cossack communities living along the Terek and Yaik river frontiers (near the present-day border between Russia and Kazakhstan). While there, Yemelian Ivanovich Pugachev noted the high levels of poverty and general discontent among local Cossacks. Encouraged by the ubiquity of 'false tsar' rumours, the old soldier tried his hand.

Pugachev presented himself to locals as the resurrected Tsar Peter III. Peter had been deposed and died in mysterious circumstances. Tsarina Catherine, later to become known as Catherine the Great, reigned in place of her husband. She was German-born and so held under suspicion by Cossacks. Her martyred husband, having introduced limited reform in the legal status of serfs, was held up as a quasi-supernatural protector.

Pugachev arrived at Yaitsk (modern Oral, in Kazakhstan) and learned about recent uprisings. A series of punitive measures from distant imperial authorities had pushed local Cossacks to the brink of revolt in the preceding years. The restriction of local fishing rights; Cossack conscription into the Imperial Army; and enforced beard-shaving (contrary to sacred Old Believer practice). The political grounds for rebellion were already fertile. The mysterious newcomer merely gave them focus.

With the local *ataman* (leader) deposed and exiled, Pugachev began to spread the story of his alternative personality, but was soon captured himself. Early subscribers to 'Tsar Peter' sprung him from prison. His resolve hardened by this show of support, Pugachev decided on rebellion. A 1773 manifesto promised loyal followers 'the river from the heights to the mouth, and land, and grasses, and money and lead and powder, and bread provisions'.[1]

Word spread. With little military expertise or hardware for conventional battle, Pugachev concentrated on building manpower and spreading propaganda. News decrying the Antichrist Tsarina and proclaiming 'Tsar Peter' the resurrected protector, along with the promise of food, land and redemption, combined to great effect in the restless Terek and Yaik Cossack regions. Mutinies among the irregularly paid, Cossack-manned garrisons in the locality delivered easy conquests. With mutiny came countless arms and thousands of soldiers.

Revolt spread beyond Cossack communities. The legend of an avenging 'Tsar Peter', aka Pugachev, gave voice to economic, ethnic and religious frustrations of all types. Sympathetic industrial workers in the town of Orenburg brought manufacturing capacity. Rebel recruitment was also successful among the Tatars, Chuvash and Bashkirs. These tribal groups, many of them Muslim, had only recently fallen under tsarist taxation and religious persecution. With early victories, the forces of rebellion began to resemble a real army. Plunder and taxation aided the formation of a military academy. Supporting characters commanding their own branches included: Kinzia Arslanov, leader of the Bashkirs; Andrei Ovchinnikov, a talented military tactician: and Afanasi 'Cracker' Sokolov, leader of the Orenburg industrial workers.

Pugachev himself continued to play the lost tsar, imposing strict imperial discipline while enjoying a personal bodyguard, young wife and lavish life at his court. With early success came bombast. 'Tsar Peter' took every chance to expound to listeners on his plans to impose an all-conquering Cossack regime on the world. Russia's actual rulers in distant St. Petersburg received events in the Urals with displeasure. Peasant unrest, however, was neither uncommon, nor the most pressing item on the imperial agenda.

Russia had been stretched by war with the Ottoman Empire for some five years. In 1773, the upper hand was finally gained against the Turks. More energy could be allotted to crushing Pugachev. Despite repeated efforts at rebuilding his forces, he had seen the siege at Yaitsk lifted and defeat at Troitski, right on the present-day border of Kazakhstan and Russia. His rebel forces did win a victory at Osa on the Kama river and momentum seemed to have been regained when a frontal attack on Kazan was successful. However, imperial reinforcements from the Ottoman frontier ejected the rebels from Kazan and repulsed several more attacks.

With an Ottoman peace treaty signed in 1774, the full weight of imperial might was felt by the rebels for the first time. At the same time, Pugachev committed a string of fatal errors. His forces turned south after crossing the river Volga at Kazan, eschewing the chance to escalate rebellion towards European Russia. The rebels began to avoid military targets, attacking instead the prosperous towns and estates along the Volga. The imperial forces, however, inflicted a heavy defeat on Pugachev at Tsaritsyn in early 1774, killing thousands of rebel soldiers and signalling a final devastation of their scattered army. Later the same year, his 'kingdom' dispersed, Pugachev fell victim to the huge bounty offered for his capture. He found himself bound for a parade through Moscow, followed by trial and a gory execution.

In the aftermath, Cossack regions saw a mixture of reprisal and reform. Towns which had most enthusiastically assisted the rebellion suffered greatly. Rebel leaders were rounded up and executed. However, Catherine's later reputation as an 'enlightened despot' stems in part from her reaction in the Cossack lands. Given the scale of the uprising, the killings were limited. Army violence was tempered by amnesties, lowered commodity prices and the elimination of certain taxes. The rebellion's outcome encouraged the Tsarina to more rigorously organise her frontiers, with a system of smaller province boundaries and elected officials. In the same vein, Muslims were no longer forcibly converted and conditions for industrial workers improved.

Pugachev's Rebellion is not an isolated event in European history. The slow and painful transformations which brought feudal societies into the modern industrial age bombarded peasant communities with devastating change. Where the human and material costs proved unacceptable, and given the means to do so, violent revolt was the result. Certain events – the 1525 German Peasants' War and the Peasants' Revolt in 14th-century England (see *Summer in the City*, p 130) – were organised, sustained and unlimited to one class or ethnicity. Countless other peasant uprisings were minor affairs; swiftly suppressed and consigned to the dustbin of history.

Pugachev's rebellion, having involved tens of thousands of soldiers and briefly threatened European Russia, ranks toward the higher end of the scale. The would-be tsar joins Stenka Razin and Bohdan Khmelnytsky as the last in a series of three major 17th- and 18th-century Russian rebel peasant leaders. They shared much. Their rebellions all originated in expansions of Russian state power over its people. All had focused on tension between centre and periphery. All had ended with a redefinition of that crucial relationship.

This tradition continued in the 1770s. 'Schismatics', as Old Believers were pejoratively labelled by the rest of Orthodoxy, became a minority within their own religion. Their perceived honour and faith, allied to a legacy of poverty and banishment, linked Old Believers in later artistic imaginations to an ancient and truer sense of the Russian nation. Dostoevsky made use of their image of political marginalisation. He named his anti-hero in *Crime and Punishment* 'Raskolnikov'; from the Russian version of 'schismatic' *(raskolniki)*. Nicolas Roerich used his impression of pre-modern rural Russia to style the 20th century's most scandalous artistic performance: Diaghelev and Stravinsky's 1913 *Rites of Spring*.

The cult of the tsars grew with the wealth and power of imperial Russia. The 19th-century tsars from the Romanov dynasty became embedded in Orthodox mythology. Assassinations carried out by godless revolutionaries – of Alexander II in 1881; of the entire family of Nicholas II in 1918 – only augmented the process. Pretenders claiming inheritance to the Romanov dynasty emerged throughout the 20th century. None mustered the following of Pugachev.

Meanwhile, Cossack identity has become fused with that of Russia. Cossack cavalry, officers and border guards led the establishment of Siberia and the consolidation of Russia as a major 19th-century European power. With the preponderance of fur hats, brightly dyed robes and gymnastic folk dances in popular depictions, the gap between Russian and Cossack cultures is now indistinguishable. Antichrist, husband-murderer, or otherwise, Catherine's reforms drew Cossacks closer to the heart of imperial Russia. They would never again attempt to break the connection with such conviction, or in such numbers.

The Liberator's Liberator
GRAN COLOMBIA 1820S

Nature, or Pacha Mama, where life is reproduced and occurs, has
the right to integral respect for its existence and for the mainte-
nance and regeneration of its life cycles, structure, functions and
evolutionary processes.

That's Chapter III, Article 71 of the current Ecuadorian constitution. In 2008, these lines became the first of any national
constitution on earth to provide for the legal rights of nature.

This small, otherwise innocuous South American state can
boast a surprising number of such historical landmarks. It was
the Galapagos Island finches, after all, which helped Charles
Darwin develop his theory of evolution. In 1929 Ecuadorian
women became the first on their continent to obtain the
right to vote. And some hundred years previous, Ecuador
proclaimed its freedom from Spain before any other South
American country.

However, it's the meeting of two legendary revolutionary leaders in the current Ecuadorian city of Guayaquil that
crowns the country's record of political mavericks and marks
the true dawn of the independence era for South America. The
year was 1822. Though they had never previously met, José
de San Martín and Símon Bolívar were long-time allies, celebrating joint victory over common enemies at the close of an
odyssean revolutionary war.

San Martín had marched 5,000 troops from his native
Buenos Aires across the Andean mountain range to win

Chilean independence from the control of the Spanish king. Successfully establishing Chile, San Martín had then fought his way north, partially liberating Peru and entering present-day Ecuador. Bolívar had been fighting the same monarchist forces since 1809. Starting at the opposite end of the continent, his army united the disparate forces of independence in the huge Spanish vice-royalty of New Granada (comprising much of the north-western part of present-day South America).

After winning his revolutionary war, Bolívar had renamed New Granada, Gran Colombia. He became the new state's first leader, publishing for it a progressive liberal constitution. The new laws ended slavery, handed freedom to the press and gave citizenship and suffrage to blacks and native Indians. By the time of his commune with San Martín, who soon after retired to Europe, Bolívar felt his informal but universal title of 'The Liberator' was justified.

But before settling into presidential life, Bolívar ran into a problem: he fell in love. Manuela Sáenz, a vivacious member of Ecuador's *Creole* elite, began a passionate affair with the victorious general after meeting him at a ball. Sáenz was from a rich, local family but held roots in peninsular Spain. She had been the product of a brief and ungodly union, so colonial etiquette dictated her father was not expected to acknowledge nor support her. He did both. Sáenz received a privileged convent education followed briskly by marriage to an older man. Sedate city life with Englishman James Thorne, however, did not appeal to this lover of horsemanship, drama and high political intrigue.

She left her husband and, even before encountering Bolívar, had become politically active. She ran an informal espionage network amid the revolutionary fervour swirling across New Granada. After their meeting, 'The Liberator' had been forced to fight on, stamping out remnants of royalist resistance in Peru and Bolivia. And so Sáenz's relationship with Bolívar largely remained one of yearning; based on long-distance letters and snatched encounters.

While she awaited her lover, Sáenz was far from the model of feminine passivity. She energetically promoted the cause of Gran Colombia, defending Bolívar from detractors. Sáenz was not the pliant mistress of South American tradition ('The Liberator' had already enjoyed enough of those while campaigning anyway). Her political instincts remained sharp and spirited, even after settling down with Bolívar in the Gran Colombian capital, Bogotá, in 1827.

Warranted or not, it was a period later used to attach to the reputation of Sáenz a certain predilection for wild behaviour. She faithfully, and sometimes violently, protected Bolívar. The most prominent legend – that Sáenz saved Bolívar's life from assassins – is true. On the night of September 25th 1828, clasping a sword and still in her nightclothes, she diverted a group of assassins for long enough that her lover could make his not-so-presidential escape from a bedroom window.

The attempt on Bolívar's life had come as a result of the growing fragility of Gran Colombia. Well-versed in political theory and history, 'The Liberator' had originally conceived of the new country as a Latin American version of the USA: liberal, democratic and uniting several states under a federal umbrella. But former allies did not share the vision. The *criollo*, *llanero* and *pardo* factions which had fought together so effectively to achieve independence, peeled away as the 1820s wore on.

Gran Colombia's continued existence relied on Bolívar as figurehead and enforcer. More committed to the security of its immediate future than its liberal constitution, however, he increasingly used dictatorial powers to bind quarrelling factions together. Bolívar's last years revealed a sad irony: the man known as 'The Liberator' had become a despot, little different to the monarchs he had spent his life battling. Under stress from Ecuadorian interests and Venezuelan separatists, Bolívar's Gran Colombian dream died with him. It split apart only months after he passed away in December 1830, far from Sáenz. The quote on Bolívar's gravestone reveals his awareness of the failure of his great pan-American project: 'All who served the Revolution have plowed the sea.'

The myths surrounding Sáenz, drawn from the drama of this period, are many. There is dispute over whether she followed Bolívar on an arduous military march in 1824. At its end, conflicting reports alternately pin the Ecuadorian revolutionary fighting on the field of battle at Ayacucho, or hundreds of miles away back in Lima. She is alleged to have had an affair with one of Bolívar's generals; to have sported a military uniform in public; to have ridden into a barracks brandishing a pistol, in an attempt to halt a mutiny. Accusations abound of heavy drinking, swearing and smoking. The explanations offered by various historians for unladylike behaviour have ranged from nymphomania, to lesbianism, to the genes of her Spanish grandparents.

Few are convincing. Most negative reports emerge from hostile contemporary sources. Faithful accompaniment of such a powerful and divisive figure as Bolívar is partly to blame. However, with no lack of opinions, nor the bravery to voice them, Sáenz was more than able to create enemies for herself. The dominant vision of womanhood in the Latin America of her day – submissive, unopinionated and committed to marriage and home-building – did little for the reputation of such a forthright personality.

This reflects a more general tendency to position women rebels behind their macho comrades. Aleida March, for example, commonly emerges from the mists of the Cuban Revolution on 'Che' Guevara's arm, rather than as the accomplished guerrilla fighter and spy she was in her own right. Rosa Luxemburg, leader of the failed Berlin Decembrist Revolution in 1919, is better known for her premature and violent death than for her ideas or actions.

Neither has the sexist streak been banished. A male writer introduced news website *Daily Beast* readers to Camila Vallejo, the leader of Chile's 2011 student protests:

> With soft green eyes, a silver nose ring, and 63,000 fans on Facebook, the Santiago-born student leader would be a better fit on the catwalks than at the barricades.[1]

The simplest explanation for the chauvinist attitudes is that journalists and historians have always been, like revolutionaries, overwhelmingly male. In fact, Latin American women have long trailed men in all public roles. Though influential matriarchs are common within the bounds of families, in creative spheres and on a local level, war and politics have traditionally been the realm of the male. Even today, deep runs the current of Catholic social teaching and the *caudillo*; the political strongman, or 'big boss'. When prominent female political leaders *have* emerged in modern times, it has most often been as widows. Both prominent examples are Argentine: Evita Perón the most famous; Cristina Fernández de Kirchner the most contemporary.

Both the study of Sáenz as a pioneering female and the practice of Bolívarian pan-Americanism have enjoyed a resurgence in recent years. In 2005 the authors of a US-published political textbook on Latin America gave their outlook for the continent:

> The peoples of Latin America have turned away from utopian ideologies towards practical efforts at the grassroots level... Almost everywhere, neo-liberal policies prevail.[2]

The timing of such a declarative statement could not have been worse. Beginning with the election of Venezuelan president Hugo Chávez in 2004, a wave of socialist and left-leaning governments have arrived at and then consolidated, a hold on power. Evo Morales became the first indigenous Bolivan to lead his country in 2006. Nestor Kirchner (Cristina's predecessor) of Argentina and Luiz Inácio 'Lula' Da Silva of Brazil, though less expressly socialist, have plainly voiced their opposition to neo-liberal economic measures imposed by the IMF and US-backed corporate interests. The resemblances to Bolívar is not accidental. Chávez and Morales have paid explicit homage to 'The Liberator'.

Fittingly, a prominent member of this new generation of South Americans is Ecuadorian. Since his election in 2006, the presidency of Rafael Correa has attained notoriety for more than his ecological constitutional clause. He has aligned Ecuador with neighbouring Latin American and Caribbean states – the 'Bolivarian Alliance for the Peoples of Our Americas' – and launched verbal broadsides against *imperialismo* in the hemisphere. Measures to counteract the freedom of the press, presumably designed to avoid the end which befell Gran Colombia, suggest more than a touch of Bolívar's despotic leanings.

As for Sáenz, the record of her later life was quite empty until recently. Her political force field was removed by Bolívar's demise and, left without allies in either Bogotá or her native city of Quito, Sáenz was indicted for 'criminal and subversive' activities, then exiled. Forced to live out her days in the remote Peruvian border town of Paita, she nonetheless continued in political activism. Sáenz met the Italian national hero Garibaldi and offered counsel to Ecuador's first president, Juan José Flores.

'The Liberator's Liberator' died in 1856. Thanks to the work of dedicated biographers and regional feminist groups, however, Sáenz has since emerged as one of history's more celebrated female resistance leaders. President Chávez had her remains exhumed and placed alongside that of Simon Bolívar in Venezuela in 2010. The reclamation of her historical reputation is the first, hopeful sign of a change in the most common method of depicting political participation and leadership by radical females.

Heaven on Earth
Taiping Rebellion 1850–61

The questions I have to ask are these –

You nations having worshipped God for so long a time, does any one among you know,

1. How tall God is, or how broad?
2. What his appearance or colour is?
3. How large his abdomen is?
4. What kind of beard he grows?[1]

So begins an extraordinary diplomatic correspondence. The captain of the British ship *Rattler*, anchored on the Yangtze river in China, is the startled recipient; the East King of the Taiping Heavenly Kingdom, the curious sender. At the time he wrote, in June 1854, the East King was Yang Xiuqing, second-in-command of a fully-functioning theocratic state in central and southern China. It had been established by the banding together of several rebel groups against the ineffectual Qing state, consolidated by an unending appetite for war and eventually felled by decisive foreign intervention.

It had been a vision by one man which first gave the Taiping rebellion life. Hong Xiuquan was a bright but frustrated young man, living in Guangdong, in southern China in the 1830s. Having failed the state civil service exams for the second and last time, he arrived home to his parents' small farm and fell into a feverous coma. As Hong would later relate, he encountered God and Jesus in the dream that followed. They gave him strict instructions to return to earth and do battle with 'demon devils'. Hong awoke and obeyed. By 1843, he had developed an evangelical version of Christianity. Along with a set of early converts amongst his family and friends, the self-appointed Heavenly King began to spread his beliefs locally.

Hong based his Heavenly Kingdom on an eccentric translation of biblical tracts. This he had been given by unidentified Christian preachers, operating in and around coastal Guangdong. Largely foreign-born, these hardy men were segregated from normal Chinese people by law. Nevertheless, they proselytised up the coastline and into China's vast, pagan interior, often sporting the silken-robed disguise and wooden shoes of a Chinese trader; the only way to avoid the capture and destruction of their biblical cargo.

By the time Hong was finalising the rituals of his minor sect, sometime around 1844, hostility to Christians on a local level was still in effect. Hong Xiuquan and his early converts of 'God-worshippers' were Hakka, bringing the concerns of a sidelined ethnic minority into line with the resentments of a stigmatised religion. The God-worshippers' zealous destruction of local idols and shrines in Guangxi resulted in harassment from government officials, militia and local landlords. This in turn forced Hong's followers to arm themselves. Their view of the ruling Qing as the same 'demon devils' from Hong's vision manifested itself in the ordinations reportedly sent down from 'Heavenly Brother' Jesus himself:

> All you young brothers must observe the Heavenly Commandments, must obey orders, must be harmonious with your brethren, must not enter villages to plunder. In fighting you should never withdraw from the field of battle; if you find money you should not keep it for yourself, but turn it over to the public treasury...[2]

Before 1850, the demesne of the 'Heavenly King' was a few backwater congregations. During that year, the Taiping rebellion leaders for the first time related to their faithful in military terms. Baptisms began to number in the thousands, rather than in dozens. By the end of 1850, Hong could challenge and defeat a Qing army in the first battle of the rebellion, at Jintian. What had transformed the Heavenly Kingdom in the interim?

The First Opium War had spurred the Taiping rebellion on a basic level. Its result had been an utter humiliation for the Qing dynasty. Their navy annihilated, they were impotent to stem the deadly poppy crop with which the British flooded the Chinese market. This served only to enhance their already widespread unpopularity. Corruption was perceived to be rife. A succession of natural disasters had ruined crop harvests and overshadowed the dynasty's claimed 'mandate of heaven'. Race also played a factor. The Qing rulers were ethnically Manchu while their imperial subjects were overwhelmingly Han.

British campaigns against local pirates operating around Hong Kong forced the bandits to move up southern China's wide rivers and mountain passes. In these lands, where Hong was busy baptising and fending off the 'demon devils', pirate junks intermingled with existing river bandits and anti-Qing secret societies, such as the Heaven and Earth Society. Bandits, ex-pirates and restless outlaw groups of different types began to slowly unite under the Taiping rebellion banner.

Conventional conflict had, however, stretched the resources of the rebel community in Guangxi to breaking point. The leadership opted to break through the Qing forces, who had by this point encircled the rebels, and march north. From the perspective of China's Qing rulers, this 1,000-mile migration, marked by both rampaging battles and mass recruitment to the holy cause, transformed the Heavenly Kingdom from a regional annoyance, to a genuinely national threat. It halted at the walls of Nanking, on the Yangtze river in Anhui province. A successful battle for the large city confirmed it as the base from which the rebellion could consolidate its swiftly won gains.

By 1851, Hong Xiuquan, only years before a failed civil service student, controlled a territory containing approximately 30 million people. He had moulded a personal religious vision, first into a guerrilla conflict, then into full-blown civil war. The large and important river trading city of Nanking, the entire upper Yangtze river, and Guangxi, parts of Guangdong, Hunan and Anhui provinces now fell under his generals' control.

In these areas, the Heavenly Kingdom's holy laws came into effect. These exhibited a curious mixture of Old Testament puritanism, Confucian traditions and the erratic personal preferences of its leaders. The binding of women's feet, for example, was outlawed (a common practice within Hakka communities from which the elite were exclusively drawn). Free commerce was severely restricted. Property was held in common by the state. The nickname of 'long hairs' for Taiping soldiers was a reference to the ubiquitous unplaited hairstyle (itself a rebellious act in itself, against the legally enforced Qing shave-and-plait).

Despite the restrictions on normal life, upper tiers of the Heavenly Kingdom took on many vestiges of dynastic imperial life. Hong Xiuquan and his fellow kings, for instance, enjoyed multiple concubines, despite the puritan ban outside palace walls on all forms of sexual intercourse (even between married couples). The merest suggestion of dissent resulted in capital punishment. Beheading was the executionary method of choice, though the horror of 'slow dismemberment' was not unknown for crimes of treason or blasphemy.

Believers or not; rich or poor; the tens of millions living within, or close to, the shifting confines of the Heavenly

Kingdom could do little to escape the harsh realities which both puritan religious law and widespread armed rebellion brought. A young man from a similar geographic and social background to Hong Xiuquan, writing after the chaos had ended, tells of the grief of a group of his acquaintances when news of the capture of a nearby city arrived:

> Some looked at the clouds and wept for their home fields, some faced their food and worried about their wives and children. Normally we would conceal our feelings in our words and faces, our hearts deep as wells; but at this point... one could see their innermost hearts. This is what is called to see people in extremity.[3]

Throughout their decade of rule, Taiping forces never ceased fighting. Whether advancing in conquest or defending entrenched positions, the net effect for the civilian was the same: food became scarce, mobility difficult and famine common. Like a latter-day televangelist, the enrobed Hong Xiuquan issued proclamations from the banqueting table of his richly decorated Nanking palace, inducing followers to sacrifice their property and produce to common grain stores.

Whether or not donations were forthcoming, armies of either side appropriated what they could. Little mercy was displayed to civilians caught up in fighting. Captured cities had resident populations purged and strategically vulnerable residences outside the perimeter walls burned. When armies retreated from an area, they destroyed any resources thought valuable, doing their best to surrender as few precious assets as possible to the Qing enemy. Regardless of responsibility, and taking into account the impossibility of achieving exactness in such calculations, the casualty figures for Taiping territories from 1850 to 1864 reach into the multi-millions, finding their only close rivals in the 20th-century world wars.[4]

How foreign powers came to view the Taiping rebellion is of crucial importance to its final failure. Confidence in the ruling Qing was almost as brittle in London and Paris as among the Chinese themselves. The Opium Wars are only the most obvious evidence of this. Early contact between the court of Hong Xiuquan and the diplomats sent up the Yangtze by Britain and France show that the foreigners were at least open to exploring dialogue with the now established rebels.

However, Christian fraternity, if that is what the Europeans expected, was unforthcoming. Hong Xiuquan and his kings either rejected or misunderstood the language of international negotiation. Taiping armies poured eastward in an attempt to overcome Shanghai, the site of not only a great metropolitan trading centre but significant overseas investment. Now it was the foreign powers whose interests were vitally threatened and who pursued directly the rebellion's destruction.

After the utter failure of the Taiping's Shanghai offensive in 1860, Hong Xiuquan found himself facing both domestic and foreign-led forces. The 'Ever-Triumphant' and 'Ever-Victorious' sections of the besieging Qing armies were staffed by Chinese soldiers, but armed and officered by the British and French.

In a bizarre inversion of the spirit of Marie Antoinette, Hong Xiuquan succumbed to food poisoning in 1861, after demonstrating in person how the starving residents of Nanking should eat weeds to combat famine. He only just outlived his fiefdom. The bloody capture of the city by the Qing lay close ahead, with its most stubborn and remotely located generals' final surrender in 1864.

Though the Qing outlived the Heavenly Kingdom of Hong Xiuquan, the Taiping rebellion stands alongside the Opium

Wars as a modern marker for the beginning of dynastic China's modern implosion. It acted as an immediate precursor to the northern Nien and south-western Muslim rebellions, and as a distant echo of the various 20th-century revolutions which would signal the country's slow resurgence.

The role of Guangdong as a source of rebellious elements is still a live issue, with prominent and violent riots occurring there throughout 2011. Internationally, Taiping was not unique as a divinely inspired Christian rebellion. The Shimabara cult had found their glorious martyrdom in a similarly closed 17th-century Japan. The successful suppression of the popular Cathar movement in 13th-century Languedoc was a founding pillar of the France we know today.

More contemporary comparisons are plentiful. From the theocratic Iranian revolutionary regime, to the infiltration of Islamists to the core of the Pakistani security apparatus, to the domination of US political debate and foreign policy decision-making by both evangelical Christians and the Zionist lobby, the world still struggles with the influence of religious extremism and millennialism over politics.

Religion is officially outlawed in today's China, suggesting Communist party leaders have learned from the lesson of the Taiping rebellion. Iconoclasts of the Falun Gong and Free Tibet movements are publically castigated, then subverted by state-sponsored alternatives. The more incendiary Buddhist and Muslim-based revolts met brute force, in Tibet (2008) and Xinjiang (2009) respectively. Marx's 'opium of the masses' is as contentious a political subject in today's China as in the days of the real opium wars and the doomed realm of the Heavenly Brothers.

History's Absolution
CUBA 1959

Ernesto 'Che' Guevara published *Guerrilla Warfare* in 1960, twelve months after his victory march into Havana. Three simple bullet points sum up neatly the ruthlessness he and his ragged comrades had applied in pitching their youthful, lightly trained soldiers against an entire army:

1. Popular forces can win a war against the army.
2. It is not necessary to wait until all conditions for making revolution exist; the insurrection can create them.
3. In underdeveloped Latin America, the armed struggle should be fought mostly in the countryside.[1]

As a soldier, Guevara became the stuff of revolutionary legend. As a martyr, his image has settled into Cuban popular folklore and reached activists around the world. Conversely, the obduracy of his revolutionary comrades in surviving to the 21st century has left their image tarnished.

Guevara was born in Argentina, to an aristocratic family of Spanish and Irish lineage, far from the peasant smallholdings of Cuba. He trained in medicine and travelled South and Central America as a young man. Touched by the poverty in which most people lived, Guevara became committed to transforming society by revolutionary means. The militant young Argentine's appetite for rebellion had been whetted while volunteering in Guatemala. He first met the Castro brothers, Fidel and Raúl, in Mexico in 1955. Having already served prison sentences for their assault on the Moncada army barracks in

Santiago de Cuba two years previously, they must have seemed seasoned veterans.

Cuba at the time was governed by Fulgencio Batista, a repressive dictator intolerant of democracy or reform. US sugar, oil, mining, tourism and gambling industries had invested significantly in Cuba in the preceding decades. This process had accelerated during the Batista presidency. American-manufactured guns, jeeps and planes armoured the trigger-happy regime and the US navy maintained a base at Guantánamo Bay in the south-east (as it does to this day).

Fidel, the elder Castro brother, was organising a new force of insurgents to liberate Cuba from the Batista regime. As a recruit, Guevara fitted the bill. Good-natured, well-travelled, he was also a qualified doctor, a multilinguist and a committed radical. A natural talent at soldiery and qualities in leadership would emerge later. 'Che', as his comrades came to call him, accepted the medic's role on Fidel's expedition without hesitation.

So it was that Guevara found himself among a squadron of 82 lightly armed guerrillas, landing on the isolated south-western tip of Cuba in late 1956. The omens were not good. Batista's army was forewarned, scattering the rebels in a hail of gunfire. For the dozen that survived this early onslaught, the Sierra Maestra mountains offered sanctuary. Its rugged terrain hid tracks. Its thick tropical foliage camouflaged camps. Its *guajiro* peasants could be leaned on for food and new recruits.

In return, the rebels offered promise of a new Cuba. Gone would be political repression, illiteracy, racism and disease. The persistent and unmasked meddling of Havana's powerful American neighbour would also be consigned to the past. Guevara, his skills having been recognised with a command post, began the process of communicating this vision of a brave new world. On condition of cooperation, locals and recruits received his medical treatment and political education for free. The roughly 10,000 cattle which the rebels 'liberated' from rich *latifundia* estates and redistributed among the *guajiro* population must also have helped to convince them.[2]

The rebels remained in the mountainous region for eighteen months. Most of this time was spent on the defensive. Any attacks were directed at local army camps, or isolated Cuban army patrols. Low rebel numbers and lack of arms necessitated this ambush style of attack. With some victories under their belt, Guevara led the guerrillas further from the foothills, directed by Fidel Castro at base camp. Entering the paddy fields, banana groves and sugar plantations surrounding the Sierra Maestra, a message of liberation advanced ahead. A bush telegraph system (*Radio Bemba*), radio broadcasts (*Radio Rebelde*) and newspapers (*Revolución, Bohemia*), all helped alert sympathy among local peasants and strike fear into the increasingly divided and demoralised army ranks.

The CIA wavered in its support for Batista but remained wary of communist infiltration of the rebel entity. Farther afield, the late 1950s had seen the cold war reach fever pitch. Ideologically charged conflicts broke out in Iran, Vietnam and Guatemala. The last thing that the USA wanted was a new battlefield with Soviet Russia on its doorstep. Political ambiguity was a skill at which the rebels excelled. The 1957 Sierra Maestra Manifesto, for example, made the first public call by several allied opposition groups for an end to Batista's rule. What would replace it was not portrayed in detail: the rebels had ensured that the text sidestepped political commitments. Chance too, played a part. A fawning *New York Times* interview with Fidel Castro was published the day that Batista lifted foreign press censorship, bolstering Castro's reputation outside Cuba and legitimacy within.

Of course, Guevara and the *ejército rebelde* did not lead all opposition. The bloodily authoritarian Batista regime's one success, aside from longevity, was in making enemies. The former president, whom Batista had sent into exile in 1952, Carlos Prío Socarrás, plied various opposition groups with funds. Police brutality helped turn many educated, prosperous and normally politically moderate Cubans against the regime. Another opposition grouping, the 'July 26' movement, which was born of the earlier attack on the Moncada barracks, counted Castro and Guevara as allies. But this alliance splintered as the guerrillas gained ground and began, increasingly, to ignore the 'July 26' movement's dictats.

The outlawed Cuban Communist party, or PSP, found influence among unions. It helped supply the rebels, maintaining ever closer contact with Guevara and Raúl Castro, the two most committed socialists among the guerrilla leadership. Using this new source of support and taking advantage of Batista's disarray, Guevara led rebel columns out of the Sierra Maestra mountains in the autumn of 1958. Fighting their way north up the flat, central plains of the island, the group met with popular support and other armed groups as they went. By December, Guevara had conquered Cuba's second city, Santa Clara.

Batista panicked. In the early hours of New Year's Day 1959, his family and top brass fled the country. The rebels entered the capital city, Havana, in triumph. In an effort to court, or at least confuse, American government thinking, Castro installed prominent anti-Communists, Harvard graduates and political moderates in the new cabinet and across state agencies. The radical opinions of Guevara, meanwhile, were far from invisible. His task was to try war criminals and purge the Cuban military of Batista loyalists.

The pretence at non-alignment could not last long. In 1960, using laws drafted by Guevara, revolutionary Cuba seized thousands of acres of private property, most notably that owned by US individuals and corporations. The USSR could only afford to maintain a safe distance from such a thorn in its opponents' side for so long. Guevara had been sent on secret diplomatic missions to meet Soviet officials, after which Kremlin interaction in the Cuban regime increased steeply.

After that point, radicals took centre stage. Moderates resigned or were levered from government. Fidel Castro assumed the presidency, 'Che' Guevara took charge of economic reform, with Raúl Castro heading the armed forces. Krushchev, the Soviet leader, committed to buy the by-now nationalised sugar exports which Kennedy had already rejected. US-led arms and trade embargos followed. While uncertainty exists over the depth of KGB operations in the new government, Eastern Bloc-manufactured military hardware was sold to Cuba from an early stage. Soviet ballistic missiles were being shipped to Cuba within eighteen months of rebel victory. The resultant nuclear face-off in October 1962 – the Cuban Missile Crisis – underlined how high the stakes were that Castro and his band of former mountain guerrillas were now playing for.

No less dramatic change was happening domestically. As the government nationalised church property, ejected clergy and secularised education, Cubans were given new idols to worship. Veneration of rebel leaders took on quasi-religious qualities. Criticism of government policies was slowed to a crawl by blanket media censorship. The *contrarevolucionario* label became as dangerous as that of *fidelista* had been under Batista, with regular use of the death sentence for plotters. The revolution's various martyrs acquired mythic status to an equal degree: Antonio Maceo and José Martí, the 19th-century strugglers for independence from Spain; Camilo Cienfuegos and Frank País, casualties of the guerrilla campaign.

Not least of the Cuban martyrs is Guevara himself. Unable to settle into a cosy domestic existence, 'Che' was convinced of the pressing need to export guerrilla-led Marxist revolution to the developing world. Africa was his first choice. A disastrous period in the Congo was followed by frustration, capture and execution in the mountains of Bolivia. Guevara's ugly death, however, was merely the beginning of his wider fame.

The image of his stoic gaze, *Guerrillero Heróico*, was first captured at a rally in Havana in 1960. Today it adorns flags, graphic prints, murals and statues from Belfast to Caracas. His enduring creed of *Hasta la victoria siempre* ('Until the Everlasting Victory') does not adorn political causes alone, however. Consumer products and Hollywood movies have led efforts to gloss over his more extreme opinions and actions.

The lasting legacy of Fidel is harder to judge. Much of the benefits of the revolution he led have come at a bitter price. Economic reliance on the US came to be replaced, in time, by subservience to the Soviet Union. When that Goliath collapsed in 1991, the resulting currency shortfalls, food rationing and infrastructural problems became chronic. The hard lessons learnt fighting in the Sierra Maestra mountains led to often brutal justice for criminals, *chivato* informers and virtually any outspoken opposition to Castro's ironclad leadership.

As leader, responsibility for the lack of transparency and civil rights since 1959 falls squarely at Fidel's feet. The Cuban people, to whom elections and reform have been promised for many decades, have not been given a chance to express such opinions at the ballot box. Hundreds of thousands have instead voted with their feet, with Florida's Cuban-exile community as populous as ever.

The guerrilla war did produce some positives. Blindness to ethnicity, for example, became a major asset among a predominantly black or mixed race peasant population, well accustomed to entrenched racial prejudice. A focus on providing basic health and education, originally forged among the Sierra Maestra *guajiros*, is still in evidence in the Cuba of today. Revolutionary Cuba, by almost any comparison a small and poor country, has boasted universal health and education systems which put many richer countries to shame. Literacy and average life expectancy levels regularly outstrip that of a certain northern neighbour. The collapse in Soviet oil supplies in the early 1990s has inspired radical environmental policies which could serve as a lesson to a world hungry for alternatives to fossil fuels.

2011 saw Comrade Fidel Castro move further from the spotlight. President Raúl Castro joined an exclusive club of octogenarian world leaders. Alongside the portraits of Ernesto 'Che' Guevara and busts of José Martí, were erected new totems: posters in support of the 'Cuban Five', jailed in Florida in 2005 for espionage; speeches of Evo Morales and César Chávez, new heroes of the revolutionary left in Latin America. Misty evocations of the heroic revolution, however, do not move young Cubans as much as regular electricity blackouts and a lack of political freedoms. Major change seems unavoidable upon the Castros' demise. Only time will reveal the identity of Cuba's new heroes, martyrs and despots.

Just Violence, Radical Peace

In early 1989, with open calls for representation already having been made in the Baltic, the Soviet Union attempted elections to a newly democratised Congress of People's Deputies. The results seemed to affirm Mikhail Gorbachev's reform programme: his Communist Party won 87 per cent of the seats available, an impressive figure on first glance.[1] Back in 1849, Frederick Augustus II saw little need for such niceties when his people demanded a parliament. The Saxon king called on Prussian troops to crush the Dresden uprising.

Yet Gorbachev, in spite of reform, was still an authoritarian leader in the mould of Frederick Augustus. The Communists had pre-selected candidates for the 1989 Soviet election. In reality, they had only won around a quarter of the popular vote. With no free press to satisfy, nor higher international powers to impress, why had the party bothered with such plainly fabricated elections?

Universal electoral democracy in the late 1840s was an extreme political position to hold. Its few radical proponents could not speak about their cause in public. By 1989, a political earthquake hit the Soviet Union, but not of the type sought by the Communists in Moscow. In a succession of popular uprisings, Eastern European men and women voted with their feet. Half a dozen new democracies arose and Gorbachev, to his credit, did not order in the Soviet tanks. The revolutions remained largely peaceful. This chapter sets out to investigate how extreme cases of revolutionary violence and peace have changed the world's perceptions of people power.

A government which derives power from its population is expected to provide essential services and offer protection from threats. Twenty-first-century democratic politicians, for example, deal in manifestos and mandates. Before an election, a set of promises are laid in front of the electorate. Afterward, the winner claims popular justification to carry those promises to fruition (even if that process never actually comes about).

Leaders, however, have put such justification to many uses. From 1952–60, for example, the British government detained tens of thousands of native colonial subjects for questioning across Kenya in the wake of a series of attacks by extremists. The Mau Mau movement had indeed employed murder, rape and atrocities to voice opposition to British and white settler power. Back in London, politicians and press used shocking – and sometimes blatantly false – details of Mau Mau crimes to arouse support for a network of camps where suspects could be interrogated and movement could be controlled. The true extent of violence instituted against native Kenyans, whether proven Mau Mau or not, has yet to be revealed.

By contrast, legitimacy has long been conferred on revolutionary violence by politicians. During the French

Revolution, the storming of the Bastille in Paris was initially denounced by the National Assembly, sitting in session in distant Versailles. But as the effects of the victory began to materialise, it became, 'imperative' for the Assembly members 'to embrace the violence as a foundation of their own authority'.[2] While later violence was castigated, the storming of the Bastille became a sacred symbol of French freedom, elevated above normal violent crime by the endorsement of officialdom.

Legitimacy in China's 9th-century Tang dynasty became an increasingly elastic concept. The Mandate of Heaven slipped from a corrupt central court and was contested by a century and a half of revolutionary violence on the empire's periphery. Rather akin to the experience of Gorbachev and the Soviet Union a millennium later, a great imperium's fall – whether violent or peaceful – is signposted for a long time beforehand.

Within a modern democracy, however, political violence is much rarer. With barricades and rocks not an option in democratic, developed countries, 21st-century activists draw on past rebels who have achieved success through peaceful means. Mahatma Gandhi's teachings of mass civil disobedience have found students beyond their immediate setting in pre-1947 colonial India. UK Uncut highlight corporate tax-avoidance by setting up impromptu classrooms in banks and shopping centres.

Other innovations in peaceful revolution are born of necessity and ingenuity. When New York banned the Occupy Wall Street demos from using loudspeakers in 2011, protesters responded with the 'human microphone':

a 'callback' public address system powered by vocal chords alone. This is protest informed by Gandhi and other pacifist rebels, but designed specifically for the 21st century: non-violent; human-centred; both using and subverting the media's reach. Not having an army in 1849 left the Saxon rebels toothless. These days, peaceful actions, their effects amplified by the diversity of information available and a dynamic global audience, have themselves become weapons of revolution.

Half the World
HUANG CHAO AND TANG CHINA 874–88

With a fifth of the world's people, a 2,000-year legacy of contiguous statehood, a deep-seated cultural hold on its neighbours and genuinely continental geography, it's perhaps more useful to think of China today as a civilisation, rather than a country. The flurry of unfamiliar names, regimes and battle sites which present themselves on a first-time encounter can bewilder, such is the depth of Chinese history.

A useful memory aid is to associate each imperial dynasty – there are dozens – with a rebellion that contributed to its collapse. The Qin, for example, were upended by popular revolt on the cusp of the 2nd century BC. Within 400 years the Han were fatally weakened by the revolting Yellow Turbans. The most recent dynasty, the Qing, came crashing down amid a cluster of revolts; most notably the Boxer Rebellion and the Japanese-sponsored Xinhai Revolution.

Tang emperors were no different in this regard. Lasting from 618 until 907, their reign stands at a rough midpoint in Chinese imperial history and is marked by influential legal codification and the long-term settlement of China's borders. The age of the Tang, however golden over the course of its first half, endured a torrent of pressures in its final 150 years. This period is book-ended by two major outbreaks of mass revolutionary violence: those of the popular leaders An Lushan and Huang Chao respectively. The combined force of these two revolutions not only brought the once-mighty Tang dynasty to its knees, but have played a large part in shaping the China we know today.

It was to be a sorry end to what had been a stable and prosperous empire. In the early years, the expansionist and professionalised Tang imperial army conquered Korea and large chunks of Central Asia. Seaborne trade flung a Chinese diaspora across the world which, just as they do today, returned the wealth of new settlements to their homeland. Kingdoms as far apart as Kashmir, Vietnam and Japan sent embassies and tribute to the imperial court at Chang'an.

That city, on the rough site of present-day Xi'an, boasted a population of over one million people at its imperial peak; the largest city on earth. Hospitals, palaces and temples faced each other over wide avenues. Three urban canals met in the city centre. Just as in today's cosmopolitan cities of Hong Kong and Shanghai, world trade fuelled the empire. Commercial activity at two bustling markets was protected by layers of gated walls. Stretching away from the city, the Grand Canal and a developed postal system moved goods to other Chinese cities, lubricating trade in a large domestic market and beyond.

The Tang emperors set lasting standards in bureaucracy. The 'Equal-Field System' was a kind of government property regulation measure to forestall the power of large landowners. Civil servants took regular censuses, leaving detailed demographic data. A 'History Bureau' wrote official accounts of important leaders and state events. Travelogues of particular visitors have placed Tang China within a wider context. Ennin, a Japanese Buddhist priest resident in the capital, praised the canal network and described the security afforded foreign travellers such as him. Al-Masudi, a Persian historian, left an account of the strength of trade links with the Muslim Abbasid caliphate.

The benefits of openness to the world were not limitless, however. While Silk Road caravans had extended Chinese influence into and beyond Central Asia, they simultaneously heralded conflict with tribal nomads and the Tibetan Empire. By the middle of the 8th century, Tang emperors had found it necessary to enlist the services of Turkic nomads to guard against more malevolent barbarian penetration around China's periphery. In time, these soldiers had integrated into cosmopolitan Tang society. Soldiers became generals. Certain generals then won lucrative office as regional governors.

China's north-east was where much of the 8th- and 9th-century turmoil would spring forth. Not uncoincidentally, it also featured a high incidence of non-Chinese governors. Their control of locally produced commodities, such as silk and grain, funded a further loosening of ties with the court at Chang'an. In 755, a particularly ambitious north-eastern governor-general, named An Lushan, rebelled, leading his army on a marauding rampage across China. Though he was obese, half-blind and eventually murdered by his own supporters, it took the enlistment by the emperor of yet more Central Asian barbarian warriors – the Uighurs – to end An Lushan's assault.

An Lushan had not been the only official to rebel. Yet many of his mutinous cohorts were not militarily defeated, or even punished, but *bribed* into peace with higher office. This set important precedents for what was to come. The extra imperial soldiers who were needed to keep peace after the An Lushan Rebellion came to be stationed permanently in China's interior, rather than on the frontiers where they could protect trade and maintain the prosperity of the empire. Armies began to choose their own commanders, increasing the separatist spirit. Tang China after the second half of the 8th century became an inward-gazing, militarised camp.

In economic terms, the results of the An Lushan Rebellion were even more disastrous. The Tibetan Empire, having occupied the capital Chang'an at the tail end of the rebellion, threatened Silk Road trade and spread fear into the empire's heartland. The 'Equal-Field System' was ended, increasing pressure on small landholders. The Tang court scrambled to locate new sources of cash, with austerity for the average peasant a much easier option than root-and-branch reform. Special commissioners were assigned responsibility for improving income and efficiency. Information on taxable households which had escaped previous censuses was captured. The canal system was overhauled. Government monopolies on important goods were adopted so that prices could be fixed to benefit the coffers of the court.

It was not enough. In the intervening century between An Lushan's death and the rebellion of Huang Chao, unrest blocked the flow of trade revenues to the imperial capital at Chang'an. Insularity crept into the formerly cosmopolitan dynasty: an official crackdown on Buddhism in 842, for example, saw temples closed and monks ejected, the Japanese diarist Ennin included. Droughts and famine rolled over Central China in the 860s and 870s. The emperor could no longer afford aid, whether direct (emergency food supplies), or indirect (tax relief). Bandit armies, such as that led by Kang Quanti in the south of the country, fought for resources. Garrison mutinies became common.

In the immediate prelude to disaster, the court at Chang'an was beset by factional infighting. The elderly Emperor Yizong died in 873. With his heir still immature, a corrupt eunuch known as the Duke of Jin held effective political control, splitting the loyalties of generals and high-ranking officials further. In the wake of these dark omens, Huang Chao emerged.

A descendant of merchants, he had failed civil service examinations several times, resorting to smuggling of salt as a direct result of enforced government monopoly. His home was the same north-east where An Lushan had roamed; in the mid-870s it was beset by further lawlessness, with violent competition between imperial authorities, mutinous officials and multiple ethnic clans: Korean, Khitan, Turkic and Uighur.

After 875, Huang allied himself with a rebel general named Wang Hsien-Chih to fight his way south. His army took Guangdong province with little resistance. The rebel soldiers appeared intent on massacre and pillage. Al-Masudi, the 10th-century Arab polymath, related that, in Canton:

> The victims who fell under the swords of the rebels were innumerable; and the number of Moslims, Jews, and Christians alone, exclusive of the Chinese population, who were killed or drowned for fear of the sword, amounted to two hundred thousand.[1]

In spite of the destruction Huang *did* hold political ambitions. He was in direct contact with the Tang court throughout and appealed to the emperor for an official role, taking his lead from Wang Hsien-Chih who had successfully defected in 878.

Huang Chao's courting of his enemies, however, fell on deaf ears. The emperor dispatched a large army to bring the rebel threat to an end. Despite overcoming every imperial force sent against him, Huang Chao's troops were falling victim to tropical disease in the south of China. He looped back northward and inland. Between 879 and 881 his army fought towards the imperial capital at Chang'an, capturing cities and gathering troop strength as they went. With Huang at the eastern approaches to the city, the Duke of Jin fled, taking the teenage emperor with him.

The stated aims of Huang, the self-titled 'Commander of the Righteous Army', had been to cleanse the court of its corrupt influences. His rebellion couched in the language of high morals, Huang Chao entered Chang'an in victory. But the overall result of the battle for power was indecisive. Despite the likelihood of wider popular support among disaffected peasantry, Huang's proclamation of a new dynasty was generally ignored. The various warlords, bandits and rogue military commissioners of outlying regions were all busy sculpting their own localised power bases from the recession of imperial authority.

In any case, Huang Chao had no time to savour victory. Loyalist forces rallied, repeatedly assaulting rebel-held Chang'an. After initially repulsing them, Huang abandoned the city in 883. The emperor returned to his capital and, as had become something of a Tang tradition, used Central Asian Turkic barbarians, this time the Shatuo Turks, to hunt down his rebel quarry. Huang Chao's army disintegrated. The salt-smuggling rebel would eventually be killed by a scheming nephew in 884.

Huang Chao had mortally wounded the Tang dynasty. Many wonders of Chang'an had been destroyed. The port of Canton (then known as Kuang-fu) had been razed to the ground. With disunity came plummeting trade with Asia and the Middle East. But the dynasty was not yet dead. The last rites took 20 years to be administered. In 909AD, a participant in the original rebellion cast down the final Tang emperor, only to be overthrown himself by a coalition of Turkic groups. There followed a chaotic period. Its name explains much; it became known as the age of the Five Dynasties and Ten Kingdoms.

The revolutions of 19th-century China can parade a higher body count; those of the twentieth more ideological purity. But if one period can sum up the countless rebels who have strived against scores of Chinese dynasties over thousands of years, it is Huang Chao. He is the Chinese rebel *par excellence*, in many ways archetypal of those who had fought before, and predictive of many who continue fighting the Chinese state today.

Huang Chao brings to mind 21st-century Islamic and Tibetan struggles in Western China; a region, ironically, set within China's orbit by the once mighty Tang and populated by the Uighur ethnicity. There are echoes of the Taiping Rebellion in his failed bureaucratic career; reminders of Mao's peasant army in his motives. But most of all, the lesson Huang Chao seems to hold for a 21st-century empire is the inevitability of the end. When the time comes for a dynasty to implode, no matter its military strength or the glories of the recent or distant past, revolution will find a way to accompany corruption, famine, disease and massacre on an industrial scale.

Hungry Philosophers
EUROPE 1848

One of the lighter-hearted stories to emerge from the uprisings and demonstrations which broke out across the world during 2011 was of a foreigner travelling *to* the scene of a revolution from abroad. The Israeli newspaper *Haaretz* reported in September on the visit by Sean Penn to Tahrir Square in Cairo. The Hollywood actor waved an Egyptian flag and gave interviews, in an effort to encourage Americans that the city was safe and to return there as holidaymakers. It may not be wise, but neither is revolutionary sightseeing a new activity. A footloose *artiste*, just like Penn, introduced the wave of uprisings which broke across Europe in 1848–49.

In his youth, Richard Wagner's early-19th-century Saxony home was not yet part of a larger Germany. Although the young composer spoke the language and would probably have identified himself as a German, *Großdeutschland* would not exist for some five decades. Instead, a patchwork of German states lay spreadeagled from the Baltic to the Belgian border, sharing in neither flag nor religious denomination. An extremely loose confederation meant that each state was ruled by its own king, duke or elector.

Wagner, having shown his sympathy for democratic politics in an 1830 uprising in Saxony, travelled far and wide in the late 1830s and early 1840s. Shifting from Riga to London, Boulogne to Paris, the composer's flights were sometimes an attempt to promote work or meet more successful musicians. More usually, they represented an escape from creditors.

A notable musical product of the period was *Rienzi*; an epic five-hour opera completed by Wagner in 1840. Its account of a foiled liberal uprising appears to foretell the coming revolutions with amazing accuracy. In actual fact, Wagner was recalling the uprising of 1830. Wagner's wanderings paused when *Rienzi* was staged in Dresden in 1842. But the composer continued to be better known for his radical politics than his operatic scores.

The backdrop to 1848 saw economic depression sweeping across Europe in the latter half of the decade. Farmers faced twin pressures from crop failure and mechanisation. Food prices spiked. Famine hit Ireland and Flanders, with localised but intense shortages in countless other regions. The industrialising cities of Europe held several features in common: polluted slum areas with no welfare provision; factories with no safety legislation; child workers with few guarantees in law.

A growing class of educated Europeans experienced these depressed circumstances at first hand. Aspiring to the modes of sophisticated Europe, but barred from participation in civic life, a clamour for representative politics emerged. The 1830 uprising in Wagner's Saxony, for example, resulted in a limited constitution to underpin the king's rule. But this was far from democracy and the tranche of absolutist regimes in power from Paris to St. Petersburg suffered little in the way of compunction. The fate of Louis XVI during the French Revolution still rang loud in courts and salons, their denizens only too aware of the speed with which populist concessions could lead to total loss of control.

Having completed the education thrust upon every male Saxon child, Wagner and his peers remained frustrated by poverty. Hunger and literacy remains, to this day, a politically explosive combination. Radical publications – humanist, idealist, socialist, rationalist – circled Europe during the 1840s. Amid incendiary new philosophies, with empty stomachs, the French revolutions in 1789 and 1830 showed that tyranny could be overcome. The precedent of an end to kingship gave hope to Wagner and his Saxon brethren. This penniless anger was replicated across the continent.

Rebellion first emerged in Sicily, in January 1848. A hail of calls for constitutional unity then spread across the various kingdoms, papal states and duchies of Italy. Monarchs were deposed. Bourbon France itself saw radical worker-led 'National Workshops' proclaimed. These were subsumed into the Second Republic, led by Louis Napoleon, Bonaparte's nephew. News from Paris spread. Barricades arose across city streets. Armed revolt broke out in Prague, Warsaw, Bucharest and countless other locations. Stuttgart and Berlin saw liberal demonstrators win concessions.

Revolt was forestalled in the Saxon capital. But Wagner's seditious writings succeeded only in the cancellation of *Rienzi* at the Dresden opera house. The composer moved on, spending the second half of 1848 in Vienna. The Habsburg capital represented the dissonant hub of an empire filled with competing ethnic and religious concerns. Catholics within imperial borders identified the newly elected Pope Pius IX as a liberal, broadly supportive of national causes. Hungarian politicians called for a constitution in March. Germans and Poles, entrapped under Habsburg rule, strained to join marchers in Berlin and Warsaw respectively.

Perhaps, at some juncture during his stretch in Habsburg Vienna, Wagner spoke with another volatile young musician active in the city at the same time: Johann Strauss Jnr. Wagner left few details of his role in the Viennese street demonstrations. Either way, in a conscious echo of Paris in February, and of the

sans-culottes generations before, Viennese and Budapest marchers eventually forced the resignation of Chancellor Metternich
and extracted promises of reform from the emperor.

The result in Vienna was typical. Across the continent, the
same story emerged. Would-be European revolutionaries may
have unsettled their better armed, better prepared opponents,
but they could not unseat them. Belgian rulers, their frontier
established by uprising in 1830, had had their fill of revolution.
They suppressed demonstrations. Polish insurrectionaries were
unsuccessful in unsettling the Prussian and Russian aristocra-
cies which hemmed in their homeland. The Young Irelander
revolt was limited to the siege of a single Tipperary cottage.

The French should have studied Louis Napoleon's family tree in more detail. Within three years of his election,
Bonaparte's nephew converted the progressive institutions of
the Second Republic into the Second Empire, with he at its
head. The Swiss cantons were subsumed not by democratic
revolution but sectarian civil war. Only the Danes got to keep
the liberal concessions their protests had won.

Wagner's German Confederation ran into familiar problems when it rose up in uncoordinated fashion throughout
1848: protests remained toothless without an army. Prussian
King Frederick William IV in Berlin, for instance, simply
agreed to whatever outlandish demands were made of him.
Because the great bulk of the military had remained loyal, the
king simply bided his time. Once the dust had settled, Frederick
imposed his own laws in place of the liberals'. A Stuttgart parliament was routed by troops; the nascent National Assembly
in Frankfurt simply ignored.

As the first anniversary of the Paris barricades rolled
around, uprisings across the German states petered out one by
one. In a May 1849 Saxon epilogue, crowds of artisans, miners

and students demonstrated in Dresden in support of the tooth-less National Assembly. Wagner had returned to his home city from Vienna. He joined the protests, spending a night keeping watch in a bell tower, high over Dresden.

From there, Wagner watched the city Opera House in flames, a sight that must have conjured mixed emotions, given the building's connection to his work. Wagner recounts another man's greeting to him, on the barricades on May 8th 1849, in typical style:

> 'Hullo, conductor, your *Freude schöner Götterfunken* [a reference to a recent performance of Beethoven's Ninth Symphony] has indeed set fire to things. The rotten building is razed to the ground.'[1]

After six days of skirmish, reality dawned. The Prussian troops invited into Dresden by the Saxon king crushed the protests. Our intrepid revolutionary tourist was forced to take to the road again. The composer spent the best part of the next decade on the run in society's fringes. But time passed and Wagner's fortunes rose. By the early 1860s age had mellowed the political firebrand. Patronage of Wagner's music by Europe's aristocracy – not least the sycophantic young King Ludwig II of Bavaria – no doubt helped the transformation.

As a result of his actions in Dresden in 1849, however, Wagner's reputation among the elite circles his art drew him into was one of ongoing suspicion. Wagner found greatest fame in his last days. Based in Switzerland, he travelled across Europe for performances of his work at the purpose-built opera house at Bayreuth in northern Bavaria and in the palaces of kings and aristocrats.

In spite of his adoption by the cultural elite in the autumn of his artistic career, Wagner's earlier, politically-inspired travels across revolutionary Europe have not been forgotten. He had not been the only radical who set out to observe and influence events in the late 1840s. Karl Marx moved around Europe in the hope of testing his political theories. He arrived in Cologne disappointed to find the city's workers accepting the king's promises in good faith. The anarchist Mikhail Bakunin moved himself from city to city amid the political tumult. This wandering agent of revolution crossed paths with Wagner in Dresden in 1849, delivering speeches to the rapidly assembled citizen soldiery.

Alexis de Tocqueville, meanwhile, belonged to a different generation. He had long since completed his journey, having seen at first hand the young system of democracy in 1830s America. De Tocqueville used his impressions to publish *Democracy in America*, a classic of political studies, still featured on university reading lists. The author would participate in the government formed in France in the spring of 1848, helping to frame the constitution which Louis Napoleon would first govern under, but later usurp.

Marx and Bakunin too would offer influential but conflicting reflections of the period. Their work would go on to form the philosophical bedrock on which much of the succeeding two centuries' political battlefields would be built. Bakunin is one of the spiritual forefathers of today's anti-capitalist and anarchist protestors; Marx, along with Friedrich Engels, became the progenitor of socialism, communism and all that followed.

Richard Wagner's roller-coaster life and musical innovation remain equally divisive. His popularity among leading Nazis in the 20th century, as well as his professed anti-Semitism, have dogged his reputation. In a purely artistic sense, however, Wagner is recognised as a genius. His *Gesamtkunstwerk* compositions exceed the boundaries of music and opera, reaching creative spheres as far apart as philosophy, cinema soundtracks and heavy metal.

Liszt and Hungary; Chopin and Poland; Handel and Hanoverian England: it is not unusual for composers to become intimately associated with a nation. While Wagner's participation in the unrest of 1848–49 did not directly create a German state, in the last quarter of the 19th century, his music did become the soundtrack to the unification of Saxons, Westphalians and Prussians.

Failed revolutions do not always justify study. The European upheavals of 1848–49 represent the blinding exception. The forces of nationalism awakened by the period would shape the future to an even greater extent than the political theories of Marx, Bakunin and de Tocqueville. Many Romanians, Hungarians, Czechs, Poles and Italians would not live to see it, but their manning of the barricades during the 'Spring of Nations', however disastrous in the short term, heralded the birth of a dozen nations-to-be. The Swiss cantons came together immediately. The republican tricolour invented by the Young Irelanders is today's Irish national flag. France, meanwhile, had several further painful contractions in store before its modern birth.

A Pinch of Salt

INDIA AND PAKISTAN 1947

Ask a random passer-by on the street about the events of 1947–48 on the Indian subcontinent and the basic knowledge expressed will probably sound something like this:

1. A small, bespectacled man called Gandhi brought about independence.
2. He was then assassinated, as were various members of his family.
3. Gandhi's political tactics were based on meditation and peaceful protest.

It is true that, as a politician, Gandhi's methods and physical appearance were strikingly different to the standards of his day. The sad facts also show that 'Mahatma', having finally won his lifelong struggle, met a premature and unfair death from an assassin's bullet. Gandhi preferred peace. His courage and dignity in the face of violence tower above the story. A deeper look, however, shows that peaceful civil disobedience cannot be the only lens through which independence and partition are viewed.

India's great 20th-century anti-hero, Subhas Chandra Bose, offers a counterpoint to the received and oversimplified wisdom on the revolution which led to independence and partition on the subcontinent. Both Gandhi and Bose shared the broad aim of a break from British overlords. But the paths they took to achieve that goal diverged significantly. While Gandhi's approach is summed up by the Hindi word *swaraj*, or self-governance; *purna swaraj*, or complete independence, were the watchwords of Bose.

Of course, another clear difference between the two men was their age. Mohandas Karamchand Gandhi, later given the honorative prefix 'Mahatma', was born in the 1860s; Bose in the 1890s. Though raised in privileged circumstances, Bose's native state of Bengal saw widespread unrest in his youth, when the British divided it in two, the Muslim-dominated east shorn from the richer, Hindu western section. Gandhi, by contrast, had experienced a vegetarian childhood in a peaceful Gujarati principality.

Both Gandhi's and Bose's education included local British-administered schools, followed by a spell in an English university. Later, Gandhi spent an influential twenty-year period abroad in South Africa. Here, using his legal training, Gandhi mobilised South Africa's Indians to resist oppressive legislation, gaining notoriety across the empire. Bose's political baptism was more resoundingly domestic and, once again, linked to the cut-and-thrust of restive Bengali society. He served under the militant nationalist Chittaranjan Das, foreign travel limited to exchanges with British Labour politicians and some admiring trips to Mussolini's Fascist Italy.

Both men were spiritualists, with neither of their political visions defined solely by state structures and other such rational details. Gandhi in his early years had actively recruited for the British in India during the First World War but, with age, he rejected violence as a political tool. His peaceful civil disobedience – Gandhi called it *satyagraha*, or 'soul-force' – was designed to incline the opponent's conscience towards one's position through persuasion alone. Bose saw himself as a socialist, but one informed by the morals of ancient Hindu texts. Gandhi led three peaceful campaigns for *swaraj*. Just as Gandhi embarked on the second of these, the 1930 Salt March, Bose was using his mayoral platform in Calcutta to reject non-violent means. 'Give me blood and I will give you freedom' became his motto.

What effect did these efforts have? In the immediate sense, both men were jailed by the British on successive occasions for agitating against imperial rule. While Gandhi was first imprisoned in South Africa for defying colonial decrees, he was later targeted in India simply because of his popularity as a focus for change. Bose had been imprisoned by the British for his outspoken views on independence in 1924. Held for three years, his wrongful incarceration actually aided his reputation within the Indian National Congress (INC), the political vehicle which drove Hindu nationalism, as well as his subsequent career. Upon release, he rose rapidly through the ranks.

Both men served as leaders of the INC. As president from 1921, Gandhi had broadened the movement's appeal beyond an educated elite leadership. He also made pains to attract poorer members and women. Bose, true to form, was more divisive. After speaking publicly and favourably of the need to violently overthrow British rule, he was forced to resign in 1939. The elder Gandhi, who had originally opposed the presidency of the Bengali firebrand, looked on disapprovingly.

It is more than a little ironic then that history's most famous pacifist saw his political dreams realised by humanity's most violent conflict. The island of Britain only just escaped from the Second World War intact. After sacrificing so much to defeat the racist, imperial designs of Nazi Germany, the moral basis for continued colonial domination of India and other colonies lay shattered. In any case, the funds to support the British *Raj* were needed at home.

In India itself, the war brought disaster. A famine in Bengal in 1943 killed millions through starvation and disease.

Escaping house arrest in 1941, Bose travelled to Berlin to broadcast anti-British propaganda for the Nazis. The budding fascist then recruited pro-independence Indian soldiers from among Allied prisoners of war in Japan and set up his own liberation force, the Indian National Army (INA). Bose led them into the Burmese jungles bordering his native Bengal, where the INA was soundly defeated, in the early summer of 1945. Sensing the impending defeat of his fascist Japanese allies, Bose attempted to flee again, this time to Soviet Moscow. His luck had run out. The plane he was on came down over Taiwan and Bose's body was never recovered.

Gandhi and the Congress leader, Jawaharlal Nehru, were left to declare independence, their 'Quit India' campaign victorious. Violent upheaval, however, had only just begun. There was little real revolutionary action during 1947. But India's Muslim-dominated territories in the Balochistan, West Punjab and Sindh joined with East Bengal to establish themselves into a single, sovereign state: Pakistan. Massive loss of life occurred during the mass migrations which resulted. Some deaths occurred as a result of ethnic tension when millions of Muslims in Indian territory swapped places with Hindus and Sikhs in Pakistan. Others happened during the dispute on Kashmir, over which the two newborn states fought their first war, a matter of months after partition.

Apart from the rash of death, and aside from the changed borders, had India's independence struggle created real revolutionary change? Caste, the system of stratification between higher-class Indians at the top and 'untouchables' at society's base, outlived colonisation. It was still in effect after the seventeen-year premiership of Nehru; this in spite of his stated 'socialism' and his introduction of legislation to tackle the issue. Differences of caste remain pronounced in India to this day, nowhere near fully resolved by the recent growth of the country's stature on the world stage, the surge of modern digital industries, or the mutation of isolated villages into mushrooming cities.

Was it the revolutionary model of Bose or Gandhi – violence or peace – which had the lasting effect on India? In later years, and even recently, followers of Bose alleged that 'Netaji', as he is known, had not died, but was living as a wandering Hindu ascetic. The All India Forward Bloc, the political party he founded after his ejection from Congress, is still extant in Bengal. Independence in 1947, furthermore, has not healed West Bengal of violent revolutionary urges. In 1967, the Maoist Naxalite movement was born in its interior. Representing marginalised peasant farmers, Naxalite guerrilla terror campaigns against state representatives have seeped into virtually every impoverished corner of rural India since then. Set against a background of declining rural living standards, a Marxist state government was elected in West Bengal in 1977. The Marxists, though advocating a less confrontational approach to revolution than the Naxalites, went on to enjoy 34 years of uninterrupted electoral success. It was May 2011 before they were dislodged from power in West Bengal.

The wider success of mass civil disobedience appears to demonstrate that, globally at least, Gandhi's philosophies have won out over those of Bose and his ilk. Martin Luther King made pilgrimage to independent India to study *satyagraha*. His Civil Rights campaigners were effective adherents, as were copycat gay rights, feminist and anti-war movements during the 1960s. Whether conscious or not, a host of later protesters – environmental, animal rights, anti-nuclear – were influenced by Gandhi's teachings. The year 2011 saw dozens of interrelated protests occur across the globe. The vast majority of groups took special pains in their manifestos to profess a strict policy of non-violence and map out a strategy of civil disobedience. All the evidence suggests that *soul-force* as a revolutionary tactic is here to stay.

Her Majesty's Witchdoctors
THE MAU MAU 1952–60

> When they want you to think that a certain person, or a certain
> area, or a certain group, is involved in the actions of extremism,
> the first thing they do is project the images of that person in the
> image of an extremist. And then anything that he does from then
> on, is extreme. It doesn't matter whether it's right or wrong. As
> far as you're concerned, if the image is wrong, whatever they do
> is wrong.[1]

'They', as the speaker later put it, were 'racialist' political leaders.
The date was 1964. The speaker: Malcolm X. The iconic proponent of black rights knew full well the risks associated with
bearing a reputation for violent extremism. At the time of this
speech to Oxford University Union, he was under surveillance
by the CIA. Locked in a public war of words with his former
comrades, the Nation of Islam, within ten weeks Malcolm X
would be assassinated by gunmen in New York.

The propaganda war during a revolution can be fiercer and
more influential than that played out on the battlefield with guns
and gas. Nelson Mandela knew this. The same year Malcolm X
addressed the students of Oxford, the ANC man chose to defend
himself at his trial in Johannesburg, knowing 'the sheer freedom
that the opportunity to expound afforded'.[2] Winston Churchill
recognised the power of negative portrayal too, most infamously
expressing his displeasure at watching 'a *fakir*… striding half-
naked up the steps of the Vice-regal palace'.[3] The name of that
'seditious lawyer'? A certain M.K. Gandhi.

Manipulation of public image is just one of the revolutionary themes that converge in colonial Kenya in the 1950s. For the best part of a decade, insurgency and counter-insurgency raged across the country. The rebels aimed their attacks at fellow Africans, white settlers and the British colonial authorities. The administration, in turn, meted out severe punishments. The era remains a disputed one. Conflict has emerged in contemporary Kenya and Britain over Mau Mau, reflecting a wider adjustment in relations between ex-colonial states and their former masters.

The British were certainly not the first foreign visitors to Kenya. Long before the arrival of the Imperial British East Africa Company in 1888, Arab sultans, Asian traders and Portuguese explorers had tasted life at Kenya's Indian Ocean trading ports. Coffee, spices and slaves were traded. Indelible cultural and linguistic footprints remained. 'The Company' handed over control to the British crown after 1895. Britons and other Europeans were attracted to the fertile and sparsely populated inner highlands region. Its clemency suited the climactic tastes of both the settlers and their lucrative tea crop.

Of course Kenya's best soils had not been left untilled before 1888. Tribal groups had farmed the land for many thousands of years. As the number of settlers grew in the early 20th century, newly landless native Kenyans found jobs as servants in European homes; or exchanged their labour for the right to work fields considered valueless by settler farmers. Some squatted. Many more were forcibly moved to rural districts ('reserves') set aside for Africans. Still others exiled themselves to Kenya's cities: Nairobi in the interior; Mombasa on the coast. Everywhere they went, native Kenyans in the first half of the 20th century were introduced to the pillars of British colonial civilisation: taxes; missionary instruction; and military conscription.

By the early 1950s, society was cleft. Native Kenyans could be labelled by tribe membership or religious affiliation; or by social status, as landless squatter, farmer or city worker. They could harbour nationalist aspirations, or loyally serve benevolent masters and a distant Queen. Some did both. White Europeans were split between comfortable rural settlers drawn from the British upper classes and urban-based administrators of lowlier origins. Colonial secretaries wrote ordinances from Africa House, far away in London. Just as in the South Africa that Gandhi visited as a young man, a minority Indian labouring class, originally drafted in to work on the railway to Uganda, defied any clear settler/native definition.

Intra-tribal tension and designs on settler farmland had been building for years. It burst out at the village of Lari in March 1953. Huts containing men, women and children were set alight; their occupants burned to death. Any survivors were gunned down or hacked with knives. Both perpetrators and victims were members of the Kikuyu tribe. A secretive society of landless malcontents, the 'Mau Mau', as they were known, represented the radical youth wing of Kenyan nationalism. Lari set the scene for years of bloodshed. A stated aim of ejecting the British is confounded by indiscriminate killing: white children; Kikuyu village headmen; police; members of rival tribes. British church missions were targeted and two Nairobi mosques were gutted.

How did Britain react to the violence? Details of Mau Mau oath-taking ceremonies, emotively worded and often bloody, were relayed:

> I speak the truth and swear before Ngai [God] and before everyone present here that if I am called upon to fight or to kill the enemy, I shall go, even if that enemy be my father or mother, my brother or sister.[4]

Oaths were also re-imagined. Oliver Lyttelton, Secretary of State for the Colonies, speaking in parliament, gave this as an example: 'when the reed-brick horn is blown, if I leave the European farm before killing the European owner, may this oath kill me.'[5] The government-commissioned Corfield Report (1954) alleged that:

> The use of menstrual blood and public intercourse with sheep and adolescent girls were a common feature of most of these ceremonies… Concoctions of the foulest and almost unimaginable ingredients were eaten and drunk.[6]

A one-sided portrayal of the conflict also appeared in the British press. The *Daily Mail* described warlike conditions for British settler communities, with 'wire over domestic windows, guns beside wine glasses, the charming hostess in her black silk dress with an automatic pistol hanging at her hip.'[7] Front cover *Daily Express* headlines from 1953 include: 'Mau Mau Kill Boy of Six: British couple, son butchered'; 'Babies Die in Mau Mau Massacre'; 'Mau Thugs Kill Chief in Hospital'[8]

In the light of the early years of Mau Mau terror, British journalists and commentators found little space for analysis of the rebels' rationale, nor of the failings of colonial policy as a whole. Even filmmakers got in on the act. *Simba* (1955) was an adventure story set in contemporaneous Kenya, starring Dirk Bogarde. Produced in Britain, *Simba* was released while the conflict was at its height. According to one analyst, the actions of the film's white settler and European characters represented 'modernity, reason, order, stability'; with those of its black Kenyans representing 'backwardness, irrationality, chaos and violence'.[9]

Spurred by earnest pleas from settlers for protection and by the volume of headlines, the Kenya Administration imposed a state of emergency on the colony. Under this cloak of martial law, the British struck back: 20,000 police and 25,000 Kikuyu loyalists hunted Mau Mau suspects. Unregulated settler militias dished out death sentences on flimsy pretexts. Conventional military forces swept Nairobi and Mombasa, arresting suspects in their thousands. Many Kenyans, previously uninterested in the conflict, were forcibly relocated into 'fortified villages' in an effort to contain the forest-based rebels. The effect was negligible. Many converts to the Mau Mau cause came about as a direct result of their 'relocation'.

Though Mau Mau operations were effectively ended by the 1956 capture of leader Dedan Kimathi, martial law rolled on. A network of camps played host to the detention and, in theory at least, rehabilitation of Mau Mau suspects. The reality was somewhat different. Interrogations featured physical abuse and forced confessions. Witchdoctors were employed to 'cleanse' rebels of their blood oaths to the Mau Mau cause. The camps were a logistical nightmare, with growing detainee numbers hampering court proceedings. Insanitary conditions were rampant; outbreaks of typhoid and dysentery common.

A multitude of migrant British administrators, camp guards and orderlies kept the 'Pipeline', as the network of camps was known, running. Many of these were ex-soldiers, decommissioned since the end of the Second World War. Others were ex-British policemen. Barack Obama's grandfather was one of many thousand Kenyans who remained in custody without charge or trial for months on end. Those who did enter a courtroom received rough justice. Over a thousand Kikuyu had death sentences carried out by hanging.

After nine Mau Mau suspects were beaten to death at the Hola camp in 1957, whistle-blowers came forward. Critical reports found their way into the British press; at first in church, socialist and local papers; then later into more conservatively minded broadsheets. MPs, such as Conservative Enoch Powell and Labour's Barbara Castle, asked questions in the British parliament. Left-wing politician Fenner Brockway organised a mass petition for Kenyan independence.

Even though the rebellion had been defeated militarily, mass detentions and widespread abuse by the British galvanised pro-independence opinion. Kenya won freedom on 12th December 1963. The state's first president, Jomo Kenyatta, had been tried for Mau Mau involvement, then jailed and exiled during the late 1950s. A Kikuyu, but a political moderate, he sidelined Mau Mau fighters and pursued conciliation between tribes and existing settlers.

A Kenyan national celebration of Kenyatta was replaced in 2010 by a public holiday known as 'Heroes' Day'. This acknowledgement of the Mau Mau's role in bringing about independent statehood remained tacit for the simple reason that the period's ghosts have yet to be put to rest. Even a rough figure for extra-judicial killings is not agreed upon. Despite the rhetoric employed by certain newspapers during the conflict, only a fraction of the deaths during the rebellion were of settlers (32 in total). The vast majority were native Kenyans, whether rebel, loyalist, or innocent bystanders. Virtually all were killed, maimed or jailed outside the bounds of law. No British representatives, administrative or military, have ever been tried for crimes committed during the Mau Mau period.

A 2005 book on the Mau Mau Rebellion accrued both prestige and controversy. The author, Caroline Elkins, is an expert witness for a civil case taken against the British government by tortured and mutilated Mau Mau veterans. The case, without denigrating the individual experiences of the plaintiffs, is backed by a Kenyan government which has integrated the

Mau Mau into national historical narrative only at a distance from the event itself. Anti-colonial sentiment is a useful distraction in a country still quivering from the ethnic unrest which followed the 2007 elections.

Bruce Berman argues that collective amnesia, similar to that practised over detentions and abuses in Kenya, led to similar mistakes at Abu Ghraib and Guantánamo in later years. Echoing the words of Malcolm X, the political scientist questions the way that the term 'terrorist' is applied to those groups driven to challenge colonial agendas through violence, without recourse to the social roots of the problem, suggesting that: 'Mau Mau was the face of terror in the 1950s as Al-Qaeda is today.'[10]

The full implications of such a statement are challenging. For much of the last decade, for example, the Taliban have become a byword for sub-human terror in much the same way that the Mau Mau did during the 1950s. Now that NATO has signalled its intention to withdraw from an unwinnable war in Afghanistan, the formerly unthinkable tactic of negotiation with the group has been raised. Talks with the Taliban, if indeed they do occur, will join the Mau Mau court case during 2012 in bringing into stark relief the lasting power of language in conferring value.

Velvet and Iron

THE SOVIET EMPIRE 1988–91

We have become deeply involved in building a socialist state
based on the rule of law. Work on a series of new laws has been
completed or is nearing completion. Many of them will enter
into force as early as in 1989… Soviet democracy will be placed
on a solid normative base. I am referring, in particular, to laws
on the freedom of conscience, glasnost, public associations and
organizations, and many others.[1]

When Mikhail Gorbachev addressed the United Nations
General Assembly in December 1988, he couldn't guess quite
how decisive the following year would prove to be, nor in which
direction the tide of change would eventually flow. Throughout
the early months of 1990, the Soviet leadership was forced to
coalesce with a ring of proud republics neighbouring the USSR.
Within two years, the collapse of the Soviet entity itself would
raise a dozen new flags over ancient capital cities.

Milestones along the path to the final crumbling of the
Communist Eastern Bloc reach deep into history. In 1956,
Imre Nagy had led his Hungarian countrymen in demanding
greater freedom from Soviet control, only to be imprisoned and
later executed. During the 'Prague Spring' of 1968, Alexander
Dubček, another daringly reformist Party leader, had declassi-
fied reports on official corruption and infighting among the
Czechoslovak Communists. In Poland, under the yawning
shipyard gantries of 1970s Gdansk, the Solidarity trade union
had demanded the right to strike, the easing of press censorship and the release of political prisoners.

Moscow's response was forceful. In 1956, military units drawn from across the Eastern Bloc engaged the Hungarian army and unarmed protestors with equal force. The summer of 1968 in Czechoslovakia came to a close with civilian barricades torn down and street battles between Soviet Army soldiers and demonstrators. Solidarity was outlawed in 1980. Its leader, Lech Wałęsa, was jailed and Poland was blanketed by martial law.

Mikhail Sergeyevich Gorbachev lived through all of these events. Aged 25 in 1956, it's possible he may have failed to notice the tremors that Soviet intervention in Hungary sent across the world, veiled by Soviet censorship and distracted by his daughter's imminent birth. The responsibilities of a regional agricultural role in Gorbachev's native Stavropol in the late 1960s, by contrast, were probably not enough to drown out news of the drama happening over two thousand miles away, in Prague. In 1980, as the Soviet press denounced Solidarity, Gorbachev's career took on real significance.

His appointment to the Politburo of the Communist Party in Moscow represented the law graduate's first taste of power. This organ was where central policy for the fifteen republics officially under Soviet control was formulated. More clandestinely, it was also where guidance for the authoritarian governments to the west of the USSR emanated. The decisions of this small collection of unelected technocratic officials decided the shape of some 400 million people still living under Soviet Communist rule.

The system was creaking by the time Gorbachev became General Secretary in 1985. Factories and other businesses in the Soviet system didn't work according to demand, but to order. During the early Soviet era and in the 1950s, central planning seemed to offer the world a reliable method of distributed prosperity. In harder economic times, as occurred during the stagnant 1970s and 1980s, quotas on production figures led to gross inefficiencies. Managers were pushed to falsify output figures. Shortages in basics would become chronic while over-produced goods lay stockpiled and useless. To make matters worse, a slowdown in the Soviet oil industry coincided with a virtual halt of Romanian petroleum production. The resultant energy crisis was felt keenly across the Eastern Bloc.

The German Democratic Republic (GDR) was consid-ered neither a democracy nor a republic by anyone outside the most blinkered of Communist party cadres. For leaders of the Eastern Bloc's prized industrial show-house, the noisy success of their western neighbours was both an economic *and* political problem. Soaring West German growth rates and living stand-ards from the 1950s onwards – the vaunted *Wirtschaftswunder* – were facts of life not easily hidden from the millions of *ossis* who picked up stray television and radio signals from across the border. Such was the demand for Western-manufactured goods in the GDR and elsewhere across the Soviet sphere, that many a Levi's-wearing, Marlboro-smoking traveller to 1980s Minsk, Kyiv or Leningrad turned a holiday into a profitable business trip.

Economic factors, as ever, tell only half the story. From the beginning of his leadership, Gorbachev initiated a public reform policy of *glasnost* and *perestroika* ('transparency' and 'restruc-turing' respectively). Open elections were held to Soviet assem-blies. Relaxation on press controls allowed for public criticism of Communist Party officials. Nuclear arms reduction deals were signed with the USA. The number of political prisoners dwindled.

These radical social changes coincided with serious chal-lenges to authority on the Soviet fringe. During 1988, the Soviet Army's withdrawal from Afghanistan heralded a chas-tening military defeat and a markedly softer foreign policy line. The same year, ethnic rioting between Azeri and Armenian groups initiated nationalist demands all across the Soviet Union. Tallinn heeded the call, demanding of its Moscow overlords a constitution with local control of the economy and a guarantee of private property. The first act of Estonia's 'Singing Revolution' was a warning shot of changes to come.

From there, events moved quickly. The Polish government lifted an eight-year-old ban on Solidarity activity in April 1989, allowing the popular reform movement to rout the Communists in free summer elections. Hungary unsealed its border with Austria in September that same year. Because several other Eastern Bloc countries shared open frontiers with Hungary, East Germans and Czechs could now move unrestricted into Western Europe for the first time in decades. Hundreds of thousands seized the opportunity.

Gorbachev watched as the trickle of change at which his reformist rhetoric had hinted, rushed out of control. Alongside the passage of migrants, the reburial of Imre Nagy, the martyr of 1956, became a focal point for popular protest in Hungary. The Budapest government was forced into granting rights of free association, independent trade unions and the promise of truly democratic elections. Unlike in the 1950s, the Politburo held the Soviet Army back.

In Prague, protests by students came under attack. At memorials for the victims, trade union members joined the calls for independence. These marches were attacked in turn. Gradually, those beyond the confines of universities and union offices actively participated. At each attack, as news seeped in of developments elsewhere across the Eastern Bloc, protesters rebounded, newly emboldened. A broad coalition united behind the 'Charter 77' demands for civil rights. The apex of protest was a general strike in November, after which government authority disintegrated.

On the evening of November 9th 1989, a West German news-reader stated incorrectly that border controls in Berlin were no longer in effect. Expectant East Berlin crowds surged to check-points in a state of boisterous delirium. Ill-prepared to use their weapons, and with little direction from superiors, the outnumbered border guards lifted barriers. All hope of stemming the exodus from the GDR had now faded. Within months, the Wall had been demolished and Germany was well on the road to reunification. Across Europe, the force of peaceful demonstration had won out.

Gorbachev, his rapidly disintegrating Soviet Union and the rest of the watching world, were stunned. As much as the peaceful revolutions puzzled politicians, they delighted journalists. One by one, the communist governments of Soviet satellite states had been brought to their knees. The events had everything a newspaperman dreams of: sledgehammers and tears atop the Berlin Wall; the overthrow of tyrannical rule by the long-oppressed; not to forget a shared 200th anniversary with the Bastille – 1789 and all that.

Timothy Garton Ash, London *Independent* correspondent at Berlin's Brandenburg gate on that November 9th, has noted the rich vein of irony at work. In Poland, a genuine workers' movement had brought a workers' state crashing down. Across a continent, the long-held communist utopia of an international revolutionary wave was finally realised, only to sweep away communism itself.[2] Today, historians join the ranks of analysts puzzled by what actually took place. Did 1989 represent a restoration; a 'return to Europe'? Or a true revolution; a new 1917 or 1789? The dust from the Wall is as unsettled as the fineries of the debate.

What didn't happen in 1989 is as important as what did. In June, metal tank tracks had crushed a pro-democracy camp in Beijing's Tiananmen Square. Mikhail Gorbachev, harbinger of Soviet cataclysm, was visiting Beijing at the time. He stayed as quiet on the matter as the Chinese government press did. Protestors were *not* rescued by popular support or foreign condemnation. But within months the Soviet premier was withholding Soviet Army intervention in Berlin and Budapest. Though the revolutions of 1989 were not entirely peaceful, by and large they earned their velvet sobriquet.

Elsewhere, those in power watched, learned and acted with decisiveness. Factions among the ruling Communist parties in Bulgaria, Romania and Yugoslavia pre-empted change. Enlisting the help of the military, committed Leninists became born-again democrats overnight. As the USSR collapsed, Party elites in Belarus, Ukraine, the Caucasus and the 'Stans' of Central Asia hijacked independence fever. They guilefully seized power and natural resources without any reference to the democratic source of the revolutions in the Eastern Bloc and the Baltic states. The partial reform promised by Moroccan and Saudi kings during 2011 proves that trade in counterfeit political change is still a vibrant industry.

The theme of systemic change raises perhaps the most salient questions for our era. A network of authoritarian Communist governments was consigned to history from 1989–91. In 2011, a collection of Arab rulers with similarly undemocratic traits came under intense pressure from a succession of peaceful revolutions. Rather like the Kremlin's clampdowns across the Eastern Bloc, the USA's strategic goal for this region in the late 20th century was to maintain stability rather than promote democracy. If Gorbachev was the human face of the Soviet empire at the centre of the Eastern Bloc client states, is Barack Obama the latter-day equivalent? There are alarming parallels.

Just like the late-20th-century USSR, the USA of the early 21st century has witnessed a marked reduction in its global influence. The financial might which underpinned 'the American century' has been eroded. Competition for energy supplies has led to conflict in the Middle East and Central Asia. The consequent military stalemates have undermined the USA's wider moral standing. Pressure has been increased by the growing power of China and a wave of hostile socialist governments across Latin America.

Echoing the tone of Gorbachev's 1988 speech, the US President had both conciliatory and provocative words for the Islamic world in 2009:

> You must maintain your power through consent, not coercion; you must respect the rights of minorities, and participate with a spirit of tolerance and compromise; you must place the interests of your people and the legitimate workings of the political process above your party. Without these ingredients, elections alone do not make true democracy.[3]

Within two years, Egypt had ejected its US-aligned despot, Hosni Mubarak. By the autumn of 2011, Cairo University, where Obama made his speech, was hosting forums to decide the future composition of an elected Egyptian parliament. Just as democratic contagion, begun on the Soviet fringes in 1988, eventually reached the heart of Moscow, so too have major demonstrations now occupied city centres across America. Nothing about the situation suggests the USA is about to suffer implosion on the scale that the USSR did during 1989–91. American policymakers, however, would do well to heed the lesson.

The Hidden Hand

Revolutions are far from exclusively human affairs. The wrath of the gods, portentous astrological alignments and extreme weather patterns, have long been blamed for the downfall of civilisations and the rising up of new ones. Neither are revolutions generally restricted to defined borders, nor to a homogenous set of protagonists. The cast list of foreign subversives and domestic traitors is long. This chapter charts five revolutions – or near-misses – where the trajectory of the rebels cannot be fully explained using the normal framework of ideas, leaders and tyrannical kings.

Agents provocateurs are a regularly cited source of political unrest, particularly by its opponents. But this is an undocumented force invisible to analysis. Are there really hidden teams of conspirators at work behind enemy lines? As the Ottoman Empire faded from power in Arabia, the British, superpower of their day, sent the dashing Oxbridge adventurer, T.E. Lawrence, to incite trouble. Imperial bounty leased the services of camelback Bedouin rebels. But it was Lawrence who linked these privateers on the holy sand oceans of the Hijaz, to British supply ships on the Red Sea, and ultimately, to victory. Why does this matter? The Arab Revolt of 1916–18 offers a rare example of insurgency whose foreign funding is well-established. Until the same thing is applied to more recent uprisings in the Arab world, accusations about scurrilous *agents provocateurs* will continue to fly.

In the 1st century BC, the eruptive countryside around southern Italy gave Spartacus his chance to strike back at Rome. The revolt led by the iconic slave general demonstrates how a landscape can take centre stage in a revolution. His band of escaped gladiators raided villas, rested on volcanoes and recruited in vineyards, burgeoning into a great revolutionary army. Its story could simply not be told except without the gifts of the *Mezzogiorno*. This is important because, in modern times, the expected setting for revolution has become street barricades and cityscapes. Spartacus' hidden collaborator was the land. Naples and Campania have continued to produce anti-authority figures ever since.

Powerful natural elements – plague and seasonal high spirits – combined to produce the Peasants' Revolt of 1381. London's affinity with crowd violence, in a pattern repeated up to the current era, falls into a seasonal cycle. The summer has traditionally played host to boisterous Londoners. More awake than in winter evenings, often drunker and more saturated with sunshine, English capital dwellers have long used the slow-fading light of summer to put aside revelry and dabble in direct action.

The hidden influences on revolution, or lack of them, do not always originate from external sources, however. The blunt interjection of ancient tradition into everyday modern life is a defining feature of Japan. This theme also echoes in the appeals to the eternal uttered by a coup leader on an army barracks window ledge in 1970. Yukio Mishima's insurrection was doomed to fail by design. But his effort at playing the *samurai*, captured on television news by circling helicopters, captures well a society of inherent stability, geared to avoid revolution.

The hidden hand spreading the agenda of Mexico's EZLN to a global audience in the early 1990s was a little-known communications network called the Internet. As the first revolutionary movement to effectively harness its power, the EZLN campaigns demonstrated remarkable foresight. Today, the EZLN is no longer unique in using the black magic of electronic campaigning. Use of digital tools for political activism has gone truly mainstream, with Barack Obama 'crowdsourcing' his election funding and 24-hour cameras webcasting city centre occupations in high definition.

Other provocative forces massing online are largely masked. The full identities of web-based activist networks, such as Wikileaks and Anonymous, remain mysterious. Their agendas, however, are crystal clear: to disrobe malevolent political forces at work in the world, but hidden from view by official secrecy and obfuscation. Unfortunately, even if this ambitious quest for truth achieves success, meteorological elements and deeply embedded cultural influences will continue to affect unexplained revolutions.

Rebel City
Spartacus' Revolt 73bc

On an otherwise unprepossessing street corner, from a traditional wall-mounted Christian shrine, Naples' favourite rebel son beams down. Diego Armando Maradona's beatific countenance smiles at gawking tourist and adoring Ultra alike. And why not? During the 1980s Maradona earned the idolatry, thrilling his way to World Cup glory with his native Argentina and captaining local club SSC Napoli to the Italian championship for the first time. 'El Diego' did it his way too, with match-fixing allegations (which he strongly denied), fast cars, cocaine abuse, stratospheric charity donations and a plentiful scoop of bombast.

It is not difficult to encounter other Neapolitan rebels. The city is full of them. Taxi drivers race each other down narrow alleyways. Laughing teenagers on ranks of mopeds block the wide bayside boulevards. Clifftop streets are thronged by passionate lovers, embracing beside mountains of uncollected rubbish, a result of the Mafia-infested waste collection industry. Naples feels like a city engaged in a passionate battle against its own system. As Maradona put it:

> When the Neapolitans love you, they really love you!... I couldn't go to buy a pair of shoes because five minutes later the windows would be smashed and a thousand people would be in the shoeshop.[1]

One must move one hour north into the Campania countryside, to the city of Capuá, to meet a progenitor of this unique brand of southern Italian chaos. It was here, in the spring of 73BC, that a man named Spartacus rose from the rank of lowly slave gladiator to generalship of a large rebel army. Defeating the legions sent against him by Rome, sweeping across a broad expanse of what today makes up southern Italy, Spartacus secured a permanent space for his name in the annals of history.

The boot-shaped southern Italian peninsula across which Spartacus and his rebel slave armies pillaged appears alien to 21st-century eyes. In 73BC, Capuá, and the regions south of the city, were influenced heavily by the culture of the old Greek seaborne empire, Magna Graecia. By the time Spartacus fought his first amphitheatre duels, Capuá, along with the neighbouring cities of Neapolis (Naples), Metapontum and Egnathia, maintained strong trade links with Greece. Travelling farther south on the Appian Way, the paved road which skidded south from Neapolis, Rome's political and cultural orbit stretched, then disappeared almost completely.

The revolt began in humble circumstances. Though dozens of gladiators conspired to escape their confines in the amphitheatre at Capuá, only a handful finally succeeded. Spartacus led this group in routing a local militia before embarking along the Appian Way. Not only did they find olives, vineyards and livestock in the bounteous countryside there, but also converts to their cause from among the farm slaves. Encamped atop Vesuvius, the crested volcanic leviathan of the Neapolitan coast, Spartacus' band began to assume a different form. From their base, they successfully escaped the first proper military force sent against them, that of Caius Claudius Glaber, in late 73BC. Just when defeat seemed inevitable, Spartacus and his men fashioned ropes from vines and abseiled off the bare volcanic cliff face. Glaber's militia was then taken by surprise and routed from the rear.

The winter of 73–72BC was spent in camp. Spartacus organised the escaped slaves, rural outlaws and disgruntled army veterans into a proper army. Emboldened by repeated successes against the Roman commanders sent against them, larger towns were attacked. Further conquest, of Nola and Nuceria, delivered new armaments and an ever-growing line of recruits. With such success, however, differences emerged over strategy. Crixus, leader of a Gallic faction, was for a more adventurous and aggressive approach. Spartacus, by all accounts, was more cautious. A split occurred that winter, when Spartacus moved south and Crixus continued north.

The Roman historians Plutarch, Florus, Appian and Sallust express differences over the motives in Spartacus' mind, his choice of tactics and even about the existence of certain battles. Twentieth-century accounts allude to Spartacus' proto-communism. A Hollywood version directed by Stanley Kubrick and starring Kirk Douglas linked the slave revolt to the later fate of Christianity under Rome. The question marks swarm: was Spartacus a criminal, a prophet, a general, or a revolutionary? Did he aim to march on Rome, or was he looking for an escape route?

This last query, at least, is answerable. Spartacus never turned towards Rome. After following Crixus north, observing his defeat and winning several large-scale battles himself, the slave army again turned south, where they were finally defeated by the rival legions of Crassus and Pompey, in 71BC. Perhaps aware of his force's weakness, the gladiator-general had never attempted the 'sack', that barbarian cataclysm so ingrained in Roman consciousness from raids of the past. The Roman historians had expressed fears that Spartacus would do just this; and that tens of thousands of slaves in Roman fields and homes would look up from their toil to join a vengeant orgy directed against former masters. Peter Stothard expressed the cogency of a paranoid slave-based society watching a marauding slave rebellion inch closer:

> It was as though some ordinary stuff of life, bread, flower, olive oil, were suddenly discovered to be… the most inflammatory explosive.[2]

Rome faced many other revolts during its thousand-year imperium: Iberian Goths; Gallic Celts; Caledonian Picts; Majorcan pirates; Thracian bandits. Indeed, even as Spartacus fought on, a renegade Roman general called Sertorius attempted to establish an independent republic in Hispania, and King Mithridates tormented Roman legions in the Black Sea area. Rebellions led by slaves, however, seemed to grab the attention of Rome like no other type.

Though modern conceptions of Spartacus' personality and background were largely formed in the bitter inkwells of his Roman enemies, the forces of socialism enthusiastically adopted the historical allegory of a slave uprising during the 20th century. The attempted left-wing revolution in Berlin in 1918 was conducted by a group known as the *Spartakusbund*. Hollywood's interpretation was the first major film release to involve a scriptwriter previously 'blacklisted' by the FBI during the McCarthyite era of the cold war.

In early life, Spartacus was probably married, his wife possibly joining him in captivity and maybe also in rebellion. The mystery woman's name is unknown. It is safe to assume, however, that the origins of Spartacus lie in Thrace, one of the many peripheral lands to the east over which a young Roman republic had established dominance, and whose native sons were often captured during war for shipment to the slave markets of Rome.

It is tempting, too, given his army's later levels of both formal organisation and strategic accomplishment, to assume that Spartacus had received some degree of military training previous to that of gladiator school and the amphitheatre. Other than this, however, few biographical details can be stated with certainty. No firm records of Spartacus' gladiatorial bouts exist and we are missing contemporary descriptions of his exact age, physique, temper and style of speech.

The most obvious, but likeliest, truth is that the escaped slaves fought for freedom. Once free, they hungered for food. Once sated, they desired women. Even allowing for the astute leadership of the army's gladiator-generals and its victories against battle-hardened legionaries, it is difficult to read anything else into the episode. Despite the size of his army – it numbered in the tens of thousands at its peak – Spartacus never settled to develop a town, keeping on the move for two summers and winters. Nor did he court political power aside from military rule, as his eventual conquerors, Crassus and Pompey would do on their return to Rome.

Do particular places breed political volatility, as they do accents and slang? The landscape over which slaves briefly ruled commands more certainties than their identity or motives. Leaving aside Maradona and his anarchic worshippers at the San Paolo stadium in Naples, the volcanic rebellious energy of Campania emerged again in the 19th century. After 1861, the success of the nationalist unification movement, the *Risorgimento*, had benefitted few in the formerly independent and prosperous regions around Naples. As lower-ranked soldiers filtered back to their home regions from battle elsewhere, they found themselves unemployed and disenchanted, with unwelcome new taxes to pay and with light arms slung, unrequisitioned, on their backs.

Peasants and other downtrodden southerners joined the soldiers to become *briganti*; outlaws against the new Italian state. In Naples, a well-defined path led these guerrilla rebels into the foothills around Vesuvius. The very same region that had harboured the escaped gladiators of two thousand years before, played host in the 1860s to an extended period of lawlessness, with the *briganti* preying on the handsome palaces, vineyards and estates of Campania. From a northern Italian perspective, the effort to cleanse the south of its brigands became a battle between 'civilization and barbarism, reason and violence, humanity and inhumanity, social order and crime'.[3]

Today, romanticised images of the *briganti* adorn the same Neapolitan streets that once played host to 'San Diego'; but the fly-posters mention little of their violent suppression. Just as thousands of Spartacus' soldiers met a gruesome end, crucified along the Appian Way, the *briganti* and their supporters suffered mass execution and exile. In contrast with Spartacus, the executed 19th-century *briganti* and San Paolo, Napoli's patron, the sainted Maradona is still very much alive. Today he holds an uncompromising and sometimes contradictory view of the political world; his autobiography is dedicated to both Cuban Communist Fidel Castro (see *History's Absolution*, p 73) *and* Argentine Perónist Carlos Menem (see *Human Capital*, p 33).

After Spartacus, with the growth of the Roman Empire and even through its later conversion to Christianity, the practice of slavery continued unabashed. In modern times, the slave trade was outlawed by the British Empire in 1807, with full abolition in 1833. France made slavery illegal in 1848, and Tsar Alexander II emancipated the Russian serfs in 1861. America fought a bloody civil war to decide the matter. The anti-slavery north won out and the US Constitution was duly amended in 1865.

Despite these rightly famed steps, slavery lives on, with a healthy connection to the land of Spartacus' revolt. The modern port of Naples, one of Europe's largest, is a huge conduit for trade in illegal cargo. Local *Camorra* mafia, inheritors of the *briganti* mantle, source much of their financial muscle from sales of the untaxed and unrecorded shipments arriving there. In recent times, the *Camorra* have formed partnerships with gangs of Eastern European people-traffickers. The control of unwilling sex workers in Europe is a large and vibrant industry. The International Labour Office, a UN body, estimated 12.3 million people was the *minimum* amount living in a state of slavery worldwide in 2005.[4] Some academics put the figure much higher.[5] Thus the cycle of slavery and lawlessness that afflicts Neapolitan life is perpetuated. In a tradition already several millennia old, Naples awaits its next rebel.

Summer in the City
THE REVOLT OF 1381

> It was summer, people had nothing to do… If it happened now, less people would be involved – 70 per cent of people wouldn't be there. The people who were there, they don't have work, so they just take the money or get arrested. They don't care.
>
> (Young person, Tottenham)
> Report on *The August 2011 Riots in England*[1]

Moral custodians outraged by the riots which engulfed London in August 2011 need not delve deep into the past to find precedent. Spring and summer days have long brought disorder to the English capital's highways and byways. The pattern is the same: beckoned to socialise *en masse* by the sunshine, Londoners are stirred by alcohol and shaken by the hot political topic of the day. The most notorious recent cases of crowd violence on London streets have occurred between the months of April and October: Trafalgar Square in 1990; Broadwater Farm in 1985; Brixton in 1981; Ladbroke Grove in 1976.

Back in late medieval times, one such outburst – centring around the midsummer Corpus Christi festival – resulted in one of England's most lastingly relevant outbursts of popular political anger. The origins of the Peasants' Revolt of 1381 can be traced alongside that of the Black Death. Bubonic plague had decimated the population of England in the 14th century. The somewhat perverse result for those who survived, was improved conditions. Fewer of their own peers meant higher demand for their services as millers and cobblers, herders and kempers. Monopolies allowed labour rates to be pegged high. As plague graves filled up, fields, hovels and cottages emptied. And so rents fell away almost as fast. Late-fourteenth-century English peasant farmers were more literate, had smaller families, drank more ale and ate more red meat than their predecessors.[2]

However in important areas of life, for a significant rump of the populace, things didn't improve. Poll taxes of 'three groats a head', imposed in 1380, had heavily overburdened the incomes of average labourers. Another government measure – a maximum rate for labour – caused further aggravation. This added to the long-term, negative effects of wars being fought in France and Scotland. Clans threatened from the north and privateers raided the south-eastern coastlines. Kentish and East Anglian people had borne the brunt of the problems paralysing England. They had contributed their sons as fodder for continental cannon and were located too close to the capital's roving eye to forego the increased duties. Still, many tried. The arrival of government fiscal collectors, hastily assembled in May 1381 and sent out into Kent and East Anglia to collect outstanding monies, represented a final straw.

Bands of working men rejected their authority, harrying officials into empty-handed retreat. The first recorded violence against the courts occurred in Essex. But it was in Kent, to the south of London, that roads and river crossings were first occupied. Within weeks, large portions of southeastern England stood outside royal control, with representatives of the rebels passing from town to town to spread news of revolt.

John Ball was a rebel priest who recruited many to the cause. His railing political missives, often signed pseudonymously, denounced the state of England, its monied elite, the church and the corruption of those at its head:

The matters goeth not well to pass in England, nor shall not do till everything be common, and that there be no villains nor gentlemen, but that we may be all united together, and that the lords be no greater masters than we be. What have we deserved, or why should we be kept thus in servage?[3]

Primary among the lords mentioned by Ball, was John of Gaunt. The Duke of Lancaster was not only the richest man in England in 1381, but also a key counsellor to his nephew, Richard II, the pallid boy king. While loyalty to the monarchy proliferated in Kentish and East Anglian minds, John of Gaunt became a hate figure. The king's uncle was a strong adherent of war with France, the main expense necessitating the detested poll tax. 'We will have no king called John', became a rebel password. Similar infamy was reserved for virtually anyone connected with the collection of taxes, from the royal treasurer, Sir Robert Hales, downward.

Who else featured on the rebel side? Wat Tyler was a middle-aged Essex labourer who rose to leadership from among the disenchanted Kent men after crossing the Thames Estuary in the opening stages of revolt. Jack Straw, about whom even less is known, led the Essex throng. As the festival of Corpus Christi approached, these two elusive figures, along with John Ball, better preserved for historians as a result of his preaching, marched on the capital city in the warm summer months of 1381. Their intention was to lobby the king for change.

Capital of England for less than 50 years, London in the 14th century would appear alien to today's tightly-patrolled residents. Londoners of the 1380s could still traverse hedgerows around the great abbey and political centre at Westminster. Names, extant today, then carried significance for their surroundings: swampy ground still stood outside Moorgate;

crusading knights still prayed in the Temple Church. The City of London, England's commercial hive of activity, then as now, was a walled enclave. Only one bridge allowed a crossing over the Thames.

Wat Tyler had settled his Kentish men in Greenwich, a few miles downriver from the City. He was among the throng when the king approached the crowds, massed by the river at nearby Blackheath:

> When they saw the king's barge coming, they began to shout, and made such a cry, as though all the devils of hell had been among them... And when the king and his lords saw the demeanour of the people, the best assured of them were in dread... And the king demanded of them what they would... and they said all with one voice: 'We would that ye should come aland, and then we shall shew you what we lack.'[4]

Alarmed at the large numbers and cohesive demands from the crowd, the king and his advisers sailed straight back to the Tower of London, the royal headquarters. With his demand for an audience with the teenage king rejected, Tyler shifted his forces to the gates of the city. As these angry crowds approached London Bridge from the south, groups of East Anglians arrived at Aldgate, to the east. Aldermen, holding the advisers arrayed around Richard II responsible for their own over-taxation, allowed the passage of the rebels into the City.

What followed draws intriguing comparisons with later unrest. Beginning on the eve of Corpus Christi, June 12th 1381, the Kentish and East Anglian crowds joined with locals in a storm of violence. Palaces and brothels, selected in connection with wealth and power, were looted and burned. The Tower of London and Marshalsea prison were first besieged, then overrun. Fired up by the sermons of John Ball, rioters dragged their victims – Archbishop Sudbury, royal treasurer Hales, jailer Richard Imworth – from church sanctuary. After an impromptu execution, 'the rebels fixed the heads of the archbishop and the others on stakes and carried them through the streets of London as though they were celebrating a famous victory'.[5] King Richard managed only a narrow escape.

Set against the bloodlust, the demands presented to the king, when he finally granted an audience to the rebels on June 15th at Mile End, were surprisingly rational. Tyler called for a cancellation of the poll tax, the repeal of repressive labour laws, an end to maximum wages and no further role for John of Gaunt. However, little of substance was offered in return. The levels of unrest increased. Discipline quickly unravelled. Under the cloak of political protest, foreign traders were murdered, drunks looted and gangs settled personal vendettas.

Where were the truncheons, Black Marias and kettling which greet modern protesters? With the establishment of 'the Met' still over 450 years away, Londoners of the 14th century did not enjoy the protection of any recognisable public security force. Moreover, the royal household maintained no professional standing army of its own, relying on the militias of loyal knights to fight its battles. At the time of the revolt, many such soldiers were engaged overseas, or at the Scottish frontier under the command of John of Gaunt.

Once the teenage Richard II could regroup some semblance of military force, however, he struck decisively. A third audience between Wat Tyler and the king, at Smithfield, was booby trapped. Beckoned to come forward and speak with Richard, Tyler was killed with a combination of grocer's dagger, knight's sword and executioner's axe. John Ball had already fled northward from London. The rural rebel bands had endured a week of unwashed and largely unrewarded residence in London. Left leaderless by Tyler's slaying, they scattered. Though the revolt seeped northward, with serious unrest across Norfolk, Hertfordshire, Cambridgeshire, Leicestershire and as far north as Yorkshire, the spread was temporary. Ball was caught and gruesomely executed. The Peasants' Revolt of 1381 crashed to just as ignominious an end. With London safely back under royal control, the spiteful Richard II sent out justices of the peace and several battle-hardened militias to bloodily reign in his most disloyal subjects.

Wat Tyler's hordes were not the first, last, least successful, nor the bloodiest visitors to pass through England's capital. Eighty years later, Jack Cade and the Cornish marchers would expunge memories of 1381. Roman 'Londinium' had hosted Boudica and her Iceni. Saxon 'Lundenwic' suffered regular Viking pillage. However, it is interesting to note the parallels between events in 1381 and those of 2011. The initial, rational demands of Wat Tyler were swiftly transformed into something uglier. The August 2011 riots saw something similar occur. A local protest against alleged police brutality led swiftly to burning cars and raided warehouses. The best hope for those rebels unlucky enough to be caught in 1381 was a quick death. Perpetrators in 2011, if apprehended, faced a 21st-century version of rough justice: in one case, six months' imprisonment for stealing bottled water worth £3.50.

When Wat Tyler and his rural bands crowded around Aldgate and London Bridge, they only gained access because of the distaste for Richard II's court held by certain City aldermen. In late 2011, the City itself became a target. A few months after the riots, an anti-corporate camp appeared outside St. Paul's Cathedral to protest the proximity of the publicly subsidised financial sector to the levers of political power. The resultant friction between the church's protest supporters and its hier-archy was reminiscent of 1381. Geoffrey Chaucer, a witness to the Peasants' Revolt of 1381, later satirised the corrupt author-ity held by friars and church officials. John Wyclif, a dissident theologian and court appointee to Richard II, publicly echoed John Ball's low opinion of the church elite and proposed egali-tarian reform of texts and vestments. Wyclif was also an out-spoken pacifist, his description of the war with France in 1378 as 'the sin of the kingdom' would have found favour with the Kentish lands targeted by French raids.

What became of the three central characters? After the boy king Richard II became a man, the England he ruled descended into further tyranny, chaos and war. The last of the Plantagenet kings, his reputation was lastingly savaged by Shakespeare. The great villain of events, John of Gaunt, never inherited the throne himself. But his son eventually became King Henry VI and Gaunt's bloodline ran through every monarch of England down to Elizabeth I. Wat Tyler, celebrated in cockney verse for centuries after his death, has taken a spot alongside Robin Hood, Ronnie Biggs and the Kray twins in the pantheon of heroic English outlaws. The only lasting moral of 1381 seems to be that those perceived as victors or villains during a rebellion do not always stay that way as time unfolds. Which legacy the August looters and cathedral campers of 2011 enjoy remains to be seen.

A Guerrilla Tradition
THE ARAB REVOLT 1916–18

> The Turks were stupid; the Germans behind them dogmatical. They would believe that rebellion was absolute like war, and deal with it on the analogy of war. Analogy in human things was fudge, anyhow; and war upon rebellion was messy and slow, like eating soup with a knife.
>
> *Seven Pillars of Wisdom* (1922)

The author of these words, though dead for over 75 years, continues to advise today's military theorists. The aura surrounding his personality, similarly, has transfixed historians for nearly a century. More commonly referred to by the title of his 1962 Hollywood portrayal, several strains of modern manhood appeared to converge in the eventful life of Lawrence of Arabia. A colonial intellect worthy of Kipling collided with Hemingway-like grit and the bohemian abandon of James Dean. The spectacular results – an Arab nationalist uprising in the baking deserts of the Hijaz – continues to unfold on news channels to this day.

At first glance, a museum in Oxford may not appear an obvious birthplace for sandblasted rebellion. However, it was amidst the musty shelves of that learned city's university that the seeds of the Arab Revolt were sown. Here Lawrence, as a precocious military-history student and talented linguist, laid the basis for his future engagement with Arab culture. It was also here, via well-connected senior professors, that the young man built important bridges to British military intelligence.

Lawrence initially arrived in British-controlled Egypt during the First World War to engage in archaeology. However his talent for mixing with locals quickly came to the attention of a special section of the British secret service. The 'Arab Bureau' had been established to offer covert resistance to the Ottoman Empire on the Arabian peninsula. Plans were devised for a native Arab uprising deep in Ottoman territory. The prize was great. Control of the region would act as a diversion to deflect Ottoman forces from Britain's struggling tsarist allies on the Eastern Front. It would also give unfettered access to the eastern Mediterranean, securing the recently discovered Arabian oil reserves in the process.

Sherif Hussein, the influential leader of the Hashemite tribe, earmarked to lead the revolt, nevertheless had close ties to the Ottoman regime he would eventually help overthrow. Hussein and his four sons claimed direct lineage from the Prophet Muhammad and so commanded respect in the Ottoman capital of Istanbul, where they had resided up until 1912. After that date Hussein moved back to the Hijaz, the western portion of Arabia containing the holy cities of Mecca and Medina. Prodded by both the French and British, and aided by their loyal armed bands, his sons carried out attacks on Ottoman-controlled towns, beginning in June 1916. By September, Mecca and Taif had been won, but Medina and the port of Jeddah remained out of reach.

At this point Lawrence entered the equation. Successfully befriending Hussein's son and general, Feisal, he recalibrated rebel strategies. Owing to their limited numbers, the difficult desert terrain and their strong but static enemy, a guerrilla campaign was launched. Camels were used to increase mobility. Frontal assaults on heavily defended towns were discouraged. The success of lightning raids on isolated Ottoman forts played a large part in winning the confidence of other Arab and Bedouin tribes, who joined the fight. (Herds of camels, loads of dynamite and sacks of gold provided by Lawrence's British overlords also helped.)

To maintain momentum, Lawrence made several daring moves. He skipped his rebel forces around Medina, instead concentrating on the 800-mile-long Hijaz railway line. Ottoman reinforcements and supplies heading south on trains from Damascus were vulnerable to attack. When Ottoman commanders deployed thousands of troops and large guns to the railway's 77 stations, the rebels attacked them too. The Bedouins could sustain long rides across open desert, sometimes appearing in ambush far from where their camp was assumed to be. Trenches and fixed artillery placements were no match for such mobility. After the capture of Jeddah, Ottoman towns at the south end of the railway were completely cut off.

In its early stages, the lowly camel cavalry's fight against the German-armed Ottomans may have echoed that of David versus Goliath. But as victories stacked up, the British military behemoth swung around behind Lawrence and the Hashemite fighters. The desert-dwelling rebels were resupplied by the Royal Navy via the Red Sea. Partially staffed with British imperial troops, the Hashemite brothers Abdullah and Feisal remained at the head of an organised army.

With the Hijaz and Sinai won, cracks appeared in the Ottoman defence of Palestine and Syria. The combined Arab-British forces swept up along the Gaza coast and River Jordan throughout 1918. The defenders of Damascus were defeated with ease. Lawrence and Feisal rode into the city on October 1st 1918, to be welcomed by Arab nationalist flags flying. The Arab Revolt had not been a popular revolution, however. Some Arabs, loyal to the Sultan, had fought willingly for

Ottoman forces against the Hashemites. Popular protest, too, had played very little part. It had been a military campaign, initiated as a guerrilla war which was then adopted as the flank of a larger movement of conventional British forces into the southern reaches of the Ottoman's Arabian regions.

The Arabs' northward break out of the Hijaz holy region had important antecedents. In the 620s the Hashemites' holy ancestor, Muhammad, had followed much the same route. Though the Prophet's goals were very different, he had manned his holy army from the same source: the nomadic tribes who ranged their caravans up the paths from the southern tip of Arabia, through Mecca and Medina, to the north. Once the unfriendly elements of the tribes had been either defeated or converted, militant energies of the faithful had been turned outward. Successful invasions of Syria, Egypt, Mesopotamia and Persia had followed. In under a century Islam had transformed itself from a disgruntled rabble in the barren hills of eastern Arabia to a powerful political confederation.

The immediate results of the Arab Revolt were largely the same. The fall of Damascus began the steep terminal decline of Europe's 'Sick Man'. The Ottoman Empire surrendered in November 1918, along with the rest of the Central Powers. Ottoman authority across the Middle East had crumbled. Lawrence accompanied an Arab delegation to the Versailles Peace Conference the following year, optimistic of a Hashemite-led Arab state. However, the earlier British promises of support clashed with a secret Franco-British scheme. While Abdullah did receive the kingdom of the new state of Jordan, its borders did not extend over the West Bank and into Palestine as he would have wished. This area fell under British mandate.

The other son of Sherif Hussein, King Feisal, survived only months on the Syrian throne before his unceremonious ejection by France. The British then installed him as the first puppet king of their freshly created Mesopotamian entity, Iraq. The short-term result of this illogical choice – a Sunni puppet ruler for an occupied Shia majority – became murderously clear after 1920. A new guerrilla insurgency gripped the Middle East. Baghdad, Basra and innumerable smaller settlements within Iraqi borders were rocked by nationalist attacks. Harsh British reprisals continued for years. Longer-term, the legacy of the British-installed Hashemite rule is equally disastrous. Just like Feisal before him, Saddam Hussein persecuted Iraqis who did not share his Sunni background. The latest and ongoing foreign occupation of the country has produced an insurgency carrying the sectarian stamp of post-Versailles foreign meddling.

Secular rule and the contemporary Middle East have rarely sat together at ease. Perhaps one explanation is offered by the *caliphs*, the Muslim rulers of those first holy kingdoms. They were called 'Commanders of the Faithful', a term which captures nicely the troika of political, military and religious power they embodied. Prominent among *caliphs* was Hussein. Just like his Hashemite descendants and 20th-century namesake, the Prophet's grandson was as much a rebel as a religious leader. The circumstances of Hussein's martyrdom – leading a small army against the Umayyad dynasty at the Iraqi city of Karbala – bears more than a passing resemblance to the Arab Revolt itself.

Of course the relationship between Islam and revolutionary politics extends beyond guerrilla warfare.

> Those who are ruling over the people by usurping the authoring of God cannot be made to abdicate their authority by mere persuasion and appeal.[1]

These are the words of Sayyid Qutb, an influential 1960s theorist who welded Islam's political tenets to Marxist revolutionary rhetoric. He was not alone in doing so. The Indian Abul Mawdudi was influenced directly in his approach by Lenin, coining the term 'Islamic revolution'. The founder of Egypt's Muslim Brotherhood tackled both poverty and colonialism via Islamic social reform. Most well known is Ruhollah Khomeini, the icon of the 1978–79 Iranian Revolution. He elevated the Shia concept of *itjihad*, or 're-interpretation', to new heights. The Deobandis; al-Fatah; Hezbollah; the Taliban Mujahaddeen: the list of 20th-century Islamic resistance movements is extensive. It is also growing.

There is no point, however, in pretending that Islam is inherently revolutionary. Just like the multiple denominations of other ancient belief systems, Muslim internal debate is alive and well. While some Muslims have advocated social change or radical action, the opposite is equally true. Some theorists pull Islam back from the political realm altogether. Conservative movements such as Tablighi Jamaat exert significant influence despite grabbing fewer headlines than Al-Qaeda, Hezbollah and their ilk. Other movements, such as the microfinance Grameen Bank of Bangladesh, can effect revolutionary change with reference to a tradition of Islamic social justice but no recourse to violence.

Just as secular politics contains left, right and centre ground, so practising Muslims will disagree with the beliefs of many of their co-religionists. Puritan Saudi Wahhabism, for example, carries serious differences of opinion with almost all other Muslim forces it encounters. It frowns on secularised but traditional Sunni Muslim societies like Syria, vies with Shia states for regional influence and doesn't even dignify the Sufis with recognition as common Muslims. Such diversity of opinion in today's Islamic civilisation is too often ignored.

Nor is it the case that a conflict in contemporary Arabia guarantees mounted guerrillas. Recent uprisings were carried out by unarmed civilian groups. Rather than attack an army camp in 2011, dissenting Bahrainis occupied a roundabout. Unlike Lawrence's joust through Dera'a, in Syria, in 1916, the people there had no military answer to King Assad's shelling of their city in 2011. Moreover, the insurgencies which plagued the American occupation of Iraq display significant differences to the Arab Revolt of 1916 and have more in common with anti-Feisal, anti-British insurgency in the 1920s.

The Arab Revolt of 1916 reminded a new generation of political extremists that conventional armies could be subverted from a position of apparent material weakness. Cuban, Vietnamese and Angolan bush warriors would later swallow whole the advice of Lawrence. A large number of conflicts were fought during the 20th century from deserts, jungles and backwoods by amateur soldiers. For all that Lawrence and the Hashemites lowered the odds ranged against them through daring and innovation, however, their reward was the backing of British troops and artillery. Today's guerrillas, cast in the mould of the 1916–18 Arabs, tend to fight with no Red Sea resupply route nor gold bars to bribe the locals.

Though Lawrence's writings do little to dispel the notion, he had been far from the only Allied agent at work in Arabia during the First World War. His actual contribution is still debated. What is unquestionable, and true to the life he had led, is that Lawrence's star exploded rather than faded out. His death in a motorcycle accident at the age of forty-seven contributed much to his immortality. Peter O'Toole's camp 1960s Hollywood portrayal guaranteed it.

Sun and Steel

JAPAN 19TH AND 20TH CENTURIES

The Japanese Tohoku earthquake and tsunami of 2011 led to destruction on an unprecedented scale. Nearly 20,000 people died, with many more left homeless. The estimated cost to the economy measures in the trillions of yen. There was, however, a notable lack of political fallout from either the natural disaster itself, or the resulting Fukushima nuclear meltdown. Even after evidence of cover-ups and official obfuscation emerged, public protest has been limited. Although his popularity had fallen in opinion polls, the resignation of Prime Minister Naoto Kan in August 2011 was not directly linked to the earthquake, nor its aftermath.

It is illuminating to occasionally guess at why historical events *didn't* happen rather than why they did. All the 'ingredients' conducive to revolution elsewhere in the world have long existed in Japan. In many ways, the speed of the country's development since the 19th century should have made unrest *more* likely. Japan developed from a feudal position to industrialised nuclear power faster than any other country on earth. *Samurai* knights still ruled over Japanese peasants in the 1860s; a point in time when Britain, a similarly proportioned island nation, ruled a global empire and had already extended the vote to most working-class males. From this delayed starting point, Japan emulated and accelerated the longer processes of transformation experienced by European and American countries. Emulated, but not replicated: to this day, Japan has never witnessed a popular political revolution. Why?

The extraordinary life and strange death of Yukio Mishima (1925–1970) explains something of Japanese exceptionalism. Mishima excelled in many roles. He became a novelist, poet, playwright, essayist, film-maker, bodybuilder and, finally, albeit most unsuccessfully, a revolutionary. On November 25th 1970, Mishima and a group of followers entered a Tokyo army base and took its commander hostage. Their intent was to exhort an insurrection against the government. After his failure to arouse the soldiers, Mishima returned to the commander's office and committed suicide by disembowelment – the traditional *samurai* fashion.

To outsiders, the appearance was of a bizarre and rather pathetic attempt at revolution. Mishima's supporters, the Shield Society, had made little effort to win support for their activities among either the public or the military ranks. The leader himself had pre-prepared funds for the legal costs of his cohorts, seemingly more focused on the nature of his death than the coup's ultimate success.

The key to Mishima's act, and to a more general under-standing of the protest tradition in Japan, is in the statement distributed to the barracks corps from a first-storey balcony:

> We will rise together, and, for what is right, we will die together. We will die to take Japan back to its true self… Now, even now, we mean to demonstrate for you the existence of values higher than life. Not freedom, not democracy. Japan. Japan, land of the history and the tradition we love.[1]

Mishima's coup was not an attempt to overturn tradition, but to restore it. He expressed common cause with the oppressed through emotional loyalty to his nation, not its usurpation. His fascination was with the aura of death, rather than the promise of renewed life and the creation of a new political world; the messianic vision common to revolutionaries elsewhere.

Where do the roots of such an act lie? Clues can be found among the patriotic rebellions which preceded Mishima. Just over a century earlier, in 1868, a pre-modern Japan had opened its doors to the world and attempted to kick-start modernisation. The Meiji Restoration put an emperor back on the throne after centuries of feudal rule. It changed Japan beyond all recognition. A country which for centuries had restricted visits by foreign ships, now opened itself to overseas influence. American merchants, French civil servants, English naval advisors and German military consultants arrived on the Tokyo docks. Japan embraced the industrial world and modernised its structures of state.

The changes were not to universal taste. Within ten years, a *samurai* noble called Saigo Takamori headed the Satsuma Rebellion with the specific aim of reimposing a code of honour on Japanese society's heart; a motive Mishima would undoubtedly have approved of. The rebellion was short-lived; crushed by the new efficiencies of the Meiji military. Takamori eventually committed suicide in the same manner as Mishima would later do.

The Satsuma Rebellion, however, was not simply a doomed uprising, a case of out-of-touch traditionalists raging against modernity. Takamori, the old *samurai*, had actually played a major part in implementing the Meiji Restoration in the first place. After Commodore Matthew Perry had led a convoy of American 'Black Ships' into Edo harbour in 1853, the seven-hundred-year-old feudal system received a shock from which it would not recover. Leading *samurai* nobles, Takamori included, recognised that Japan needed radical change. Along with other regional lords and their domains, Takamori led his native Satsuma in opposition to the then dominant *shogunate* system of government. The *shogunate* had been, essentially, a primitive form of dictatorship, with a hereditary figure exerting strict rule over multiple regional warlords. The model that many reforming *samurai* looked to was that of even older tradition: of an all-powerful Japanese emperor reinstalled as ruler in accordance with ancient Confucian and Buddhist rites.

Indeed, in this, Takamori partially succeeded. Emperor Meiji – a human whose divinity was candidly believed to originate in an ancestor's sexual encounter with the sun – reigned from 1868 onward. The last Tokugawa *shogun* had fallen. What Takamori does not appear to have conceived of, in bringing this event about, is that the entire feudal system would be wiped away with the *shogunate*; his own *samurai* class included.

In 1873, still in government in Edo and four years before his rebellion, Takamori had made a remarkable offer to Meiji officials. With the objective of provoking a war with Korea and recreating lost honour for his *samurai* class, Takamori wanted to sacrifice himself by leading a military mission across the Sea of Japan with no hope of success. When this offer was rejected, Takamori realised the scale of the threat to his entire way of life from the nation state being assembled under Emperor Meiji. He resigned from his official role and returned to his homeland, from where similarly ostracised fellow *samurai* nobles would nudge him to the head of another suicidal revolt in 1877.

These seemingly paradoxical motives hint at how the Japanese culture of protest would develop in the 20th century. The curtain had fallen on one period of change but, with the world wars around the corner, the new century opened to one of tumult. Tenant farmers, feminists and labour forces placed repeated stress on the Japanese state. 1925 was a key year. To placate popular demand, all men over the age of 25 received the vote. To eliminate the threat of left-wing usurpation, a special police force, the *Koto Keisatsu*, was formed to control seditious social movements. Restrictive legislation was passed, effectively outlawing communism.

1925 was also the year of Mishima's birth. His later writing and political activity was shaped by a childhood spent mostly in seclusion, devouring the library of his grandmother, who had related her memories of the Taisho period: the decade and a half after Emperor Meiji's death in 1912 when Japan brushed closest to a 'classic' revolution. During Mishima's youth, Japan turned away from democracy. The size and political power of the military expanded. Korea had been annexed since 1910 and, in 1931, Japan occupied Manchuria in northern China. A full-scale invasion occurred in 1937. The dreams of the old Satsuma rebel, Saigo Takamori, had been realised: warrior codes ruled Japan again, but this time in the form of modern tanks, fighter bombers and a huge, mechanised army.

Watched carefully by Mishima, military officers attempted coups and assassinations throughout the 1930s. Ultra-nationalists took the traditions of *samurai* culture as inspiration, but their efforts to hijack government were suppressed as ruthlessly as any hint of pro-democratic dissent. By the outbreak of war with the USA and her allies in 1941, government control was total. During the Second World War, Mishima's writing began to gain a following. After Japan's surrender, he published novels and plays. His country too entered a new world, first under US occupation, then under a democratic constitutional monarchy after 1952.

The social changes were akin to those after the Meiji Restoration. Once again, Japan imported foreign ideas, augmenting overseas technology and profiting from a reputation for excellence in engineering and design. The Japanese mirrored their former Axis allies in Germany. Both economies underwent a post-war 'miracle' resurgence. But once again the changes were imposed from above. The *zaibatsu* were a group of big businesses which had encouraged state control of the economy during the 1930s. Having benefitted from expansion into Korea, China and, later, elsewhere across Asia, they had survived the war and played a key role during the rebuilding of the 1950s, even though the empire and the nationalists had gone.

1960s Japan appears familiar. Automotive and electronics exports bankrolled infrastructural development at home. New high-speed 'bullet' trains criss-crossed the islands. During this period, Mishima became Japan's most successful literary export. His three Nobel prize nominations, his large international readership and the consequent financial rewards, however, were not enough. Having established a radical youth group which espoused ultra-nationalist sentiment – the Shield Society – Mishima planned his final act. Mishima, however, was not a true revolutionary, but a playwright. His coup attempt was a scripted drama, an epilogue to earlier events, with himself in the lead role.

A similar analogy could be made about today's Japan. Tenets of public loyalty to leaders, honour for elders and respect for authority underpin society. This has had many positive effects. Japanese cities, for example, remain the safest in the world to walk at night. In governmental bodies, unions and the family, *keigo* grammar grades the level of respect to be shown by Japanese speakers in conversation; far outstripping the honorific strata of Latinate languages. Nowhere else on earth do ancient traditions meet the cutting edge of 21st-century life so gracefully. The concept of community still holds genuine relevance. Social cohesiveness in the face of adversity helped the people of Japan work together in 2011 to aid rescue services, find survivors and comfort the bereaved.

Loyalty and hierarchy, however, render Japanese democracy something of a sham. The Tohoku earthquake, Japan's 'toughest and most difficult' event since the Second World War, according to Naoto Kan, has so far changed little in Japanese political culture or energy policy. The same political party which took office in 1955 was voted out only in 2009. Hierarchy, patriarchy and conformism permeate government institutions. The *zaibatsu* corporate giants – familiar to many through public brands such as Mitsubishi, Mitsui and Nissan – have evolved, but maintain significant leverage over politics.

From *Madama Butterfly* to the masochistic game shows shown on American television, Japan has long served as a means for the West to define what it is not. The European revolutionary traditions stand confounded in Japan:

> This loyalist is right-wing because of his fidelity to the Emperor, left-wing because of his attachment to the oppressed and hungry peasants. In prison, he is ashamed of being better treated than the communists, who are viciously beaten up.[2]

Mishima's attempted coup; the Satsuma Rebellion; the many and various attempted coups of the 1930s: these prominent eruptions, during periods of potential disruption and instability, had explicitly loyalist and nationalist goals. A true Japanese popular revolution remains far off. This exceptional society will continue along a predetermined course of stability. Having ruled for centuries, *samurai* codes remain ingrained.

Digital Renegades

The Zapatistas 1994–present

In 1916 'Irish rebels used a ship's wireless to make... a diffused broadcast in the hope of getting word to some ship that would relay their story to the American press.'[1] What a difference a century makes. Ever since Marshall McLuhan coined the phrase 'the medium is the message', in 1964, modes of political communication have come a long way. Before Iran erupted in 1978, it was a novel and easily smuggled gadget called audiocassette which spread Ruhollah Khomeini's messages of sedition into markets and madrassas (see *Rightly-guided*, p 26). American organisations bombarded opposition networks in 1980s Communist Poland with newfangled fax and Xerox machines, in an effort to combat government propaganda.

A remote corner of south-eastern Mexico is the unlikely location of the latest development. Chiapas is a backwater among Mexican states. In a total area only slightly bigger than Lithuania, there are few large cities. Yet, over the last two decades, and helped in no small part by the growth of the internet, a radical guerrilla resistance movement has emerged from its jungles to global prominence. The Zapatista Army of National Liberation (EZLN) take their name and ethos from Emiliano Zapata, the guerrilla who fought across southern Mexico from 1910 until 1917 (see *Dying on its Feet*, p 170). Like Zapata, the EZLN demand land rights, recognition of indigenous Mexicans and wholesale economic reform.

Who, or what, have the Zapatistas struggled against? That the state of Chiapas at the end of the 20th century had changed little since the era of Zapata provides a clue. Rates of infant mortality were as high as literacy was low. Clean drinking water was scarce. All the while, Mexican and foreign companies extracted oil, timber and other natural resources. Much of the state's agricultural bounty followed the same export route. By the time of the EZLN's emergence, the Institutional Revolutionary Party (PRI) had long occupied national power. The entire Mexican political system was tilted in the PRI's favour. Corruption of public officials was rife. Advocates of reform, however legitimate, had their complaints stamped out. Most notoriously, troops turned guns on Mexico City protestors in 1968.

The massacre provoked a philosophy student at Mexico City's UNAM university into radical activism. By 1984, Rafael Vicente had moved to Chiapas to help develop a guerrilla movement in the jungle. By the early 1990s, the hoped-for revolution among Chiapas' indigenous residents had not arrived. Still based in the jungle, but now the spokesperson of the nascent EZLN, Vicente watched as Mexico's leaders reduced government regulation and liberalised controls on cross-border trade and currency flows.

The model was inspired by the 'Chicago School', an economic philosophy evolved amongst a small group at the University of Chicago. Milton Friedman, the pivotal intellect of the movement, had directly advised US President Ronald Reagan and Chilean dictator Augusto Pinochet. His indirect influence was even stronger. Successive Mexican governments adopted the Chicago model, cutting spending, privatising state industries and energetically loosening controls on financial transactions.

On New Year's Day in 1994, hundreds of armed Zapatistas advanced out of the jungle to take over the cities and towns of Chiapas. Though initially successful, their takeover was brief.

Within days, a concerted repost by the Mexican army had killed scores and forced them back into the jungle. Far from hurting their campaign, however, the clashes had aided the main rebel objective: making headlines.

It was no accident that the Zapatistas announced themselves in the same hour that the North American Free Trade Agreement (NAFTA) came into effect in Chiapas. Freshly agreed by the governments of Mexico, the USA and Canada, its clauses lowered mutual tariffs and eased transnational labour; a classic Chicago School document. However, NAFTA also eradicated land guarantees for indigenous Mexicans, won for their constitution by the original Zapata, in 1917. It was on this basis that the Zapatistas justified their attack.

In terms of stated goals, the effort failed. The EZLN held no hope of rolling back NAFTA. But as an exercise in public relations, it was a masterstroke. Chiapas, lucky under normal circumstances to be mentioned even occasionally on Mexican airwaves, was suddenly thrown into the global media spotlight. Vicente, by now a permanently masked rebel, answering only to the name 'Subcomandante Marcos', claimed the rebels fought on behalf of all indigenous Mexicans against central government in Mexico City; indeed, in a succession of communiqués, Subcomandante Marcos appealed over the heads of Mexican politicians to all victims of globalised capitalism.

Though EZLN rhetoric discussed guerrilla tactics, the January 1994 attacks would remain the sole experiment with violence. In retreat, Marcos and the rebels fell on a support network constructed since arrival in the jungle ten years earlier. With official state government in the remote state capital, localised Zapatista-organised assemblies took over. Derived from indigenous community decision-making, anyone could speak on any matter; the size of the meeting small enough that collective votes could be taken with a show of hands.

The EZLN boasted another weapon lacking from the armoury of Emiliano Zapata: the internet. Their emergence had coincided with the birth and popularisation of a free and globally linked communications network. Marcos put the technology to good use. Reacting to his communiqués, international activists established direct communication via email. In embassies and on university campuses around the world, EZLN demands were translated and repeated. Indigenous rights groups from elsewhere in Mexico, documentary film-makers and representatives of Non-Governmental Organisations (NGOs) travelled to Chiapas. Fertilised by cheap digital technology, a global support web sprung up to match that of the jungle.

Meanwhile, communications technology had developed just as vital a role in the growth of the globalised economy. Starting in the early 1970s, information on stocks and shares began to be broadcast electronically. This allowed international investors to buy and sell at speed and across borders. The cost of computing plummeted in line with processor power: IBM's 5100 'desktop' computer weighed 22kg and cost $20,000 in 1975. Within six years, a smaller, more powerful unit cost less than a tenth of that price. Coupled with the advent of 'floating' currency rates and the popularity of Chicago School market liberalisation, the ease and potential benefits of global financial trading increased massively.

Unfortunately, so too did the risks. Thanks in part to the Mexican government's strict diet of deregulation and liberalisation, the value of the *peso* currency collapsed during 1994. The disastrous results, known as the 'Tequila Crisis', reflected similar shocks during the late 1990s to economies of ex-Soviet and south-east Asian 'Tiger' states. Amid unease at globalised finance, several meetings of the Chicago School's institutional cheerleaders were disrupted on the eve of the 21st century. Violent clashes erupted between demonstrators and security forces outside Group of Eight (G8), International Monetary Fund (IMF) and World Trade Organisation (WTO) conventions. Global media outlets reported on the 'Battle of Seattle' at the 1999 WTO meeting and the killing by police of a young man at the G8 summit in Genoa in 2001. The burgeoning anti-globalisation movement was handed wide coverage.

In among the black flags and 'Che' Guevara T-shirts sported by protestors, a common sight were the emblems of the EZLN. The Zapatista strategy of building internet-based alliances with NGOs had borne fruit. The Mexican government found its portrayal of the group as terrorists circumvented. Though state military incursions into rebel territory continued, the EZLN's profession of democracy and human rights had gained them a wider legitimacy. As an American study put it:

> No matter how small a territory the EZLN held in Chiapas, it quickly occupied more space in the media than had any other insurgent group in Mexico's if not the world's history.[2]

Furthermore, the EZLN subverted normal funding routes, drawing income through unexpected sources. Naomi Klein noted the range of branded merchandise available to supporters of the Zapatistas in both their online and real-world shops: 'Black T-shirts with red five-pointed stars, white T-shirts with ELZN printed in black. There are baseball hats, black EZLN ski masks, Mayan-made dolls and trucks.'[3]

After the previously immovable PRI party was finally dislodged from power in 2000, the Zapatistas encountered a chequered period. A temporary halt in the communiqués of Subcomandante Marcos led to speculation about his whereabouts and health. In the 2006 presidential contest, the EZLN campaigned separately, often criticising the left-wing candidate. An indirect result was a split in the left-wing vote and a return to power for the PRI. Nevertheless the movement still commands support among the indigenous people of southeastern Mexico, as it does among the revived anti-globalisation movement. This has come about in spite of EZLN's seeming contradictions: a leader who has never publicly shown his face; armed guerrillas who don't engage the enemy; anti-capitalists running a network of retail outlets; a democratic manifesto that ignores electoral politics.

The internet became more than merely a medium for change during 2011. Whistle-blowing organisations released highly sensitive government data. Hackers shut down, among others, the CIA website. Anti-corporate protestors carried the *#Occupy* hashtag symbol out of social media and onto placards. Their direct, participatory democratic meetings mirrored the form of the Chiapas assemblies; in this instance streamed live from capital cities around the world.

Milton Friedman died in 2003, still confident the free market approach would continue to helm the world's finances. It is a pity the theorist of money supply could not have lived to see another recent internet innovation. Gaining its first mainstream publicity in 2011, Bitcoin offers the prospect of digital encryption as an alternative to controls on currency by central auditors i.e. banks and governments. Limited by design to a finite reserve and, theoretically at least, more secure as more people sign up, it is tempting to speculate that Friedman would have invested at least a little time to investigate the revolutionary potential of the world's first peer-to-peer currency.

In any case, since the global economic crisis of 2008 the Chicago School model has been further re-examined, with Friedman's philosophies criticised. Zapatistas, however, would find it hard to disagree with his concept of liberty:

> Literally millions of people are involved with providing one another with their daily bread, let alone their yearly automobiles. The challenge to the believer in liberty is to reconcile this widespread interdependence with individual freedom.[4]

Marcos, the EZLN and the rest of the anti-globalisation movement rely on free access to email and uncensored websites to spread their message. Much the same statement, strangely enough, could be made about the continued operation of modern financial markets. In order to trade, investors require up-to-date information and deregulated, but secure, communication systems. Balancing personal freedom with financial dynamism and social interdependence is the challenge of the new century. How digital communications technology is policed in the future will influence both economic stability *and* the culture of protest.

The Revolution
Eats Itself

Pol Pot; Joseph Stalin; Muammar Gaddafi; Fidel Castro: some of history's most notorious dictators began their political lives as revolutionaries, fighting for liberty. What happened? Are freedom and power irreconcilable? Why don't revolutions invariably lead to democracy? How can revolutionaries of the future avoid the temptation to stab their comrades in the back? This chapter aims to answer all of these questions by exploring the different ways in which the course of a revolution can be diverted.

Lessons on what not to do are many and various. Since the terror of the guillotine gripped 1790s France, virtually every major popular movement has been diverted from its original course by violent in-fighting over the details of the post-revolutionary world to be built. Violence edges closer as formerly united comrades achieve power.

Oliver Cromwell famously defeated and killed his king, then shut down Parliament, purged his army and ravaged the upstart Irish. His example stood as a model prototype for all post-revolutionary terror to come. In the Mexican Revolution, successive generals fought their way into Mexico

City, only to turn despot and train federal guns on the rest of the country at the first opportunity.

General Suharto is another rebel-turned-dictator. After fighting for Indonesian independence, he ejected the president and assumed murderous control. The 2004 Orange Revolution appeared to herald a new democratic era for Ukraine. Since then, press and political freedom have been curtailed.

Eliminating leaders altogether would be one solution to this age-old recurrence. Horizontal, grassroots assembly structures were visible across almost all major arenas of protest during 2011. How that system might translate onto the national level is debatable. History again provides a warning. In 1936, Spanish anarchist unions successfully defended Barcelona and several other towns and regions from fascist attack. They turned to implementing collectivised, leaderless systems within their territory. The experiment lasted only a year. However it was not the fascists who dealt the mortal blow, but the anarchists' fellow left-wingers, the moderate socialists.

Spanish fascism in the 1930s, with its grassroots structures and goal of re-making society, carried many hallmarks of revolutionary movements discussed elsewhere in this book. In other parts in Europe, in the same decade, the German Brownshirts and Italian Blackshirts erased the status quo, radically remodelled their economies and set their countries, and the world, on a new course. Both Hitler and Mussolini enjoyed genuine popular support in their endeavours.

So are revolutions actually bad for democracy? There is no guarantee that successful rebels will create free societies. However, less obvious, longer-term effects can take hold.

Cromwell, England's early modern dictator, left behind powerful, competing interests which were forced into a unique political arrangement. The 'unwritten' British constitution which emerged from the island's revolutionary 17th century has since gifted several centuries of stable, peaceful, parliamentary democracy.

The destructive modern revolutions of Mexico, Spain and Indonesia consumed their countries many times over. In all three, 20th-century upheaval descended into extended undemocratic interludes. Spain endured 35 years of fascist rule after defeat for the Republic in the civil war. Mexican governments held token polls after the 1910–20 revolution, but the same party won each presidential election between 1926 and the new century. Both Indonesia's rich ecological resources and human population have been the victims of its own post-revolutionary nightmare.

These cases will do little to reassure Ukrainians, whose 2004 Orange Revolution demanded immediate democratic change. Much the same is true of Egyptian protestors, who spent much of 2011 attempting to move reform from a promise into effect. Both groups will have to face the fact that brave new worlds are not built overnight. Balancing grassroots democratic structures with strong checks on the conduct of national leaders is a long and painful but nevertheless obligatory lesson for any revolution that wishes to outlast the average. The founding creed of few popular uprisings have survived intact beyond their first years. If Ukraine, the new Arab democracies and other revolutionaries of the future can learn properly the lessons of the past, they may yet buck the trend.

Not Just English;
Not Only a Revolution
ENGLAND AND SCOTLAND 1640–1707

Writing about Scotland's relationship with England in the *Guardian* in the August following the May 2011 election to the Scottish parliament, playwright David Greig portrayed the moment as the point in a marriage when 'the wife looks at her husband and realises – suddenly and clearly – that it's over'.[1] Soon after victory, the Scottish Nationalist Party (SNP) pledged to hold a referendum on full-blown Scottish independence. Though the outcome of such a poll during the SNP's tenure of Edinburgh's underling parliament is far from certain, the 17th-century roots of British union may yet be exposed to 21st-century light.

The marriage began over three centuries ago. Since then, England and Scotland have shared monarchs, a central parliament in London and a now-defunct empire. A unique constitutional settlement stitched together the deal. The 1707 Act of Union was forged at the close of a traumatic and revolutionary period. The 17th-century era had seen as much war, massacre and famine as it had revolution. However, several genuinely popular movements spurred its radical changes. Their influence lasts to this day.

In the early 1640s, the two countries were not yet united in law, political power in each kingdom rested on starkly contrasting religious loyalties, born of the previous century's Reformation. The Westminster parliament was summoned at the king's whim; its members exclusively English, Protestant, male and propertied. Power in Scotland resided in the two dominant churches: Anglican and Presbyterian. The religious tension embodied itself in Charles I, King of England, Scotland and Ireland from 1625 onward. Though baptised a Protestant, his Stuart family traditions and French wife were Catholic.

When Charles imposed a 'High Anglican' liturgy on the fiercely democratic Presbyterian 'Kirk', rioting broke out in Scotland. The king sent forces north, only to be defeated by a united Scottish army. Charles then called on the Westminster parliament to fund his fightback. He failed. When he tried again to subdue the Scots, his forces were not only defeated, but his discourteous subjects north of the border marched over the River Tweed and occupied English soil.

Left with no funds and little choice, Charles was forced to recall worthy members of parliament again to request their financial support. The king, however, had long engaged in imprudent wars with little clear gain and much expense. Charles' money-grubbing habits and perceived 'papist' sympathies had drained reserves of goodwill. An East Anglian member of parliament named Oliver Cromwell, having earlier undergone evangelical conversion, was typical of the Puritan suspicion that prevailed. Parliament went further than simply refusing Charles' pleas: it demanded an end to royal absolutism and a permanent role for elected government.

It was at this crucial point, in late 1641, that a full-scale revolt broke out across Charles' third kingdom. Ireland's population was split between the more numerous Catholics and the more powerful 'planted' Protestants. Catholic gentry were embittered for much the same reasons as the English parliamentarians: the Stuart crown's partiality to abrupt demands for cash; and a lack of recognition of their faith. Backed by popular support and Vatican funds, Catholic militias attacked

Protestant settlements across Ireland. Word of massacre and mayhem, not all of it unembellished by hearsay, reached London. Whereas one of the reasons for the Irish Catholic rebellion was the perception of a king under the sway of powerful Protestants, Oliver Cromwell and other radicals, automatically assumed Charles' malevolent involvement on the side of the rebels. Mutual suspicion deepened when the king's attempt to try several parliamentarians for treason failed. In January 1642, Charles and his most loyal followers fled the English capital for Oxford. Decades of revolutionary havoc had begun.

The ensuing English civil war was, in actual fact, three wars spread across three kingdoms. In the first chapter, 'Cavalier' royalists won early victories, mostly concentrated across the centre of England, only for their lines of supply to be stretched by the better-organised 'Roundhead' forces of Parliament. The year 1645 proved decisive. The Roundheads concentrated their energies in the recently formed New Model Army and routed their enemies.

North of the border, Scotland saw its own conflict. A highly mobile Royalist army roved the Highlands and won victories against the Parliament-aligned Presbyterians. After a short lull in 1647, and as the power of Cromwell's Puritans grew, Charles befriended the Scottish Presbyterians, persuading them to switch allegiance. He then instigated Royalist uprisings in Parliament-controlled southern England and once again attacked.

Though the king held a special talent for persuading diverse groups he had their interests at heart, the Parliament forces' upper hand on the battlefield began to show. In the second part of the conflict, the New Model Army won battle after battle, finally purging the Royalists at Preston in 1648. With Charles' seeming total defeat, Cromwell affirmed his new found stature by stamping out dissent in Westminster. He pushed for the trial of the king. Charles was duly found guilty of treason and publicly beheaded in January 1649. Little did Charles' executioners know that the regicide was but an *aperitif* for the violence to come.

While all this carried on, recognisably democratic and, for the era, radical political elements emerged at ground level. While they couldn't vote, women played a prominent role in the many and various protest movements of 1640s London. The Thames Watermen – the tube drivers of their day in a bridge-deprived London – instituted full-suffrage elections to their guild council. The Levellers spread a message of political equality and moderation with their pamphlets. Clubmen formed defence committees to protect local lands from both sides in the civil war. Both reforming Puritans within the Anglican Church, as well as Presbyterian congregations outside of it, relied on assemblies of leading members to make decisions, rather than the centralised and autocratic power of bishops.

Elections for the 1641 'Long Parliament', so called because it sat in session for nearly eighteen years, had been limited in franchise. But they had beckoned real political debate out into the open. A plethora of dissenting Protestant sects emerged. From chapel to street corner came the pacifist Quakers. Diggers initiated agricultural communes. The millennial Fifth Monarchists foretold coming doom.

A myriad of religious radicals carrying potent political messages followed. Prominent was 'Free-born' John Lilburne. His outspoken demands for freedom of worship and the restriction of bishops' power gained him a significant following. Riots had occurred when Lilburne encouraged crowds to storm the Archbishop's palace in 1637 and again when Charles attempted to levy new taxes in later years.

In the third instalment of civil war, the outer kingdoms came into play again. Angry at Charles I's execution, Scottish Presbyterians had crowned his son King of Scotland. An uneasy alliance under Charles II then emerged between Irish Catholic lords and the remaining English Royalist generals. Cromwell and his New Model Army eradicated both in extended Irish and Scottish campaigns from 1649 to 1651. With biblical zeal, and exaggerated reports of Catholic massacres fresh in the memory, the Puritans laid waste to the Irish towns that refused to surrender. Thus Cromwell's lasting two-way reputation was sealed; spittle-worthy war criminal across the four provinces of Ireland; father of parliament and protector of liberty in his native Albion.

Both reputations are not without irony. Cromwell may have defeated the absolutist tendencies of Charles I, but he repeatedly restricted the power of parliament when its members differed, by force if necessary. Grassroots democracy within his own New Model Army, too, posed big problems for the Machiavellian Puritan. What began as England's first professional fighting unit, mutated into a potent revolutionary force in its own right. A salaried, mobile soldiery untied to a particular town or garrison was a significant departure from the norm. So too were promotions on the basis of merit rather than social standing. Radical Levellers disseminated their pamphlets amongst the New Model ranks. The army councils to which each regiment elected representatives contained a fair share of radical voices. Cromwell and his loyal commanders came down hard on Leveller-inspired mutinies, dispersing the main force of internal opposition through executions, expulsions and foreign expeditionary missions.

By 1650, Cromwell reigned supreme. Over the next decade, he led a military dictatorship (the Protectorate) which set in place the early foundations of the constitutional framework still governing the United Kingdom to this day. Cromwell united English and Scottish government in London, denying the Scots their parliament after 1653. For the first time, these domains fell under a common set of laws (as opposed to a united crown, as had been the case under Charles I).

When Cromwell died and Charles II was restored to the English throne in 1660, Scotland again regained its independence. Scottish demands for an accountable king had helped bring about the whole conflict originally. These demands now came to an end. Charles II died in 1688, succeeded by his Catholic brother James. This led to what in England is often called the Glorious Revolution; it was neither a revolution nor a particularly glorious event in itself, but an effort by Protestant interests to swap a Catholic monarch with a Catholic heir, for a reliable Protestant prince.

William of Orange's coup at the expense of James, however, did lead directly to a series of political documents which capped the revolutionary changes of the previous century. The English 'Bill of Rights' ended the lasting power of absolute monarchy. The Scottish 'Claim of Rights' earned space for a Presbyterian-inspired democratic system under the new king. The Act of Settlement enshrined a Protestant monarch at the centre of an unwritten parliamentary constitution; all this before the 1707 Act of Union united territory. The effects have proved durable: England and Scotland remain bound together in law; British monarchs remain figureheads of the Anglican Church; the UK has never enjoyed a Catholic prime minister.*

Just English, or not; full-blooded popular revolution, or not; the drama played out on the western edge of Europe in the

---

* Openly, at least. The most recent of borderline cases was Tony Blair. He was baptised a Catholic in the same year that he left prime ministerial office.

mid-seventeenth century has riven wide and deep influence. In Ireland, punitive settlements imposed by Cromwell set centuries of sectarianism in train. Similar chasms opened up across Scottish society and have, arguably, yet to be patched up. A positive response to the SNP's independence referendum would not necessarily result in the break-up of the United Kingdom. Whatever the result, however, the prospect of an independent Scotland has certainly not been as seriously considered for over 300 years.

Meanwhile, the grand finale to 17th-century revolutions and war in England and Scotland was an ocean and a century away. Tenets of the most extreme dissenting radicals found their ultimate realisation in the late-18th-century New World. With victory over the Levellers, the Puritan sects and the Scottish Covenanters, Cromwell had blocked from power the most extreme ideas born of the period. Those who could, took their leave across the sea. Presumed lost, the wildest Scottish and English practitioners of godly people power scattered to a savage western colony called America.

Dying on Its Feet
MEXICO 1910–17

Atop a cantering steed, over a barren horizon, the hero
approaches… José Doroteo Arango Arámbula, aka
Pancho Villa, became the most famed rebel on the
planet when a Hollywood studio filmed, on location with real
battle scenes incorporated, a sensationalised account of his part
in the Mexican Revolution (1910–17). *The Life of General Villa*
was released in the USA before fighting in Mexico had ended.
In the movie, naturally enough, Villa wins. The reality, though
even more dramatic, did not boast such a happy ending.

Villa had grown up fatherless, in the direst poverty. He
enjoyed little basic education, let alone a grounding in politics.
But the Durango native possessed the independent *vaquero*
'cowboy' spirit of the north in abundance. The young Villa
quickly established himself in a roving bandit gang, acquiring
the nickname '*La Cucaracha*' ('The Cockroach').* After rising
to leadership, a fateful encounter directed Villa's core skills of
horsemanship, gunslinging and ingenious military strategising
towards revolution.

A political agent in Chihuahua state successfully persuaded
Villa to support Francisco Madero's bid for the presidency.
Madero, an educated member of a northern establishment
family, cut a rather unlikely rebel figure. He was, however, also
an enthusiast of Mexico's liberal 19th-century constitution.
To its letter, Mexico was a democracy. In practice, however, by

---

* The folk melody of the same name is itself linked to the Mexican Revolution.
Both rebel and government soldiers invented new verses and characters to fit
their political views.

1910, Porfirio Diaz had occupied the presidential throne in Mexico City for 30 out of the previous 34 years.

Madero's anti-government broadsides had found common cause among many besides Villa. Diaz successfully fixed the 1910 election in his own favour and imprisoned his opponent, but Madero escaped and fled across the border to Texas. It was from here, in November 1910, that an open revolutionary appeal was proclaimed. Villa and many other armed bandits across Mexico heeded the call. Diaz's armourers in Washington and London wavered, however, and the president's military stayed loyal. Expectations of success were not high. His own grandfather thought the physically unimposing Madero's fight against Diaz akin to that of 'a microbe's challenge to an elephant'.[1]

Mexico's geographic diversity played a large role in the decade of revolutionary conflict that then unfolded. Dixie accents and US dollars, for example, were plentiful around the corrals, cotton fields, inland mines and offshore oilfields of the north. In the southern coffee- and sugar-producing states, little had changed for the labouring masses since the Spanish conquests of the 16th century. Plantations – the *haciendas* – either hired or forced local villagers into cultivating cash crops. Unlike the north, where those of native or mixed blood were in the minority, Indians made up the bulk of the poor. Southern landownership and wealth was either concentrated in the rich plantation owners or dissipated along communal lines in rural villages.

Another star-crossed Mexican rebel, more comfortable in stirrups than on his own two feet, emerged from the south. Emiliano Zapata was born into a relatively prosperous family in the subtropical southern state of Morelos. Repeated encroachments by a local *hacienda* onto the land of his local village acted as the spark for Zapata's revolutionary awakening. Unlike Villa's marauding *vaqueros*, however, Zapata based the success of his campaigns on guerrilla strategies. This suited not only the heavy southern vegetation and steep crags in which his rebel cells operated, but also their peasant backgrounds and relative dearth of military experience. Zapata had already attacked and beaten several federal forces by the time of Madero's 1910 call to arms.

In the north, Villa was building his own rebel army. His simple but effective formula had been to hitch resentment to President Diaz, his tyrannical state governors and local landowners to gun-toting *vaquero* culture. At the decisive Battle of Ciudad Juarez in 1911, Villa's ingenuity came to the fore. His ranks defeated seemingly stronger government forces, using dynamite to blow through the mud walls of adobe houses adjoining a besieged citadel. By the time Zapata had pushed his way north from Morelos into the suburbs of Mexico City, Diaz had already fled power. Madero became president. A new era had dawned.

Or so Mexico thought. With Diaz gone, Madero's inherent moderation kicked in. Conservation of the old regime's social and military structures satisfied neither Villa's calls for liberty, nor Zapata's ideals of communal living and indigenous rights. Counter-revolutions by Diaz loyalists broke out in several Mexican states. Madero entrusted their suppression to his military head, Victoriano Huerta, who promptly turned on his boss in 1913. Madero was first imprisoned and then murdered. The reactionary, ultra-conservative President Huerta was even less acceptable to Villa and Zapata as leader. Rebel guns had hardly had a chance to cool before they were raised once again, this time against Huerta. And so the assassination of Diaz marked not a final act, but only the end of the revolution's opening stages.

An increasingly attritional revolutionary war then unfolded. The middle stage of the revolution (from 1913 until 1917) was marked by bloody assaults, treacherous double-crosses and innocent victims caught in the crossfire. In the south, faced with overwhelming government opposition, Zapata rallied his peasant armies to unlikely victories. Government arms stores were looted. Taxes were extracted from *haciendas*. On occasion the region's cities were even captured and held by rebels. However, Zapata's gains were unsustainable and he had little time to implement his radical vision of society. Better armed federal forces showed no hesitation in gunning down the peasants of the southern states, believing them complicit in the rebellion.

Meanwhile, Villa attacked corrupt churchmen and *haciendas*, redistributing wealth among the Chihuahuan poor and gaining a new nickname: 'the Centaur of the North'. He also won famous victories. Sometimes, as at Ciudad Juárez in November 1913 when his troops used a government train as a 'Trojan Horse', wit was the weapon. Elsewhere, brute force won the day. The merciless battle of Tierra Blanca rendered Villa master of Chihuahua and paved the way for Huerta's defeat and exile in 1914.

In one of their few meetings, Zapata and Villa entered Mexico City in triumph that year. Side-by-side on horseback, the contrasting styles of the two rebel soldiers was clear: Villa wore the khaki of a career general; Zapata sported a cravat and the white cotton garb of his peasant guerrillas. Their endorsement of a new national leader, Venustiano Carranza, was short-lived. Once again, demands for land reform were rejected. Carranza went one step further by trying, but failing, to demob their troops.

And so civil war continued. Northern and southern rebels faced similar obstacles: the military challenge of building, maintaining and controlling professional armies; and the social challenge of retaining the trust of townsmen and rural poor simultaneously. Carranza's cold-blooded policy of executing all prisoners of war was soon mirrored by the rebels.

Aware of their fate if captured, soldiers on both sides battled with fierce intensity.

Lack of resources was a constant problem. Arms, medical supplies and food were the most pressing requirements. The outbreak of the First World War, in the midst of the revolution, favoured Carranza in one respect: the import duties and export revenues of Mexico's main Atlantic and Pacific ports were controlled by his government. In return, the conflict in Mexico played a major part in the outcome of the First World War itself: in 1917, a German message – the infamous 'Zimmerman Telegram' – encouraged Mexico to attack the USA. It was intercepted by British cryptographers and its contents published widely. The fallout saw the American public, formerly isolationist, swing behind the idea of combat.

South of the Rio Grande, with both Villa and Zapata ostracised from the presidency of Carranza, their rebellions limped on. Weakened by yet another 'scorched earth' campaign, Zapata was finally assassinated in 1917. Villa lost crucial battles against Carranza forces and retreated back to a life of sporadic bandit raids across the northern plains. Even after the 1920 assassination of Carranza brought relative stability, Villa's status as an icon of resistance remained dangerous for the new regime. A government-appointed death squad gunned down the perennial rebel in 1923.

With Carranza's downfall, the revolution came to an end. Mexico, however, was a wreck. The capital's commercial and cultural riches had been looted under successive military occupations. The anti-Spanish xenophobia common to rebel areas had been extended to Chinese and other foreign moneylenders, pawnbrokers and shopkeepers. In Morelos and across the south, peasants drifted back to the deserted *haciendas*. Entire towns and villages had been wiped off the map. Influenza and other diseases ravaged those lucky enough to emerge from war unscathed.

And still Mexico rebelled. The government defeated twin revolts in the mid-1920s: the Cristero Catholics fought and lost a three-year battle against state anti-clericalism; the Yaqui Indians demanded the promised land reform their fathers had fought and died for, only to be crushed themselves. Hence, 1920s Mexico retained its peculiar pre-revolutionary mix of absolutist politics, foreign corporate penetration and anti-quated social strata. The federal system remained in place, just as it does today. Mexican elections retained their characteristic opacity, as they continue to do. The corruption-riddled political bloc born amid the revolution's aftermath became known as, without a shred of irony, the Institutional Revolutionary Party (PRI). It won every presidential election until the year 2000.

What did the revolution change for the better? The immediate answer is depressing. Zapata, perhaps the event's only true revolutionary leader, lay murdered. Although certain individuals who had opposed Diaz 'won' in the end, they could hardly still be called rebels. It had been a revolution of unilateral *pronunciamientos*, of splintered legitimacy and the all-too-familiar story of the double-crossing strongman winning out. Given the number and complexity of protagonists at work, the true aims of the victors (beyond naked ambition) were never clear. Perhaps only military historians will find cause for celebration. A sideshow to First World War theatrics, revolutionary Mexico proved an effective laboratory for innovators in death. Generals waged prototype chemical, trench and aerial warfare. The rattle of early machine guns and the boom of dynamite permeated thunderous battlefield soundscapes.

Even trains became weapons. Rebels could see that railways allowed federal conscripts and artillery to transverse the thick southern jungles and vast northern plains with equal speed. They slit these arteries whenever they could, bending track and lifting sleepers. If sabotaging or hijacking a locomotive was not an option, carriages were either bombed or packed with explosives and sent slamming into fortress walls, as first occurred at the First Battle of Rellano in 1912. Villa devised another ingenious use for the railway while attacking Ciudad Juárez, in 1913: his troops hijacked a government coal train, filled it with troops and snuck into the city incognito. Despite the levels of military innovation during the Mexican revolution, other legacies emerged.

Important artistic and urban labour movements flourished in Mexico during the 1920s. Moreover, the country's economy and population saw dramatic expansion as the 20th century wore on. However, the Tlatelolco massacre of student demonstrators in central Mexico prior to the 1968 Olympics showed that the repressive counter-revolutionary methods of the century's second decade had been learned well. Corruption and cover-ups tainted the subsequent investigations. Thus Ciudad Juárez's latter-day *femicido* cases – a twenty-year string of unsolved serial murders linked to the region's massive narcotics and human trafficking industries – find themselves reflected back through Mexico's violent 20th century.

What is clear, as the blood-soaked centennials of Mexico's revolutionary decade accumulate, is that both Villa's 'Land and Freedom' battle-cry and Zapata's rural communal utopia, remain distant dreams. Since 1994, the EZLN movement in the southern state of Chiapas has consciously echoed Emiliano Zapata's call for land reform, native Indian rights and an end to exploitative preferment for foreign corporate investment (see *Digital Renegades*, p 151). If victorious, their ongoing struggle may one day become a truer and less contested legacy than that of 1910–17.

Zero Sums

Spanish Revolution 1936–38

I want you, each and every one of you, to have a reason to be out-raged. This is precious. When something outrages you, as Nazism did me, that is when you become a militant, strong and engaged. You join the movement of history, and the great current of history continues to flow only thanks to each and every one of us.[1]

So goes *Indignez Vous!*, the personal manifesto of protest written by Stéphane Hessel, a 94-year-old former French Resistance fighter. His pamphlet sold so well in 2011 that it was translated into nine languages and became the unofficial bible for anti-corporate demonstrators around the globe. Participants in Spain's 15-M protest movement were inspired directly by the message of Hessel, as their *Los Indignados* ('The Indignant') nickname shows. Taking to *plazas* in Madrid, Barcelona and dozens of other cities, *Los Indignados* protested against record levels of youth unemployment and the disconnection of ordinary people from parliamentary politics.

The original Spanish revolutionaries of the 1930s came from two very different political traditions. A nationwide right-wing military coup, led by Spain's eventual dictator, Francisco Franco, aimed to wipe away the country's republican democratic system, restoring the monarchy, respect for the church and military prestige. In Bilbao, Barcelona and other Spanish cities, the radical anarchist left took up arms in opposition. In a twelve-month-long experiment in collectivisation, the theories of Marx and Bakunin leapt out of the philosophical realm and into reality. The process stands, almost uniquely in history, as a genuinely popular and sustained libertarian revolution, meriting greater attention for the indignant of today.

The civil war and the revolution sprang from the same source: zero sum politics in Spain's Second Republic. By 1936, three elections in six years had delivered nothing but political extremes: socialism and anarcho-syndicalism on one side; conservatism and authoritarian Catholicism on the other. The end of Primo de Rivera's dictatorship ushered in two years of leftist rule from 1931. The socialists upset more than just the devout with swingeing taxes on the ringing of church bells and funeral processions. Right-wing Falangists then won power and promptly reversed the previous government's policies.

The cosy political centre ground, target of contemporary 15-M protesters, did not exist. Left opposed right with seething vehemence. The feelings were returned with interest. Socialists, anarchists, urban labourers, peasants and miners faced down landowners, monarchists, industrialists, colonialists and the church, using a vocabulary of violence and extremes. A union member was immediately also a 'commie'. Being a Catholic meant also being labelled a fascist.

During the Second Republic, a number of abortive coups, plots and strikes were first launched, then zealously repressed. High-stakes ideology was the order of the day: in 1934, a certain General Franco took particular relish in defeating a miners' strike in Asturias with the full might of the military. The economy, mired in global depression, remained dire throughout. In such an atmosphere, little space existed for compromise: 'Spain, far from being a happy and blissful country, was living on a volcano.'[2]

The year 1936 brought new elections. The socialists gained power. In response, a group of officers, led by the Galician-

Franco, actively prepared to seize it back. Troops under their command received charitable donations of training and weapons from Mussolini's fascist Italy. Nazi Germany too promised support. Stalin's USSR, along with Mexico, offered the governing socialists equivalent backing. Here already can be traced the outline of the looming civil war; its international magnitude; and the reasons for its relative fame. Though fought for domestic spoils, the civil war ideologies and combatants had origins that lay beyond the Spanish frontier.

The coming revolution, by contrast, was pursued by the radical libertarian left; a demographic with few international friends beyond incidental sympathisers. Its leaders encountered severe opposition from among supposedly like-minded brethren; the governing socialists. Cosmopolitan art, memoir, photojournalism and polemic focused on the cosmopolitan tragedy of the war rather than the fratricidal outcome of a failed revolution.

With the country bristling for war, Spain's countryside sank deeper into a long-standing crisis. Its huge estates (*latifundia*) and their managers (*caciques*), represented for peasants decades of division, exploitation and frustrated hopes. Land reform had long been promised. Impatient peasant groups began to occupy the estates and fields they laboured on during 1936. When Franco and his forces finally revolted in July of the same year, with the goal of reinstating monarchy, his 'Nationalists' quickly assumed control of the rural north and virtually all of the south. Government 'Republicans', wilfully ignorant of peasant land seizures before 1936, now actively encouraged them as a bulwark against Nationalist advance.

Because the immediate threat from Franco emanated within the state's own army, the moderate socialists in government were forced to turn to left-wing militias to suppress it.

But the working-class areas of larger Spanish cities were not strongly socialist. Instead it was anarchists, normally distant and antagonistic relations of other left-wingers, who held sway there. And so the anarchist militiamen who successfully repulsed Nationalist attacks on the capital Madrid and on the regional industrial centres of Bilbao and Barcelona, held serious differences of opinion with the government they defended.

Victorious, anarchists found themselves in control of Barcelona and highly influential in several other of Spain's larger cities. Eschewing the comfortable hierarchy of the government socialists, anarchists set about a ruthless reordering of society. Factories and businesses of all sizes were commandeered. Citizen-run courts, police forces, judiciaries and prisons were set up. Barter systems and vouchers replaced currency. George Orwell, active in a Catalonian militia unit at the time, observed:

> Every shop and cafe had an inscription saying that it had been collectivized; even the bootblacks had been collectivized and their boxes painted red and black. Waiters and shop-workers looked you in the face and treated you as an equal. Servile and even ceremonial forms of speech had temporarily disappeared.[3]

On Aragonese and Basque former *latifundia* estates, where rural anarchist controls were strongest, similar exercises in experimental economic systems were taking place. Agricultural syndicates were created, with produce delivered to worker-run factories in the cities. In both city and countryside, Catholicism took the brunt of the blame for its association with hierarchy and privilege. Churches were demolished or burnt, with isolated lynchings of priests.

Franco's nightmare – of an anti-clerical, anti-monarchist workers' state – had begun to materialise. While Nationalist forces controlled much of the Spanish countryside across the north and north-west, they had failed to overcome anarchist resistance in most cities and in radicalised rural areas such as Aragón. This failure, in effect, hand-delivered power to an extreme revolutionary left who had previously refused to even contemplate its taking by electoral means.

The government, ostensibly socialist, was horrified by the changes to Barcelona society and the collectivised countryside. Seizure of property and flatly equitable salaries shook its moderate, mostly middle-class support. Anarchist unions maintained rigid control over their own food supplies and soldiers, a scenario that did not bode well for the efficient pursuit of victory in the ongoing war.

Another important factor precipitated tension in the Republican camp: to Stalin, the Soviet leader, the revolutionary developments represented a challenge to the USSR's pre-eminent ideological position. Aware of a looming threat from Nazi Germany and the consequent need to develop alliances, Stalin was keen to win friends in London and Paris by appearing moderate and supportive of democracy. Soviet arms duly arrived in Republican Spain to prop up the embattled government, though with conditions: under no circumstances could anarchist militias make use of them.

Largely responsible for defending the government from a Nationalist coup, Spanish anarchists deeply resented the split caused by Soviet arms supplies. Mutual suspicion from fellow Republican forces broadened into open hostility in May 1937. In Barcelona that month, several days of vicious street fighting between revolutionary militias and Soviet-armed government troops resulted in anarchist defeat. The circumstances of the government clampdown differed across Republican Spain. Elements of the revolutionary left survived, even prospering in some isolated rural areas such as Levante. However, Barcelona's 'May Days' signalled an end to the brief Spanish experiment in revolutionary anarchism and the writing was on the wall for Republican Spain.

Government forces, bitterly disunited, outgunned and out-fought, surrendered to Franco in April 1939. The final remnants of urban revolutionary opposition had already been crushed by Nationalists across Catalonia earlier the same year. Franco led the new dictatorship. With total defeat of the Republic came Nationalist reprisals. Many Republicans unlucky enough not to escape the country were killed or sent off to Nazi concentration camps. With a particular hatred for secularism, regionalism and anti-traditional forces, Franco focused his vengeance on the former revolutionary power bases: Catalonia, Aragon and the Basque country.

Herein lie the beginnings of a great forgetfulness which, in part, still reigns over Spanish history. Circumstances had changed drastically for the war's foreign proxy combatants. Franco's fascist aides had ceased to exist. The USSR, free of Stalinism after 1953, remained understandably reticent about its role in suppressing leftist revolution. The Republican exiles and International Brigadiers in France, Mexico and elsewhere *did* publish memoirs, print photos and paint pictures. Orwell's *Homage to Catalonia*, in which the English writer lambasts the Spanish socialists and Soviet Stalinists for crushing the popular revolution in Barcelona, is perhaps the most famous work on the revolution in the English language. However, there is no photo which captures agrarian life on anarchist communes as the *Falling Soldier* of Robert Capa does the agony of the civil war; no painting explains the revolution quite like Picasso's *Guernica* sums up the butchery of the Spanish, or any other, modern conflict.

At home, however, Franco permitted only *his* kind of history after the Nationalist victory. Catholic kings, a colonial greater Spain and a general rejection of liberal values remained at the heart of Spanish curricula in schools, churches and the majority of homes. Common graves of Republican war dead – peasants, teachers, soldiers – were left unrecognised. All this took place while Nationalist victims were elevated by officialdom to the status of saints. Industrialisation and mass tourism in the 1960s brought limited social change, but historical narratives changed little until the dictator's death in 1975.

Since that date a more open appreciation of Spain's revolutionary past has come about. Pioneering researchers and government initiatives have led to an accommodation of multiple narratives of the past. The *pacto de olvido* ('pact of oblivion' or 'pact of forgetting') drawn up in 1977 offered participants on both sides of the civil war blanket amnesty for crimes committed. After 1978, devolved governments of the newly autonomous Spanish regions, such as Catalonia and the Basque country, engendered memories of the previous, revolutionary governments. Although in Spain the war 'retains a burning relevance', open discussion of its socialist revolution no longer invites danger.[4]

With censorship on sensitive subjects relaxed, the arts embraced a new era of creative possiblity. Pedro Almodóvar, Julio Médem and Vicente Aranda, for example, all offered challenging cinematic interpretations of the turbulent 1930s. They introduced themes of regionalism, feminism and homosexuality, all of which were issues left strictly 'off the table' during the Franco era.

Fast-forward to 2011: the 15-M manifesto vociferously rejects any suggestion of influence by left or right; socialist or anarchist. So venomous was the left-wing infighting that ended the revolution; so bloodthirsty was the civil war, and so deafeningly monotonous became the Francoist narrative afterward, that the outflanking of traditional political poles by today's radicals is to be expected. The ghosts of the past are here still clearly visible.

Yet 15-M has embraced direct 'bottom-up' democracy; a clear link to its revolutionary antecedents. It rejects former models of parliamentary democracy: the 1930s vintage, which failed so spectacularly to contain political extremes; and the 21st-century version, which has failed to deal with economic problems or capture the imagination of Spain's youth. In this adherence to core democratic values, 15-M and its Indignados steer a route clear of 20th-century trauma, towards a more inclusive future.

A Dutch Revolt
INDONESIA 1945–49

In 17th-century Netherlands, it seemed for many that 'the passion for tulips would last for ever, and that the wealthy from every part of the world would send to Holland, and pay whatever prices were asked for them'.[1] A speculative bubble in early modern Dutch flower prices may seem like a strange time and place from which to embark on a potted history of popular revolution in 20th-century Indonesia. The two countries, however, have shared much; not all of it on equal terms, nor unrelated to ill-thought gambling practices.

The Dutch East India Company (VOC – the Dutch abbreviation) was the first corporation to issue public stock for sale. It used the proceeds to build ships, recruit staff and bring goods from distant lands back to the Netherlands. One of these lands was Java, an island in south-east Asia where, in 1619, VOC staff established a thriving trading post. Soon, a network of Dutch ports was extracting the plentiful supplies of spices, rubber, timber and copper from the forests and islands around Java. Such raw materials were highly valued back in Europe; the prices of VOC stock soared.

Beyond Java, the VOC found an archipelago of over 6,000 islands, inhabited by a plethora of trading principalities, sultanates and tribes. *Kampung* villages had their own gods, customs, identities, languages, traditions and rulers. Landscapes ranged from the forests of Borneo to the crags of Papua. Religions ranged from pagan animism to Sunni Islam, from Balinese Buddhism to the missionary Protestantism of the Dutch mother country. Before the colonial era, the Betawi,

Banten, Javanese, Sundanese, Sumatran, Irianese and Banjar ethnicities treated one another in much the same manner as they did European arrivals.

Dutch colonialists gradually unified the diverse islands under the Dutch royal standard. They used military force to crush opposition. In the process long-term resentment brewed among the defeated elites and a military class developed among the native Javanese and Sumatrans who made up the bulk of colonial soldiers. Administrators, however, pacified the Dutch East Indies not only through force, but through education. Nineteenth-century progressives thought the Netherlands, as elsewhere, justified colonialism by the perceived positive effects it delivered to natives. And so, out of the limited colonial education offered, a literate generation of native clerks, secretaries and teachers appeared.

One such was the schoolteacher father of Pramoedya Ananta Toer. The man who would later become Indonesia's independence and literary icon was born in Java in 1925. As a result, he attended school, just like his father and the small portion of his fellow colonial subjects permitted to do so over the first half of the 20th century. During Pramoedya's childhood, proponents of the 'Nationalist Awakening', as it was later called, began to portray the archipelago as a singular entity.

Consuming this patriotic, anti-colonial message, a young and dissonant Pramoedya lent his support to the Japanese invasion during the Second World War, hopeful it would bring an end to Dutch domination. Though Japanese stewardship displayed little improvement over the Europeans, it fostered military training for nationalist forces. After Japan's surrender in 1945, the forces of the Netherlands government crept back. But the Japanese-trained rebels took up arms and declared independence.

The ensuing National Revolution of 1945–49 was, in truth, an anti-colonial war rather than a popular event of barricades and marchers. In the early part of the conflict, Pramoedya produced propaganda for the Nationalists. In a fate shared with many others, however, Dutch advances in Java led to his capture and imprisonment. The Netherlands' bid to regain its colony, supported initially by the British, looked like it would succeed. The Dutch forces were better-armed and much more experienced than their opponents.

But early Dutch gains came at a cost. Massive disruption of normal life did much to alienate those Indonesians not yet under the sway of the Nationalists. Alleged atrocities led to condemnation at the United Nations. By 1949, the Netherlands had negotiated a route out and recognised independent Indonesia. A behemothic new state was born, boasting the largest territory and population in south-east Asia and the most Muslims on earth.

The country's first president, Sukarno, like Pramoedya, was the son of a Javanese schoolteacher. His brand of revolutionary nationalism aimed to unite the disparate forces of Indonesia in what was referred to as a 'Guided Democracy'. It was Sukarno's influence, for example, which halted post-revolutionary mob violence against European colonial settlers, Chinese migrant populations and elite groups who had profited under the Dutch. Sukarno also developed a standardised version of the Indonesian language, hitherto impossible among the hundreds of island dialects.

Pramoedya watched these events with general approval. Having written his first novel while imprisoned during the National Revolution, he became a journalist at its close. He saw Netherlands society for itself in 1953, spending a year there with his family. Even though Pramoedya was broadly a supporter of Sukarno, his early work critiqued the less digestible results of independence. A 1954 novel, for example, was named *Corruption* (*Korupsi*), drawing the temporary ire of the authorities.

The military and the communists had emerged from the National Revolution as the two most powerful forces in Indonesian society. Sukarno had aimed to steer a course through the precipitous minefield of cold war diplomacy by avoiding commitments to either the capitalist West or communist USSR and China. But in the 1960s atmosphere of cold war suspicion, the split became dangerous. Communist and anti-communist army factions spun out of Sukarno's control. The president's former comrade from the 1945–49 war, General Suharto, plotted with the USA. Indonesia received its second president not by elected vote, but via a 1965 *coup d'état*. Sukarno was deposed and placed under house arrest until his death in 1970.

The 'New Order' regime of President Suharto blamed the communist PKI for the 1965 coup. Suharto rounded up and executed suspected leftists. Total victims have never been confirmed, but range from the hundreds of thousands into millions. As part of the anti-communist purge, Pramoedya was bundled off to a forced labour camp on the remote island of Buru. With many of his friends dead, and his published work censored, Pramoedya sunk from public consciousness.

Within two years of gaining power, Suharto invited foreign corporations to feast on Indonesian natural resources. Extraction and processing of tin, nickel, timber, bauxite, copper, rubber, coal, crude oil, natural gas, silver and gold were all privatised:

An American and European consortium got West Papua's nickel. The giant Alcoa company got the biggest slice of Indonesia's bauxite. A group of American, Japanese and French companies got the tropical forests of Sumatra, West Papua and Kalimantan. A Foreign Investment Law, hurried on to the statutes by Suharto, made this plunder tax free for at least five years.[2]

As an example of feckless corporate exploitation, Indonesia under Suharto cannot be bettered. Investment levels by foreign bodies were huge, but profits, products and materials were overwhelmingly drawn out of the country. With existing levels of poverty high, wages and work conditions remained medieval. The 'Made in Indonesia' tag became synonymous with 'dollar-a-day' sweatshop labour.

Indonesian democracy, a sham before 1965, became a travesty afterward; Suharto won unopposed election victories six times over his thirty-year reign. Wooed by Suharto's openness to corporate free reign, blinded by his combatting of radical Islam and Soviet Communism, the USA armed and abetted the dictator's frequent and vicious subversions of human rights. The World Bank and the IMF bankrolled the regime. With billions of dollars of loans in hand, Suharto invested in American and British arms. West Papua and East Timor were duly invaded and overpowered.

Resident in a forced labour camp or under house arrest for 22 years until 1991, Pramoedya used his storytelling skills to good effect. His written work from the period examines history and challenges colonialism, both that of the Dutch and of the later, Sukarno-era variety. His four-volume masterpiece, the *Buru Quartet*, was begun as an oral history of Indonesia. Banned from writing anything, Pramoedya relayed the semi-autobiographical tale of a Nationalist journalist back to his fellow prisoners to steady morale. Later, he was able to record it. Finally, in the late 1990s, the political change needed to uncensor and publish Pramoedya's works came about.

Completing a cycle begun by the Dutch in the 17th century, Suharto's downfall was brought about by aggressive foreign speculation and investment. Akin to the later eurozone debt crisis, the late 1990s crash in the 'Tiger' economies of southeast Asia saw inflated currency values collapse, international investment flee and debt burdens multiply. The crisis quickly spread to Indonesia, where food prices and unemployment rocketed. Student pro-democracy protests transformed into street violence. Restive forces among the ever-powerful military forced Suharto to resign in 1998.

Democracy has, superficially at least, now been restored to Indonesia. But the looting of one of the planet's richest ecological states continues apace. Palm oil, to take one disastrous example, is an ingredient in many processed ice creams, chocolates, cosmetics and biofuels. NGOs report that palm oil cultivation has grown massively in the last 50 years.[3] In large part as a result of the palm oil industry's insatiable appetite for its habitats, the Orang Utan in Indonesian Borneo has become critically endangered. Peat swamp forests – essentially, giant sponges for carbon dioxide – are clear-felled to make way for palm oil plantations, releasing massive amounts of CO_2 into the atmosphere. The Netherlands, ironically, is one of the world's largest importers.

It seems that environmental and military atrocities will haunt Indonesia for many years to come. The actions of Suharto's special forces in Aceh, Papua and Timor hark back to the vicious lessons imparted during the Dutch East Indian empire and the National Revolution. One episode in particular, in the Javanese village of Rawagede, continues to receive attention. In September 2011, a Dutch court ruling opened the way for widows of 341 murdered villagers to sue the Netherlands government. Whether similar proceedings emerge in Jakarta over alleged atrocities in Timor and West Papua will be a genuine test of how far Indonesia's three 20th-century revolutions have brought the country.

What of Pramoedya Ananta Toer? He predeceased Suharto by two years, in 2006. By that stage, the writer had won his battle against censorship and imprisonment. After 2001, the *Buru Quartet* Pramoedya had completed while in enforced exile joined his back catalogue of work from the Sukarno period in general release across Indonesia. Widely read, Pramoedya won awards and was translated into many foreign languages. His rehabilitation mirrored Indonesia's partial awakening from half a century of stolen independence.

The last words belong to the writer and are as applicable to Java in the 17th century as Borneo and other corporate-occupied territories in the 21st:

History teaches much about the power of capital. Free peoples are enslaved; artless people are transformed into compradores; the unemployed become paid murderers with uniforms and badges of rank; vast forests are torn apart by infrastructure; cities and ports spring up out of nothing at its command; labor force is sucked in from all over, even from remote hamlets whose names no one has ever clearly heard. The governments of so many states it turns into mere instruments of its will; and when they are no longer wanted, they are overthrown.[4]

More Than One Viktor

UKRAINE 2004

I t's just before midnight on a cool December night in Las Vegas. Orange and white confetti rains down on a boxing ring at the Mandalay Bay Hotel. The fight is over. Arms aloft, a world championship belt around his waist, the winner parades the ropes. A microphone is passed. The champion makes a speech:

> I want to say thank you very much to everyone in Ukraine who fights for democracy, who fights for the future, our future, our children's future.[1]

This was no ordinary boxer. The date was December 11th 2004 and the orange sash which swayed from the Ukrainian's shorts throughout his victory carried revolutionary significance. The new heavyweight champion was Vitali Klitschko. Before a worldwide audience the boxer had dedicated his victory to the peaceful pro-democracy movement then sweeping his country.

Far away in Kyiv, the capital of Ukraine, thousands of protestors were enduring a third week at their camp on Independence Square. Even with the temperature well below freezing, the students, workers, pensioners and families showed no sign of giving up. Mid-December 2004 was a crucial stage in what would come to be known as Ukraine's Orange Revolution. Having forced a re-run of the contested presidential election run-off, protestors hoped they were drawing closer to their goal of a democratically elected leader, a rewritten constitution and ultimate victory. How this point was reached, and how the revolution has fared since then, emerges in the details of Vitali Klitschko's story.

Born in 1971 in Kyrgyzstan, Klitschko's father worked in aeronautics. Industrialised Ukraine, rich in minerals and highly populated, was then an important part of the Soviet Union. The Klitschko family moved around the USSR, not living in their homeland permanently until 1985. The early 1980s saw economic stagnation severely affect living standards across the USSR. Everything from electricity to toothpaste was rationed. Yet Ukraine remained the jewel in the Soviet crown. Even as the Chernobyl nuclear disaster unfolded in the late 1980s, Moscow did its utmost to maintain close political control of Kyiv. Other republics strained at the Soviet leash, but Ukraine's dissident movement, *Rukh*, emerged much later, and weaker, than similar groups across the Eastern Bloc.

As a young man, Klitschko was more interested in sport than politics. His successful amateur kick-boxing career was just taking flight when the parliament in Kyiv declared itself independent in 1991. Ukrainian independence arrived virtually without a shot being fired. In truth, the country's new leaders were convincing neither as freedom fighters, nor as democrats. Former Communist Party *apparatchiks* had bluntly rebranded themselves free marketeers and reformers. Elections, theoretically democratic, were fixed; dissent silenced. The death of an opposition presidential candidate in 1999 was not the only one to deliver politically convenient results for the governing regime. Corruption became endemic. Journalistic freedom and judicial independence, delicate to begin with, were increasingly compromised. To make matters worse, the economic adjustment to market forces caused unemployment, shortages and inflation to outstrip even 1980s levels.

Vitali Klitschko fought on. Having converted to the more lucrative boxing codes, the heavyweight was in possession of not only his first world boxing title by 1999, but also a PhD in Sports Science. Living and training in Hamburg, Klitschko became a celebrity in both his adopted and native homes. He travelled between Germany and Ukraine, no doubt noting the stark differences in political culture. While a succession of efficient coalitions occupied the Bundestag, the corrupt habits of Ukrainian government only increased. Illegal arms deals with Saddam Hussein's Iraq were revealed in 2002. Important state assets in the mining, energy and military manufacturing industries were sold off for set prices, the buyers often maintaining close links with both organised crime and the political insiders who fixed the auctions' outcome.

Against this backdrop, the main actors in the Orange Revolution took centre stage. Both Viktor Yanukovych and Viktor Yushchenko had already served as prime minister when they contested the presidential election of 2004. Similarities, however, end with the shared first name. Yanukovych was a former Communist, a favourite of the incumbent president and, in his youth, a twice-convicted criminal. Yushchenko, meanwhile, had been a banker and outspoken supporter of democratic reform.

Just as in former elections, the first round of voting saw widespread fraud. State-controlled television coverage centred on Yanukovych and ignored the pro-Western reform bloc led by Yushchenko, *Our Ukraine*. Opposition voters were intimidated. Government employees, military conscripts and students were pushed to vote for Yanukovych. Exit polls were suppressed. Unlike in other Ukrainian elections, however, a broad and committed pro-democratic resistance emerged. The movement was instigated and organised initially by the political youth organisation *Pora!*, backed by *Our Ukraine*.

Predictably, Yanukovych and the incumbent president denied all knowledge of irregularities. The government also laughed off suggestions that poisoning was the reason behind an unexplained illness that had disfigured Yushchenko's face badly in the run-up to the poll. Fraud was more brazen during the second-round run-off between the two main candidates. Even before government-controlled state media had declared Yanukovych the winner, leading *Our Ukraine* figures, including Vitali Klitschko, called for demonstrations to protest the result.

Pora! erected a protest camp in central Kyiv and invited Ukrainians to join them. Though Independence Square saw the main groundswell, demonstrations were not limited to Kyiv. Ukrainians wearing the orange campaign colours of *Our Ukraine* flocked to the centre of other towns and cities. Cracks began to emerge in the government's version of events. Election commissioners broke ranks and revealed changed vote tallies. Dissident police officers confirmed the allegations. A section of Ukraine's foreign diplomats disowned the governing regime. Broadcasters began reporting without bias towards the government. Sympathetic city authorities accommodated demonstrators with Portaloos, rubbish collection services and ambulances.

Emergency medical attention, thankfully, was not needed. The army surrounded Independence Square at one point, but crucial elements of the military and intelligence sided with the massed demonstrators and the protests remained peaceful. International pressure on Yanukovych from the USA, the Council of Europe and neighbouring EU states increased. Klitschko's world title fight was broadcast across Ukraine on December 11th, the same day that a toxicology report on Yushchenko's illness was released: it confirmed he had been poisoned. Ukraine's Supreme Court nullified the declared election results and a new poll date was set. Klitschko flew home, appearing in Kyiv to 100,000 cheering protesters.

Our Ukraine topped the rescheduled poll, with Viktor Yushchenko becoming president. A landmark event had been reached. Ukraine had missed out on the popular revolutions which swept across other ex-Communist states in 1989, such as Poland, Czechoslovakia and Hungary. After two decades of misrule by a powerful anti-democratic, ex-Communist clique, an opposition candidate had obtained the presidency. More importantly, support for the Orange protestors from the normally pliant judiciary, as well as from certain prominent journalists and diplomats, suggested the autocratic system had lost support permanently.

The Orange Revolution was primarily a popular reaction to electoral fraud. Looked at through a longer lens, however, several alternative angles emerge. Different areas of Ukrainian society have historically pulled in opposing directions. The extreme western areas of the country had not been part of Russia before 1945. People living to the west of the river Dnieper generally spoke Ukrainian, revered a history of nationalist literature and looked to a tradition of struggle for national independence.

By contrast, centuries of intermingling had occurred between eastern Ukraine and the Russian heartlands. Russian is still the preferred tongue of eastern Ukrainians. Russian newspapers and opinions proliferate. The Kremlin, not Brussels or Washington, is the trusted 'big brother' in foreign affairs. A survey carried out in the same year as the Orange Revolution, a full fourteen years since the demise of the USSR, revealed 13 per cent of Ukrainians still identified themselves most of all as Soviet citizens.[2]

The Orange Revolution was not merely a battle between east and west Ukraine, however. The disputed election results also set powerful forces in eastern and western Europe on a collision course. A series of uprisings in Russian satellite pseudo-democracies had occurred in the years preceding the Orange Revolution. Serbia overthrew Slobodan Milosevic in 2000. In Georgia, in 2003, the Rose Revolution had abruptly ejected pro-Russian president Eduard Shevardnadze. In May 2004, six months before the Orange Revolution, Ukrainians had watched as the European Union accepted into its lucrative club three former Soviet republics and five ex-Eastern Bloc states.

Ukraine's Russian neighbour had good reason to fear an *Our Ukraine* victory. Viktor Yushchenko was an unabashed proponent of EU and NATO membership. Russia, having fallen in status during the chaotic post-Communist adjustments of the 1990s, now grew steadily in economic and diplomatic influence under Vladimir Putin. Highly sensitive of challenges to Russian regional influence, Putin repeatedly expressed his support for Yushchenko's opponent during the campaign. Yanukovych returned the favour, travelling to Moscow to appear alongside the Russian president, in pictures broadcast across Ukraine.

The image of a Ukraine standing in solidarity with Moscow appealed to many eastern Ukrainians. A Yanukovych victory, they were told, would mean closer ties with the Kremlin and official recognition of the Russian language. Allegations of illegal foreign aid were made against *Our Ukraine*. Boris Berezovsky, the exiled Russian billionaire dissident, was accused of funding Yushchenko's campaign. Similar allegations were made of the philanthropic foundation controlled by US billionaire George Soros.

Whatever the truth behind the protests of the Orange Revolution, their subsequent reversal has been spectacular. Viktor Yanukovych, ousted by the protests, was elected as president in 2010; his former foe, Yushchenko, beaten into third place. Yanukovych appears too to have flipped his former pro-Russian stance, telling *The Wall Street Journal* in August 2011 of his intention to lead Ukraine into the EU.[3] Yulia Tymoshenko, former darling of the Orange movement, who secured a close second place in the 2010 battle for president, has suffered a still sharper fall from grace. In late 2011, in a decision criticised by external observers for its alleged political bias, she was jailed for alleged abuse of office while prime minister, a conviction that will bar Tymoshenko from contesting 2012's presidential election. Even the musical career of pop singer Ruslana, Ukraine's Orange Revolution hunger striker, is on the wane. The unravelling of the formerly united protest movement appears complete.

Alone among the Orange revolutionaries, Vitali Klitschko stands as a political success story. His bid for mayoral office in Kyiv in 2006 fell short, but the political party he subsequently founded, the Ukrainian Democratic Alliance for Reform, polled well in 2010 municipal elections. Still only aged 40, Klitschko even found time during 2011 to successfully defend his world boxing title.

The Orange Revolution was heralded as Ukraine's 1989: a belated 'return to Europe'. With the benefit of hindsight, however, the victory for democracy has proved pyrrhic. The trial and imprisonment of Tymoshenko has raised new questions over the state of press freedom and levels of judicial independence.[4] With opposition thus constricted, and the hopes of the original Orange Revolution so severely disappointed, a recurrence of protest seems likely before Ukrainians can openly reflect on a political system truly committed to the power of its own people. The spotlight will land on the country again in 2012: Ukraine will host both a presidential election and the European Football Championships. Whether it is one of the Viktors, Vitali Klitschko, or the return of mass protests that dictate affairs, one thing is certain: attention from both the rest of Europe and Russia is guaranteed.

Remembering
the Future

What results do Chinese citizens get when they enter '革命' – the Chinese characters for revolution – in a search engine? Government controls on the internet are such that only certain approved historical events may turn up; the original, sanitised Tiananmen Square protest, of 1919, for example. Absent will be any detail on the pro-democracy protest which occurred in the same location 80 years later, uncritical reports of ethnic Tibetan and Uighur uprisings from more recent years, or on the riots which briefly shook Guangdong in 2011.

Censorship of this kind is not restricted to China. Every government on earth takes similar decisions about what aspects of history to teach; which historical characters to celebrate. Equally, every country ignores less savoury stories: the famines; ethnic cleansing; the government mistakes and corruption. Historical textbooks have references to atrocities removed or glossed over. Academic research and the attentions of publishing houses cluster around the minutiae of particular, chosen events.

This chapter aims to accentuate the tectonic importance of revolutions to the creating and re-making of cultural memory. Revolutionary activities do not simply topple tyrannical rulers or produce immediate political reform. They cast ripples across history, invoking often drastic reinterpretation as both time and prevailing political environments pass. How any one revolution is remembered by the public will seriously influence its lasting effects; a process, it should be remembered, that is unconfined to the written word. Governments can do little to censor the habits and assumptions of everyday life, which are as forceful a record of events as any book. Nursery rhymes can be read as folklore; syntax and vocabulary as rite and ritual. Even attitudes to the passing of time and personal beliefs in what lies beyond life, can rest on a supporting scaffold of collective memory and recycled ideas.

Reactions to revolutionaries of the past can extend centuries beyond the end of their own lives. The distance in time between an ancient revolution and its interpretation by the contemporary world leads to serious problems. A lack of direct information about the 2nd-century Jewish rebel, Shimon Bar Kozeba, for instance, allowed modern Zionist political tastes to be projected backward onto the event. This can occur even when the gap between an uprising and its celebration is relatively short. The sectarian strife at work in Ireland at the end of the 19th century has done much to cloud the longstanding status of the 1798 Rebellion as a unitary event.

Of all revolutions, the events of 1789–99 in France probably require least introduction. Over more than two centuries, its stories have been ceaselessly remoulded. Action and reaction continue to be analysed, motives dissected. Conservative and radical intellectuals in many countries toss the heroes and horrors of the event amongst themselves, their order shuffled depending on the political machinations of the day. Abdelmajid Hannoum, writing on a revolt in 19th-century Algeria, asserts that the narrative does not actually portray truth, but 'what colonial agents, soldiers, politicians, administrators, and settlers thought was happening'.[1]

Today, the explosion in media consumption and the associated hyperactivity of communications technology has changed the way that revolutions are reported and remembered. There is rarely only one version of events to choose from. Mass literacy and the low communication costs means both sides of any conflict can broadcast their story to a global audience. A gigantic amount of information, dwarfing the world's great libraries, is collected on an infinite number of happenings each day, in every corner of the world. For historians of the Bagaudae, a broad but vaguely recorded uprising in 4th-century Roman Gaul, the precise opposite case holds true: a distinct lack of reliable sources has hampered understanding and biased the subsequent interpretation of an important event.

With wondrous new possibilities, however, come new challenges. Further restrictions on publishing, scriptwriting, even the content of game shows, were announced by the Chinese Communist Party's censorship organ in 2011. Elsewhere, the overload of information will make future interpretation of contemporary events as difficult and nuanced as any attempt to provide a modern account of the Bagaudae. In spite of the information age, and in some ways because of it, the way that history is remembered still relies to a surprising degree on assumption and re-imagination.

A Star is Born

JEWISH REVOLT OF 132–136AD

At the United Nations General Assembly, speeches by the world's revolutionaries have brought a dash of colour to often staid proceedings. In 1964, a black-booted, khaki-enveloped 'Che' Guevara rounded off a searing anti-imperialist broadside with an exclamation of 'Homeland, or death!'. The ex-Sandinista president of Nicaragua, Daniel Ortega, took the rostrum to lambast US foreign policy in 1987. In his second term twenty years later, and identifying the very same problems, he repeated the feat. Muammar Gaddafi covered a diverse range of conspiracy theories in his 2009 speech; everything from swine flu to the identity of JFK's assassin was revealed by the self-appointed 'Guide of the Libyan Revolution'.

When he made his own UN address in 1947, David Ben-Gurion had already been many things: Zionist; Marxist; lawyer; British soldier. At this point, however, Ben-Gurion was primarily speaking as a revolutionary, aspiring to establish the future state of Israel he would govern. It is perhaps surprising then, that this Founding Father adopted a conciliatory tone, his speech hinting little at the troubled future in store for the Middle East:

> We have no conflict with the Arab people. On the contrary, it is our deep conviction that, historically, the interests and aspirations of the Jewish and Arab peoples are compatible and complementary.

Of course Ben-Gurion's voice speaks from a different era. His declaration of Israeli independence was twelve months away, and a far from universally accepted concept. Arabs remained a dominant demographic in Palestine. The British and French empires still held effective military and political control over the entire region. Over the coming years Ben-Gurion would successfully carve out a Jewish homeland against the odds. The bloody 1948–49 Arab-Israeli war saw him lead his young countrymen against combined British, Egyptian, Saudi, Syrian and Transjordanian armies. Thousands of Palestinians were swept into exile and the ancient dream of the 'Promised Land' finally materialised: a revolution by any definition.

Where had the Israeli nation's driving force come from? One answer lies in an ancient insurrection on the same soil. In the 2nd century AD, Jewish populations in Palestine rose up against their Roman overlords. Though the rebel onslaught was fierce and its after-effects widely felt, details of the Bar Kokhba Revolt are less important than how its protagonists have been mythologised. Even today, the legend of its long-dead leader retains relevance for Israelis, Palestinians and their stalemated portion of the eastern Mediterranean.

Shimon Bar Kozeba led the uprising. Recent discoveries of letters have helped pad out meagre details about his origins and motives. Kozeba had military training, referred to himself as 'prince' ('*Nasi*') and was a holy man: he inclined his men to observe religious festivals and practices, such as the Jewish sabbath. In facing down the Roman Empire of the 2nd century, Kozeba broached a daunting task. It stretched south into Africa, west to Hadrian's native Iberia, east to Baghdad and north to Germania and Britain (where the most famous of Emperor Hadrian's edifications still traverses northern England). Palestine served as an important bridge between the Roman Mediterranean centre and the rim of Rome's greatest rival: the Persian Parthian Empire.

The Judaism of the era itself is barely recognisable. The destruction of the Second Temple in Jerusalem, around 60 years before Kozeba took up arms, had ushered in a period of religious persecution by the Romans. Still in relative youth in the 2nd century, the accepted practices and central texts of Judaism were at an early point in their evolution. It was 'a religion of radical messages spread by itinerant preachers'.[1] These often diverged from town to town, believer to believer. Some hundred years after the death of their own messiah, for example, Christians remained a Jewish sect. They were not alone. A multiplicity of different belief systems existed under the Jewish umbrella.

When Kozeba's revolt broke out, however, it was primarily a religious uprising, uniting the Jews of the province of Judea against perceived Roman injustices. Primary among these was the outlawing of circumcision; an important tradition, already ancient by the 2nd century AD. In addition, Emperor Hadrian had ordered the wholesale reconstruction of Jerusalem as a Roman city. This work interfered with sacred sites of Judaism and aroused great anger.

Bar Kozeba harnessed popular anger, planning and fighting a guerrilla war. Coins, minted in rebel territories, show the Star of David and mention the leader's name. Letters written by the leader show that hostilities lasted for nearly four years. That the rebels captured Jerusalem at any one point is disputed, but the large number of Roman soldiers summoned to Palestine from across the empire suggest Jewish resistance must have been well organised. The eventual fate of the rebel leader Shimon Bar Kozeba is unknown, though his rebellion's ultimate failure is clear. The site of the final annihilation was the fort of Betar, south-west of Jerusalem, probably late in the year 135.

The inevitable Roman reprisals were concentrated in Judea. Punitive measures included the banishing of Jews from

Jerusalem and the continued outlawing of circumcision. Such reprisals were only too familiar. During a widespread rebellion of the previous century (The Great Revolt of 66AD), a Jewish group known as the Zealots had unsuccessfully challenged the Romans for control of Judea. The result had been utter decimation at the fort of Masada and, as already mentioned, the destruction of the holy site of the Second Temple. Within the lifetime of Bar Kozeba, another violent upheaval fought among diasporic Jewish communities had occurred. Though initially staged in Cyprus, Egypt and elsewhere, the final, bloody act of the Quietus War had come about in Judea in 116AD. Inflecting all of these events were the distant legends of the Maccabees, the Jewish rebels who had overturned Syrian rule in 168BC, but had themselves fallen victim to Roman invasion.

Not all of Palestine had arisen to support Bar Kozeba's revolt. To the north of Judea, Galilee was less homogenously Jewish. Its population had not involved itself in the revolt to as great an extent. They were consequently spared the wholesale extermination that awaited Judea. It was from the aftermath, and in Galilee, that influential centres of learning and much of modern Jewish rabbinic tradition would spring. The opinion of those rabbis was almost uniformly negative, with later chronicles referring to Bar Kozeba's revolt as a foolish or disastrous event.

At the turn of the 20th century, however, Jewish perspectives on Bar Kozeba changed. Zionists such as Theodor Herzl and Chaim Weizmann sought to establish a safe homeland for the world's Jews. This quest led to reappraisals of Jewish history and a surge in the publication of Zionist-themed literature. The profile of the ancient revolt against Roman persecution changed. Kozeba's attack on his Roman rulers came to be portrayed as a heroic act. Novels and folklore emerged

on the topic. The most common spelling of the rebel's name –
Bar Kozeba – was changed to Bar Kokhba. A seemingly subtle
switch, it neatly incorporated his earlier laudation by the martyred rabbi Aqiva as 'the star that fell from Jacob'.[2]

After independence in 1948, the battles Ben-Gurion and
Israel fought intensified. Several full-scale wars with Arab
neighbours were won. They included the Six-Day War in 1967,
Yom Kippur in 1973 and an invasion of southern Lebanon
in 1978. What better historical model for a small, militarily
besieged country than a devout and determined rebel fighter?
In spite of the lack of real information about his life, an ideal-
ised hero called Simon Bar Kokhba began to feature in popular
songs and primary school curriculums. Even secular Israelis
came to celebrate the revolt, on the national annual holiday of
Lag Ba-Omer, because modern Jewish tradition links the holiday to the Bar Kokhba Revolt.

May 11th 1982 saw the Kokhba legend complete its journey
into public consciousness. Israeli Prime Minister Menachim
Begin witnessed a public reburial of bones, unearthed in a
Judean cave, which had been connected by archaeologists to
the revolt. The historical symmetries at work in such a scenario
are too tempting to ignore. Begin himself was a former rebel,
a more extreme contemporary of Ben-Gurion. He had led the
Zionist Irgun group in a campaign of violence against British
rule in Palestine in 1944. Moreover, he had previously been a
member of a radical Zionist youth movement, Betar, which
took as its title the name of Bar Kokhba's final fortress.

In the autumn of 2011, a triad of speeches to the UN
General Assembly heralded the possibility of revolutionary new developments in the Middle East. After address-
ing the assembled diplomats, Palestinian leader Mahmoud
Abbas delivered an official application for recognition of an

independent Palestinian state to the General Secretary. Having watched US President Obama criticise the move, Israeli prime minister Binyamin Netanyahu took the stage, ending his speech with similarly conciliatory words to those of his predecessor, Ben-Gurion, spoken some 65 years before:

> President Abbas, I extend my hand – the hand of Israel – in peace. I hope that you will grasp that hand. We are both the sons of Abraham. My people call him Avraham. Your people call him Ibrahim. We share the same patriarch. We dwell in the same land. Our destinies are intertwined.

That destiny will be either one of lasting and unprecedented peace, or a continuance of bloodshed, rebellion and religious intolerance; a path carrying heavy influence from the enduring legend of Bar Kokhba. With hope, the people of the ancient holy lands, historically called both Palestine *and* Israel, can embark on the path less travelled.

Indomitable

The Bagaudae 4th and 5th centuries

'One small village of indomitable Gauls...' – the same beginning has adorned the first page of every single English edition of the Franco-Belgian *Asterix* comic for the past 60 years. The bestselling authors, Goscinny and Uderzo, seem to revel in presenting hilarious inaccuracies. Bizarre scenarios of magic carpets and Druidic potions are often closer to fairytale than true ancient Gaul. However, real historical figures make regular appearances and the geography is accurate. Asterix's Armorican home, in which an exasperated Julius Caesar often finds himself, was one of the last Gallic regions to capitulate to Rome.

The comic riffs on the reputation for defiance among more recent inhabitants of old Armorica (an area roughly equivalent to present-day Brittany). The French Revolution is probably the most glaring source of these stereotypes, with the regular tendency of French workers and students towards strikes a more modern manifestation. Drawing on a Celtic heritage shared with brethren in Ireland, Scotland, Wales, Galicia and Cornwall, Breton nationalists continue to campaign for political recognition, a struggle which has at times become violent. Sometimes the agitative Armorican spirit has been channelled *too* successfully. In 1865, Napoleon III erected a towering monument to the chief who surrendered Gaul to Caesar after defeat at Alesia in 52BC. Within five years the emperor had led France to a similarly disastrous military defeat; this time against Prussia.

The concept of a rebellious proto-France has deep and very real roots. The year 387BC saw Gallic barbarians invade and sack Rome. They continued to raid from northern strongholds along the Mediterranean coast until Massalia (modern-day Provence) was conquered and romanised in the 2nd century BC. Roman armies then routed military roads all the way to the north through 'long-haired Gaul', carrying trade and cultural influence with its legions, to the banks of the Rhine. However, unruly Gallic tribes continually resisted incursions into and across their territories. After a series of intense military campaigns, Julius Caesar finally defeated Napoleon III's hero, Vercingetorix, in 52BC. Gaul was temporarily pacified.

Centuries passed. With Gallic frontiers under pressure from increasingly daring Germanic barbarian raids, Rome's north-western colony again proved restless. Incursions by tribes of Alamanni, Franks and Saxons increased in frequency, striking at large and prosperous Romano-Gallic towns. Suffering the brunt were trading posts and tribal centres which had been transformed over 300 years of Roman subjugation; towns like Samarobriva (Amiens), Lugdunum (Lyon) and Durocorturum (Reims). The reaction of the now-romanised Gallic society was to challenge central imperial authority. A succession of alternative Gallic emperors, still differentiating themselves as Roman but assuming the right to raise taxes and armies, ruled over Gaul. Their brief Gallic Empire gained limited support from parts of Roman Britain and Spain but collapsed in 274AD.

It is here, in the aftermath of the Gallic would-be emperors, that one of the most intriguing sources of the later French and Breton rebellious repute is apparent. Various Roman chroniclers of the 280s refer to a widespread military revolt against *Pax Romana* using the term *bagaudae*. The sources are not only vague as to the origins of the rebels, their conclusions often appear contradictory. Ordinary 'farmers', 'countryfolk', 'rural bandits' and 'shepherds' are blamed in some accounts.[1] Elsewhere the possibility of cavalry is suggested.[2]

The leader of the revolt, Amandus, appeared as 'Imperator Caesar Gaius Amandus Pius Felix Augustus' on coinage, suggesting an effort to appear as a legitimate emperor to the militias of the Rhine borderlands in the temporary absence of central imperial authority.[3] About the only element of the faceless *bagaudae* left beyond reproach by contemporary accounts is that their menace necessitated the appointment of a special 'Emperor of the West'. Maximian co-ruled alongside Diocletian, eventually quelling the unrest and returning Gaul to a relative and taxable peace.

The early 5th century sees our view of the *bagaudae* clouded even further. References to them reappear, dotted across Roman sources but still offering a generally unsatisfying account. This time the leaders offer resistance to Roman rule over a prolonged period of time in spaces as far apart as Armorica and Tarraconensis, which was in Roman Hispania (today's Tarragona in Spain). Etymology of the term *bagaudae* suggests Celtic origins. However, its wide application to virtually all Gaulish upheaval against Roman rule in the late 3rd century and throughout the 5th, combined with the romanised names of its leaders and reports of legionary deserters amongst the rebels, suggests there must have been sufficient popular discontent among the romanised natives to actively participate.

Thus contemporary historians have been left to project their own ideas onto a largely blank canvas. Writing from an autocratic Europe left quivering by the failed liberal revolutions of 1848, Theodor Mommsen cast the *bagaudae* as a *jacquerie*; a collection of disruptive peasants bent on little more than thievery.[4] Reflecting the language of his early 1950s cold war world, the Anglo-Irish Marxist historian E.A. Thompson saw the *bagaudae* as composed of 'submerged classes' who suffered unfair taxation and other unspecified 'oppression'.[5] Slightly more trust can be placed in less ideologically-tinged observations. In 1985 Raymond Van Dam linked the phenomenon to both the resettlement of Germanic tribes across Gaul and the rise in power of early Christian bishops.[6] Just about the only point agreed upon is the meagre state of the original sources!

Their role in helping create an image of unruliness apart, of what importance, the reader might reasonably ask, are the *bagaudae*? The answer lies in how their revolt fits into a broader picture of uprisings in the Roman Empire from 250AD onward. Rebel action, which we can assume broke out across Armorican Gaul but whose details will remain a mystery, was just one segment of a general crisis faced by Roman civilisation in the late 3rd century. Usurper emperors arose from amongst competing factions in the military and political elites of the empire's constituent parts. Christianity had escaped its heretic denomination and was beginning to take hold amongst Roman elites. Persian and Germanic groups augmented their strength and threatened Rome's borders. The combination of repeated defeats for the legions in Germania and ravaging outbreaks of disease tore the empire into three parts, of which the Gallic Empire was the westernmost.

The *bagaudae* of Armorica and Tarragona were not alone in banding together to face down Roman overlords during this extended decline in imperial influence. A patchwork of revolt broke out across the empire from the end of the 3rd century onwards, in concert with the eastward drift of imperial control. The Circumcellions, or Agonists, were the *bagaudae*'s North African equivalents; an extreme Christian sect who sought to eliminate slavery and bring about their own martyrdom through violent struggle. Visigoths who had settled in southern

Gaul revolted and fought a long war against Roman forces in the late 4th century. Alongside these attempts at internal revolt lay the continuing threat of usurpation by pretenders to the imperial throne, usually from within military ranks. Barbarian forces grew ever stronger, before the Visigoths successfully besieged Rome in 410AD. Within 50 years, the Vandals had followed suit. This disastrous series of events is only brought to a halt by the final collapse of western Roman authority in the 5th century.

Defining why this happened has been an obsession of the history profession. The variance in explanations for the *bagaudae* is but a drop in the historiographical ocean when compared to how many reasons have been posited for the steady transferral of Roman leadership eastwards towards the 'second Rome', Constantinople. As such, it is a topic neither easily summed up nor added to. It's sufficient in this short space to mark that the *bagaudae* fits into a sustained period of popular revolt, itself a large part of the Western Empire's closing acts. Such is the state of historical sources for the ancient world, we don't have the luxury of the rebels' motives, or anything other than the leaders' names. The general fact of their existence, however, is undoubted, as well as relevant to our world.

Do the *bagaudae* and its ilk show that revolutions occur in batches? That the western section of the Roman Empire was overcome so soon afterward begs questions to be posed about the direct relationship between localised revolts and broader system collapse. Do the 'batches' of revolution which broke out in 2011, for instance, signal the downfall of not merely national governments and their leaders, but some wider system? If so, the next query has two possible answer: is it the global economic system or existing geo-political hierarchies which are on the way out? Both of these supranational systems are linked to revolts and demonstrations in the Middle East, Europe and elsewhere. Both have been seized with crisis at the same time. Answers are impossible yet. The question is enough.

Such is the depth of modern media penetration that future historians of our interesting times will be spared the guess-work that comes with any account of the *bagaudae*. Given the weight of the world's gaze on present upheavals, they will face an altogether different problem; namely, how to liberate cred-ible historical voices from the drone of feeds, forums, videos, news footage, interviews, blogs, learnéd lectures and rumours from the street. The heirs to Asteríx have been carried into the modern day.

Popular Venom
THE FRENCH REVOLUTION 1789

Try for a moment to imagine your everyday world without any of the following: the metric system; universal suffrage; the possibility of self-improvement; the expectation of equality, human rights or religious freedom. Difficult, isn't it? This is just a sample among many philosophical, political and social innovations which sprang from the French revolutionary process, begun in 1789 and, according to some, still hard at work. Other revolutions – social, economic, intellectual, scientific or political – may have played a more direct role in bringing about the various functions and dysfunctions of 21st-century life.* However, without the events and ideas raised by the French Revolution, thereafter analysed by generations of historians, theorists and politicians, the world today would be an unrecognisable place. If you live in a democracy, speak a European language, have ever studied history, received state welfare, or been a member of a political party, the same is probably true for your life.

Explanations for France's descent into revolution take many forms. Each year countless undergraduate essays cook up some variation of volatile social ingredients to define it. Historians likewise have long debated its causes, outcomes and meaning. Arguably modern history's most important event, it is without doubt its most studied. In fact, the story of history-writing as a surprisingly new medium could be told almost wholesale through the illustrious interpreters of the

---

* These include, most notably, the Reformation, the Enlightenment, the Industrial Revolution and the American Revolution.

Bastillards, the *Jacobins* and the *Brissotins*. Given its supposed familiarity, the events which led to the world's most infamous regime collapse can still confound in their speed, depth and intensity. Helpfully, the shadow of one figure falls across the entire story, from the earliest rumblings of noble discontent to the present day.

Emmanuel-Joseph Sieyès was born in 1748, another addition to the rapidly rising population of his native France. As a teenager, Sieyès would have known well the devastating extent of military defeat suffered to Britain in the Seven Years' War. Perhaps his father, a tax collector, related the parlous state of the kingdom's finances which resulted (it's less likely Honoré Sieyès bemoaned the accompanying hiked tax rates).

Emmanuel-Joseph entered the priesthood despite an active interest in often heretical Enlightenment philosophy. Later, serving as secretary to the Bishop of Tréguier in Brittany, he would have no doubt been aware of the newly enrichened Nantes' mercantile class. They were the beneficiaries of a boom in trade not isolated to the north-west, but common to other large regional maritime towns, such as Bordeaux. Fuelled by Caribbean slave-based sugar and rum production, the steady growth in social stature for the controllers of this trade saw no corresponding rise in political representation. As a sitting member of the Breton Estates (a local council of higher-status subjects), Sieyès saw at first hand the difficulties encountered even by rich merchant commoners in making their political voice heard.

A transfer to Chartres in 1780 brought the Parisian hub of French politics a step closer. Sieyès could not have failed to notice either the tension accompanying sharp spikes in food prices in the mid-1780s, or how the democratic notions with which French soldiers were returning to France from revolutionary America seeped into society at large. Armed with years spent studying radical thought and buoyed by Louis XVI's concessionary tactic of a mass meeting of society – the 1788 calling of the Estates-General – the now titled Abbé Sieyès sent shockwaves across Parisian coffee-houses and the underground press with his thesis *What is the Third Estate?*. In it, he challenged a society which denied rights to its most productive segment (the commoners) while the idle rich (nobles and church hierarchy) remained tax-exempt. Why, the author reasoned, should the latter hold superiority over the former in the Estates-General and in society in general? It became a bestseller.

Jacques Necker was the latest on the conveyor belt of king's ministers. Despite his efforts to accommodate the Third Estate of the pamphlet's title, and its supporters by increasing its representation, Louis appeared to hover between vague blessing and blatant disregard. One day he would ignore the upstart deputies, the next he would address them. The Third Estate, including the author, elected despite his noble eligibility, quickly asserted its identity as the true representative of the nation. It became the National Assembly, rejecting the separate decision-making bodies of nobles and churchmen. Shifting chairs in the palace, however, did little to drown out developments taking place beyond Versailles. With food prices approaching a pinnacle, city dwellers procured arms from barracks, formed militias and 'liberated' grain stores. In much the same way, rural peasants violently targeted the symbols of their feudal and monastic overlords.

News of these events rushed the National Assembly into declaring an end to the favoured positions of nobles, to church tithes and to *lettres de cachet* (a system allowing the monarch to rule by decree). Although Sieyès voted against this last move, he led opposition to the king's response: the firing of Necker and encirclement of Paris by troops. Amid rumours of aristocratic plots to starve the nation and foreign influence over the king (not least by his Austrian wife, Marie Antoinette), popular venom pre-empted attack. Disorder and paranoia in Paris resulted in the desperate storming of the Bastille prison in the capital, violence which Sieyès and the National Assembly initially disavowed. The failure of the army to offer resistance, however, signalled the crown's powerlessness. The attitude of the Assembly quickly changed from one of castigation and despair to celebration and optimism. Conservative forces fled the country, leaving Louis to limp back into Paris to accept his defeat, humiliated but as yet enthroned. The first act of the revolution had played out.

And so Sieyès found himself perched close to the confluence of a remarkably powerful set of human forces: war defeat; debt; tyranny; taxes; hunger; violence. This is the template of revolutionary causes which France left behind. It is not by accident that the French Revolution is near the top of the list when students first sit down to engage with the general historical concept. Through a combination of historical writings and successor events, the majority of subsequent revolutionary action has come to be viewed, at least partially, through this founding 1789 prism. This book's chapter titles bear testament: France could have slotted neatly into any one of them. The world created by Sieyès and the National Assembly in turn created the common historical idea upon which this book is based: that popular political upheavals should follow a seldom-trodden but clearly identifiable path and be packaged and disseminated with clear beginnings, high points and endings.

More interestingly, the French template can be applied to the present day. Has Egypt, for example, recently experienced a revolution as France did? Egypt does tick *most* boxes. Mubarak plays the role of the absolute ruler. Riots for bread in both scenarios were common. Mobile phones, online social media and satellite TV are the pamphlets and coffee-houses of their day, offering novel spaces for discussion. Even the repeated occupation of Tahrir Square was seen as Cairo's Bastille, transformed into that rare species of 'revolutionary moment' which the news cameras so crave.

National symbols have also been prominent among the Cairo crowds, a signal that they consider themselves as the Parisians of 1789 did, the legitimate representatives of the nation. The similarities are many and analysts wasted no opportunity to proclaim that Egypt had indeed played host to a revolution. In some cases this happened before Mubarak loyalists had been ousted, before even the crowds, smoke and gunfire had drifted from the running battles on Tahrir.

Avid viewers of events in Egypt and elsewhere should remember that neither a burning Bastille nor Louis' genuflection brought the French Revolution to a neat and convenient halt. Though they all ended up on top, Sieyès, French republicanism, democracy and people power would have to endure much in the years ahead. During 'the Terror' of 1793 and 1794, while the Abbé survived, tens of thousands were guillotined, not least of them Louis and Marie Antoinette themselves. Several bloody conflicts were fought following the revolution, including a civil war in the Vendée and an attempted reconquest of revolutionary Haiti.

Napoleon Bonaparte, personally aided by Sieyès, declared himself emperor in 1804. He imposed stability, exported revolutionary violence across Europe, but rolled back civil liberty at home. Radical attempts to win it back were unleashed throughout the 19th century. The major re-stagings of 1830,

1848 and 1871 all suffered similarly false dawns as 1789. Indeed it was not until after 1880 that the Revolution officially colonised national consciousness, as shown by the adoption of *La Marseillaise* and the celebration of Bastille Day.

National days and national anthems are mere symbols, however. They represent the French Revolution's radical ideas more than its dramatic events. The idea that a government derives its legitimacy from the people, rather than from a god or king, for example, was a completely new one at the time. Human control of personal and national destiny too, as exemplified by developments such as the new Republican calendar and the church's forcible ejection from state affairs, was a devastatingly original concept in the 18th century. To be sure, none of these ideas was entirely unknown before 1789. However, the French Revolution did much to popularise them beyond literate and learnéd elites, in the process embedding them in the minds of the ordinary people of France, her neighbours, trading partners, puppet republics, conquered enemies and colonies.

How is the French Revolution remembered? The simple answer is: effortlessly. You probably don't have to even think without paying some type of daily tribute to the epochal gains brought about by Sieyès, his contemporaries, imitators and successors. Through the continued obsessiveness with 1789 observed by the disciplines of history, philosophy and sociology,** its ideals have become the political and philosophical bedrock behind many of the world's states and much of recent history's most prominent social movements. High examples abound: the 1951 UN 'Declaration of Human Rights' has filtered into most European national legal frameworks via

---

** The term 'sociology' is believed to have been first used by Sieyès.

EU law. It took inspiration directly from the 1791 'Declaration of the Rights of Man and Citizen'.***

Very basic illustrations of 1789's contemporary resonance are not hard to locate either. Elections, for example, offer ordinary people the chance to call their leaders to account. At a more basic philosophical level, electoral democracies purportedly offer their citizens the chance to stake a claim in how their world is shaped. The linkage to the changes wrought by the French Revolution are undeniable.

Assuming the perfection of the historical model has proved dangerous, however. With the aid of the Marxists' interpretation of France, Bolsheviks and Maoists expanded the revolutionary remit to murderous extents during the 20th century. Whatever their noble origin, Spain, in early 2011, and Greece in the latter part of the year, have shown the current crop of electoral democratic systems to be less reactive to the needs of citizens than they would like. Nevertheless, it is elections which the uprisings in Egypt and across the Middle East were fought for.

Seeking an Abbé Sieyès in Tahrir Square might just as easily turn up an Egyptian Napoleon, or even a Stalin. Revolutions of the 1789 ilk rely on violence as much as on peaceable rulers enshrined in enlightened law. As Bonaparte himself might have observed, the world is still not governed according to the universal rights of the citizen, but through the link between violence, finance and power. Until accommodation is met between these forces, the legacy of the French Revolution will remain undecided.

*** Another piece of Sieyès' handiwork. He helped draft the document.

Kidnapped!
THE IRISH 1798 REBELLION

The most poignant event during the 2011 Irish presidential campaign concerned neither the eventual winner,
nor anything directly related to the position on offer.
It came on October 24th, towards the end of a televised debate
between all seven candidates in Dublin. Martin McGuinness,
backed in his bid by the pro-unity party Sinn Féin, was asked
whether he considered those killed by the Irish Republican
Army (IRA) during the violent conflagration in Ulster from
1969 to 1998 as 'murder victims' or simply 'collateral damage'.

Having already seen his campaign waylaid by accusations
about his former command position in the IRA, McGuinness
tried to steer away from providing a direct answer. The moment
revealed much about Irish attitudes to the past. Several other
southern candidates scoffed at the Deputy First Minister of
Northern Ireland's sudden evasiveness; while the only other
candidate native to the north also avoided a cogent reply.

Amnesia and violence define both Ireland's collective
memories and her historical rituals. The 'glorious' 12th of
July sees Ulster unionism celebrate a 1690 battle with blazing
bonfires, marching and, often, sectarian songs. The Republic's
founding national myth, the 1916 Easter Rising, is conveniently
ignored by most citizens because of its association with hard-
line republicanism. Even the globally celebrated St Patrick's
Day is based on historical smudge: no snakes were charmed;
no shamrocks displayed; most damningly of all, evidence suggests Patrick's 7th-century chroniclers may have collated several holy men's lives into one politically convenient epic.

It may not be altogether surprising, therefore, to discover that the single most important event in modern Ireland's history enjoys neither national commemoration nor international profile. Instead, the 1798 Rebellion is remembered as it was fought: island-wide but on a local, often rather disjointed level. It is notable among the succession of failed Irish revolts against English domination not only for its rejection of sectarianism, but for its link to the 'enlightened' late-18th-century revolutions of France and America. Most importantly, analysing how Irish people of different traditions choose to remember and forget events tells us much about their 19th-, 20th- *and* 21st-century political struggles.

Today's visitors to the elegant centre of Dublin would be correct to imagine it a prosperous place when its finest squares and buildings were erected throughout the late 18th century. At that time, Irish agriculture found expanding export markets in British cities, in its navy and armed forces and in its growing number of colonies across the globe. Behind the grandiose Georgian façades, however, poor rural districts bore testament to the political and economic inequalities of the age. Seventy per cent of the island's population were Catholic, largely Gaelic-speaking and uneducated. While Ireland's green fields fed much of the empire, among this poorest bulk of the population, malnutrition was commonplace and famine not unknown. Penal laws repressed Gaelic culture and, until limited reform in 1793, blocked Catholic bishops from civic life.

With normal avenues to change limited, the direct route of political violence boasted a rich and bloody tradition. An extended rebellion at the end of the 16th century had led to the eradication or expulsion of much of the old Ulster Catholic aristocracy. The rebellion's defeat had led to the imposition of 'plantations' of Scottish and English settlers into Ireland, the forefathers of Ireland's Protestant communities. The Catholic uprising of 1641 had failed of itself, but had had the side effect of kick-starting the English civil war. It had also precipitated widespread sectarian bloodshed, of which the most controversial had been instigated against Catholics by English Puritan Oliver Cromwell.

In such an atmosphere in the late 18th century, even Protestants were far from a contented or united group (though their material conditions were infinitely better than most Catholics'). Presbyterian households, though generally educated and involved in enterprise, were barred from politics. A minority, they were centred in the north and were beginning to align themselves with similarly unsettled Catholic gentry. The propertied, male, Anglican Protestant elite became known as the 'Ascendancy'. Its richest members owned the vast majority of arable land, enjoyed the cream of export profits and elected their peers to 'Grattan's Parliament' in Dublin, itself a subordinate of the London government.

Ireland's restless society, however, was far from unique. For communities on both sides of the Atlantic, the era was one of great clashes between forces of change and conservatism. The nascent USA declared independence in 1776 and had won it within a decade. France descended into revolutionary turmoil from 1789 onwards, soon after declaring war on Britain (and Ireland, by proxy). Britain itself drifted into the 1790s distracted by a bitter battle between Tory supporters of 'mad' King George III and Whig manoeuvres for the candidacy of his son.

The 'Declaration of the Rights of Man and the Citizen' (1789) and the 'Bill of Rights' (1791) reached Irish eyes not long after publication in Paris and Philadelphia respectively, renewing hope for the disaffected and downtrodden. The radical humanist ideals contained in these documents were not, however, without detractors. Dublin's own Edmund Burke bagged a British bestseller with his critique of the French Revolutionaries. Tom Paine's rebuttal of Burke was even more popular. Paine's *Common Sense* found Ireland a hungry market.[1]

Pamphleteers, such as Dublin lawyer Theobald Wolfe Tone, translated calls for republican government into a specifically Irish context, appropriating and refining the general clamour for civil rights and representation. An Anglican by birth, Tone was committed to harnessing the era's *zeitgeist* by uniting 'Protestant, Catholic and Dissenter under the common name of Irishmen'. He found common cause among several domestic groups, as well as French military planners eager to puncture Britain's vulnerable Irish rearguard.

The Catholic 'Defender' group entered into a secret alliance for armed rebellion with the professedly non-sectarian United Irishmen, a group Tone co-founded with northern Presbyterians. In direct response, both the yeomanry and the Orange Order were established: the first to defend the alliance with the British crown; the second to celebrate and promote the hegemonic interests of Ireland's Protestants. The same year, 1796, Tone's French contacts despatched a large military force to Ireland's south coast. Disastrously for the waiting rebels, 14,000 battle-hardened infantry, cavalry and cannon were forced by severe gales to turn hard about and sail back to Brittany.

The failed landing provoked immediate reprisals against suspected rebels. Crown forces, among them both Irish Catholic and Protestant staff of local militia and the yeomanry, pre-emptively persecuted any suspected United Irishmen. Rebels, known as 'croppies' (because of their cropped haircuts) and 'pikemen' (on account of their agricultural grade weaponry), endured lynching, flogging and a gruesome torture known as 'pitchcapping'. Weapon stores were confiscated, printing presses smashed and property burned.

Espionage too was stepped up. By March 1798, spies had brought down Dublin's entire rebel leadership. Among them was Lord Edward Fitzgerald, the most militarily experienced rebel general. Fearful of Jacobin-inspired anti-clerical backlashes, and excepting some prominent but maverick priest rebels, the advice from pulpit and parish was to reject the United Irishmen and their ecumenical aims. In spite of these setbacks, or perhaps because of them, local United Irishmen branches spluttered rather than exploded into rebellion at the end of May.

With Dublin's uprising stillborn, action in the surrounding province of Leinster centred on the counties of Wexford, Wicklow and Kildare. There were significant, though poorly organised, attacks on the towns of Wexford, Arklow, New Ross, Prosperous, Bunclody and at the Hill of Tara. Guerrilla tactics proved more successful, with notable ambushes launched from the wilderness of the Wicklow mountains (and continuing years beyond the defeat of conventional strategies). Branches of the United Irishmen rose and fell like dominoes across the countryside.

So fierce had been the clampdown in Ulster that the northern province was dissuaded from taking a stronger lead. Even so, June saw separate risings in counties Antrim and Down. In August, the belated landing of a minor French force on the Atlantic coast helped inflame County Mayo. September saw isolated Westmeath and Longford arise in now almost hopeless insurrection. Though countless minor skirmishes occurred in all four provinces, the strength of the opposition and the near total lack of strategic direction meant a succession of inevitable and ignominious rebel defeats.

Contentious memories of 1798 illuminate better than any itinerary the contemporary Ireland the rising helped create. The rebels had come to be remembered or forgotten according to the fortunes of the religious communities from which they had been drawn. An illustrative case is that of the Presbyterian County Down rebel Betsy Gray. Only 20 when killed in the aftermath of the Battle of Ballynahinch, her renown spread quickly through song and verse.

A century later, however, a volatile political atmosphere existed in her native Ulster. A group from the city of Belfast visiting Gray's rural graveside in 1898 to pay homage, were confronted by locals. A riot ensued. The explanation, of course, was in contemporary politics rather than historical fact. The visitors were Nationalists, advocates of home rule for Ireland and largely Catholic. The 100th anniversary of the rebellion had offered an opportunity for the Irish Party to further its causes of land reform and home rule in Westminster. The Catholic church grasped the opportunity, hitching themselves to the Nationalist movement and conveniently forgetting that their priests had originally declaimed the rebels.

The locals at Betsy Gray's graveside were her Presbyterian co-religionists. By the end of the 19th century, they were strongly supportive alongside Anglicans of the continued union between Ireland and Britain. Their demands for civic representation had been largely met over the ensuing century with the granting of voting rights. Furthermore, they had invested significant leadership in Belfast's growing industrial economy. Thus their new-found political status and enhanced financial prosperity was threatened by Nationalist demands for home rule and the historical complexities raised by Betsy Gray's loyalties. Coupled with the revival of Gaelic culture and the unveiling of plaques and monuments among Catholic communities across the island, commemoration in 1898 struck a decidedly one-sided cultural and religious tone. Events since then have done little to help reconcile the formerly united traditions.

Southern Ireland's independence eventually arrived in 1921, as did the creation of Northern Ireland as a state. Although land reform and a bloody two-year guerrilla conflict contributed more to the independence struggle in material terms, the revolutionary event etched strongest in the collective memory of the Republic is the brief and localised Easter Rising of 1916. As in 1798, it too met with failure.

One of contemporary Unionism's most cherished communal memories also took place in 1916, with the slaughter of the Ulster regiments at the Battle of the Somme. Once independent, the Irish state conveniently ignored those from the south who had died in the same battle. A similar situation developed during the Second World War. It took a long time for Irish blood spilt in British uniforms to be even acknowledged, let alone celebrated in the south. Brave was the voice that queried the amnesia. As in 1898, contemporary political concerns trumped fact.

All of this is, in some respects, to be expected. Communities everywhere pick and choose from the past, loudly hailing some elements while ignoring others. Ireland is no different. Competing narratives of the past litter the historical landscape: nationalism; republicanism; loyalism; independence; unionism; partition. As a result, selective historical memory is particularly evident and often rife with hypocrisy, with value allotted to events as and when convenient.

The Troubles, for example, were still raging on the 75th anniversary of the 1916 rising in 1991. The Republic (the state at least) was effectively still fighting the IRA, a group which claimed direct inheritance to not only 1916, but all of Ireland's violent struggles for independence. A markedly muted tone emerged in official commemoration. By contrast, the 200th anniversary of 1798 chimed nicely with the freshly inked Belfast Peace Agreement. With a ceasefire in place, memorialising rebellion became kosher once again.

Stranger still is the communal forgetfulness inherent on all sides in Ireland, a product of so many religious, historical and cultural entanglements in so small a space. Unionists have developed the linguistic anomaly of Ulster-Scots to combat the Gaelic Irish revival and reinforce their version of the plantations and partition. Many southerners, in turn, will readily describe their national flag as 'green, white and gold'. This blatantly ignores the intentions of the Young Irelanders for the flag, with its origins in revolutionary Europe and the aspirational arrangement of white (peace) between green (Catholic) and orange (Protestant) (see *Hungry Philosophers* on p 92).

Such enlightened symbolism is lost on a northern Unionist community who associate the flag most strongly with the painted pavements of republican West Belfast and years of internecine terror. The tricolour of the Republic is not the only historic symbol kidnapped by contemporary politics. Sinn Féin, formerly the IRA's political arm, still celebrate the life of the 1798 icon, Wolfe Tone, each year at his graveside in Co. Kildare.

The great historian of the Russian Revolution, Martin Malia, asserted that any one country receives only one tilt at full-blown, popular upheaval.[2] The closest Ireland has come to staging such a 'classical' event came and went with United Irishmen's defeat in 1798. It is today the trauma of 20th-century partition which holds hostage the memory of this rare period of enlightened fraternity. In 2016 the memory of both sets of 1916 martyrs – soldiers of the Somme and Nationalist rebels – turns 100.

Only on the most superficial level has Ireland changed. Indeed, Ireland does not appear to have adjusted far from 1798 itself. Very many negative facets of late-18th-century life will still be at work by 2016. Churches will still control education, even as false religious frontiers separate familial cultures and very real economic borders cut the poor out of history. The island will still be, to paraphrase historian F.S.L. Lyons, disunited, wilfully forgetful and not cherishing the children of the nation equally. It will be interesting to observe whether commemorative pomp and historical obfuscation once again trump a deeper agreement over how Ireland could honour its true revolutionary moment.

Love the Future
CHINA'S 20TH CENTURY

A 300-storey 'mega-city' covers the globe. A neo-Confucian clique of warlords oversees the plunder of Africa and the conquest of distant planets. Chinese culture and language dominate. America's civilisation has come to an ignominious end; democracy a relic. This is the vision of English science fiction author David Wingrove. With China a relative economic and diplomatic weakling when the first instalment was published in 1988, his popular *Chung Kuo* series must have appeared highly fanciful to early fans. The perspective offered by two decades of unremitting Chinese growth, however, suggest Wingrove, in theme at least, may yet be proved prophetic.

If China fulfils expectations by becoming America's hegemonic successor in the future, it will have charted a particularly steep ascent. Its borders violated by preying foreign powers, its jurisdiction ignored by regional warlords, the ruling Qing dynasty limped onto the world stage in 1900. It backed the wrong horse in the Boxer Rebellion and promptly collapsed with the Xinhai protests in 1911 (see *Half the World*, p 85). Twentieth-century China then witnessed invasion, expansion, civil war, a space programme, nuclear weapons and a cataclysmic famine. Amidst such extremes, historical comparisons understandably tend to fall down. But at some point, all discussions must consider modern China's love/hate relationship with political upheaval.

Certain events, such as the 1934–35 Long March, have become sacrosanct revolutionary myths. Sacred too is the still-resonant personality cult of Mao, the country's monolithic mid-century helmsman. He helped lead the Communist Party of China (CCP) down its early, opportunistic path; at first piggybacking the Soviet-supported Kuomintang (KMT), before successfully winning a civil war against them and consolidating the CCP dynasty. Even since his death in 1976, Mao's image has loomed larger over China than any other modern figure, his most frequently expressed writings and sayings a kind of bottomless Sino-Marxist *hadith*.

Equally infinite is the list of politically sensitive historical events: 'The Hundred Flowers Campaign' (1957; encouraged open public debate, then repressed any critical opinions); 'The Great Leap Forward' (1958–61; collectivised agriculture and caused the planet's worst famine of the 20th century); 'The Cultural Revolution' (1966–76; a decade-long purge of anyone considered to offer resistance to Maoist dictates). Similarly, public discussions on the historical status of Tibet, Japanese actions during the Second World War, or Taiwan in general, are likely to induce uncomfortable conversations, at best.

A problematic recent addition to the list is Ai Weiwei. A dissident artist, Weiwei's arrest and imprisonment on charges of 'economic crimes' during 2011 received significant international media coverage. Weiwei's criticisms of modern Chinese society can take artistic forms – a Coca-Cola logo crudely embossed onto a replica of an ancient urn needs little explanation – or they can be more canny: the artist first contributed to the design of Beijing's 'Bird Nest' Olympic Stadium in 2008, then refused to participate in the opening ceremony in protest at the lack of Chinese democracy; US headlines were guaranteed. Since then, apart from a surge in demand internationally for his art, thought and services, Weiwei's Shanghai studio has been bulldozed and his right to leave the country has been withdrawn. The criticisms of the government have not stopped. Weiwei recently claimed that search-engine results of his name, accessed within China, were now blocked.

If anything, it is surprising that CCP intelligence took so long to imprison Weiwei. In 1989, pro-democracy student demonstrators were denounced by officials within days of taking up residence in Beijing's gigantic central Tiananmen Square. The protests are linked both to a growth in the country's university population over the previous decade and a general dissatisfaction among graduates towards job prospects and the lack of political freedoms. Smaller student protests had occurred in both 1987 and 1988 and, contrary to the general impression, the 1989 demos were not limited only to Beijing. Neither did the military crackdown actually take place on the square which gave the doomed movement its name. Tanks and troops attacked students and their local supporters in the western neighbourhoods of Beijing after they had been escorted from Tiananmen. Casualty figures have never been established. Record, let alone discussion, of the sad event is hidden from public view in China.

Almost exactly 70 years previously, there was another Tiananmen protest, this one as yet not historically taboo: soon after news of an unfriendly settlement at the post-First World War conference in Versailles reached home, patriotic Chinese students took to the streets. Their march spread to other cities and was supported by labour strikes. The Chinese delegation to Versailles eventually refused to sign the treaty. Leading participants went on to form the CCP. May 4th 1919: here lies a real starting point for China's century of upheaval.

Today China stands as a bewildering mix of theoretically incompatible systems. A rigidly opaque and paranoid state structure finds itself fused to a globalised economy; fattened with foreign trade reserves, but ever starved of the raw materials its insatiable growth demands. The growth of controls exerted by government over public and cultural life after 1949 is difficult to ignore. Uncensored political criticism, virtually outlawed for 50 years, has conversely often been used as a weapon by party factions to discredit internal opposition and their past policies. The 1958–61 famine, for example, cost a minimum of 15 million lives, but was not alluded to by the state except in the vaguest of manners before 1976.* Only after Mao's death and the arrest of his 'Gang of Four' allies was the depth of state responsibility even hinted at.

Further complexity is added by the Cultural Revolutionary period. This decade saw the power of the violently anti-intellectual Maoist youth, the Red Guards, supersede even that of the police. All vaguely independent public voices were forcibly silenced. The educated were prime targets for forced manual labour, social ostracism and, often, much worse. For over ten years universities effectively ceased to operate. Education – a re-education system for those unlucky enough to be tarred with the 'rightist reactionary' or *bourgeois* brush – appropriated wholesale the dogma of Mao's *Little Red Book*. A resultant gaping chasm opens when researching Chinese-penned accounts of the 20th century, not only in the dearth of independent university research, but in the minds of the people themselves, whose state education textbooks steer them away from critical analysis of past government failure.

Unlike in the realms of media and education, where the CCP has held a consistent grip since coming to power, party attitudes toward artists and their depiction of the revolution have continually undulated. While political poster propaganda

---

* Fifteen million people lies towards the lower end of famine death estimates.

arguably reached its global zenith in mid-century China, the majority of graphic art forms came to be denounced as counter-revolutionary in the final decade of Mao's rule. Western-originated art received particularly short shrift. Chinese cinema holds a mirror up to these trends. Film studios, historically centred around Shanghai, found patriotic, leftist and anti-Japanese themes received government backing after 1949. Non-political, alternative, critical or foreign pieces were banned outright. The Cultural Revolution saw film production suffocated, almost beyond the point of resuscitation. Recent treatments of history by film-makers, as well as recognition of the artistic value of previously banned works, suggest a partial relaxation towards those willing to criticise the adherents of state-dictated memory.

Amongst the many riots and rebellions which have changed their country, Chinese tongues speak little of the one event most frequently discussed abroad. Tiananmen in 1989 has proved a dominant though, at times, restrictive lens through which much of the world's media and journalists view recent Chinese history. The moves to independence were more popular, the Cultural Revolution more bloody, yet Tiananmen has proved equally magnetic for enforced domestic amnesia as it has for Western criticism. In this it fits a distinct historical pattern. While Chinese authorities employ extreme methods in celebration or expunction of revolutionary memory, foreign observers continue to devote huge energies to critiquing the process.

David Wingrove is far from alone in offering dystopias of a dark Chinese future. Each challenger to American global hegemony during the 20th century had to contend with a swathe of cultural and historical analysis, much of it penned from outside the confines of expertise. The apparent economic pre-eminence of late 1950s USSR brought with it McCarthyism and the Second Red Scare. In the 1980s, accounts from diplomatic and business insiders told of the 'unstoppable' rise of Japan (currently stopped).

Since the late 1990s, a similar weight of analysis has sprung up on China. Among allegations of copyright infringements and clashes with corporate champions, amid criticisms of free speech, democracy and human rights, lies a latent critique of China's century of change. The world remembers China's revolutions and would-be revolutions in a very different way from China itself. Moralising op-eds and blog posts from overseas are rendered all the more ironic given that foreign intervention in Chinese history has been, and remains, a constant. After all, it was the American and European First World War victors whose harsh Versailles settlement first ushered a young Mao Zedong from part-time university librarian to a life of leadership and infamy.

As usual, China's Communist Party spent much of 2011 lauding that life. However, it also took special effort to congratulate itself on 90 years of 'permanent revolution'. Unofficially of course, the policing of airwaves and search algorithms continued apace. News of pro-democracy uprisings against totalitarian rulers across the Arab world were restricted. The detention of Ai Weiwei and other prominent dissidents received similar attention.

The lack of free information and freedom of speech in contemporary China is, indeed, frightening. But in this regard, the country is far from alone. North Korea, Russia, Iran, Saudi Arabia and Zimbabwe: none leave to their public any significant space for critical opposition views. US agencies did much to limit the spread of the classified information released by WikiLeaks in 2011. Even rarefied Europe can boast a repressive dictatorship, expert in information control: the tinpot regime of Lukashenko's Belarus.

The aspect of historical memory unique to China is its authoritarian government's proven success at setting the boundaries of debate *inside* its citizens' minds. As the State Administration for Radio, Film and Television (SARFT) continued its censorship work, its most recently announced ruling – a ban on misrepresentation of historical characters – began to take hold. Targeted was the popular genre of time travel films, as were new versions of the 'Four Great Classical Novels' of Chinese literature. SARFT's aim was to suppress discussion of the dominant themes of both: a rose-tinted view of the past and violent armed rebellion against corrupt rulers.

All of China has clearly not forgotten the events of Tiananmen Square in 1989. They are uppermost in the minds of CCP cadres. As Timothy Garton Ash has noted, the leadership studied with intensity the Velvet Revolutions which spread across the former Eastern Bloc later in the same year, scrambling to avoid a similar situation developing and spreading in the wake of the student massacres in central Beijing.[1]

This represented another step in the process started by official, and infallible, histories during the many traumatic events of the Chinese 20th century. The recurring monopolisations of discussion of state events render difficult any balanced treatment of contemporary China, both within and outside the country's frontiers. It remains to be seen if foreign scaremongering over China will ring true, or indeed whether recent censorship can succeed in the internet age. What appears undoubted, however, is that the CCP has up until this point, somehow, somewhat incredibly, successfully circumscribed their public's historical imagination.

Conclusion
The Evolution of Revolution

If he were alive today, Ernesto 'Che' Guevara, the revolutionary icon of the 20th century, would undoubtedly find much to criticise in the consumerist world of the 21st. For a man who expressed such passionate opposition to capitalist domination, a website which trades off his own image might attract the strongest ire. 'The Che Store' has all that the Guevara collectible enthusiast could wish for, from signature berets to 'Che' 'bobblehead' figurines.

This is part of a broader modern sanitisation of the term 'revolution'. Marketing professionals and advertisers use a vocabulary of faux rebelliousness to channel the spirit of the *sans-culottes* into unlikely arenas. Domestic cleaning products offer us 'a revolution in the kitchen'. A new hemline promises to 'revolutionise fashion'.

As long as people live on in oppressive circumstances, however, real revolution will continue to occur and evolve. The Arab Spring is the latest manifestation of demands for genuine and radical political change. The potential of events across the Middle East to have lasting significance is clear. As yet, those events brim with immediacy, posing difficulties of definition. Is the Arab Spring a call for democracy in the form the West knows it? Is it the beginning of a new form of politics? What if a worse despot than Hosni Mubarak or Muammar Gaddafi takes power?

No single account of revolution can ever hope to offer a predictive model by encompassing each social bandit, each peaceful mass movement, *foco* guerrilla insurgency or peasant *jacquerie*. The historical examples compared in these pages have attempted to show that these elements can combine to produce all manner of outcomes. What past models can offer, and have done over the course of this book, is a useful reference point from which to begin to understand the Arab Spring.

Charting, with reference to classical models of revolution, the specific political eruption in Egypt – a strategic, geopolitical lynchpin between the Mediterranean the Middle East and Africa – offers the reader a direct connection between past and present. Exploring where events have diverged from the accepted path of revolution is as revealing as examining the parallels.

The origins of the Egyptian Revolution find plenty of antecedents. Under the Mubarak regime (1981–2011), the most populous Arab nation offered no shortage of tyranny and despotism. Set in a semi-permanent state of martial law, criticism of government was punishable by jail terms and ex-judicial abuse. Prices for basic commodities and wage levels were unilaterally set by central authorities.

Egypt's tyrannical regime did not fail to produce its martyrs: in April 2008, long before thousands demanded freedom in Tahrir Square in central Cairo, protestors marched against the removal of state subsidies on wheat in the city of Mahalla al-Kubra. They were greeted by tear gas and rubber bullets. A fifteen-year-old boy was shot dead. As revolution descended on Egypt in 2011, the self-immolation of Tunisian street vendor, Mohamed Bouazizi – a martyrdom credited as a catalyst to the Tunisian Revolution, that in turn heralded the Arab Spring

– was imitated, new casualties joining the hundreds of victims of Egyptian police brutality and the thousands imprisoned on flimsy politicised charges.

From early on, protestors colonised national symbols. Egyptian colours were painted on faces and bedecked giant flags. Leaders emerged to speak on behalf of the protesters. But while the fates of the individuals in this book's second chapter came to be entwined with their revolutions, figures such as Mohamed ElBaradei, the Egyptian former head of the UN's IAEA nuclear agency, and Wael Ghonim, an Egyptian Google executive whose anti-regime Facebook page was highlighted as a decisive factor in kick-starting protest, never claimed to command power over the revolutionary masses. This decentralised structure confounded the usual fixed gaze of journalists on icons. It also raises important questions over historical depictions of revolutions as dependent on strong leaders.

Events in Egypt in 2011 also require a fresh approach in the classical search for hidden hands. At least in the early stages, the two forces who might have traditionally been expected to play a part in manipulating political intrigue in Egypt were nowhere to be seen. US officials, despite their country's numerous vested interests in the Middle East, seemed stunned by the speed of events; President Barack Obama waited a fortnight before adhering to the practice of legitimising unrest through official proclamation and lending his voice to calls for democracy. The Muslim Brotherhood too, long the largest opposition force in the country, exercised no formal role in the unrest. Despite claims by some Middle East leaders, most notably Syria's President Bashar al-Assad in March 2011, the uprisings did not seem to be being driven by the political agendas of external *agents provocateurs* – certainly not in the fashion of T.E. Lawrence's Arab Revolt discussed earlier in this book.

Yet the Arab Spring has brought a new consideration to the fore. The exchange of information and support that flowed in and out of Egypt over open digital networks was clear for anyone to see and on a level unprecedented in any of the revolutions included here. 'The Communications Revolution' of social networking and satellite television finally caught up with its portentous name in 2011. Across the Middle East, communications technology and its adherents played an important role in popular unrest. While television news, text messaging and social media helped spread the message of the protestors, they also aided the communication of a deteriorating situation to the world. The signal of Al-Jazeera, the Qatari television news channel, was blocked at the height of protest. Government restrictions on access to Facebook, Twitter and other such social websites were an acknowledgement of their role in the two-way exchange of information between the streets of Cairo and the rest of the world. Firm conclusions cannot yet be drawn on the direct transformative power of 21st-century communication on global politics – it was, after all, the inaction of the military and a critical mass of individuals willing to risk their safety on the streets, that forced Mubarak's eventual resignation. Nevertheless, it has proved itself an active agent in large-scale popular action, whether revolutionary or otherwise, and it is important to mark the freshness of decentralised global communication; a scenario most aptly summed up by the appearance of placards on Tahrir Square in support of striking public sector workers in Wisconsin, USA.

Indeed, such displays of solidarity did much to promote the image of a peaceful protest under attack, and in the portrayal and use of violence and peace, the Egyptian revolution finds direct parallels with its historical forebears. The peaceful reputation of protestors was further reinforced as the world watched Christians protecting Muslims as they prayed and dissident Egyptian military conscripts being welcomed into camps on Tahrir Square. In contrast, in the weeks before his resignation, Mubarak appeared on television to offer conciliatory gestures – at the same time, attacks by police and the president's supporters intensified. The protestors were moved to defend themselves with force, but their persistent presentation of the focus of the movement on peaceful civil disobedience and mass gatherings was enough to gain crucial international condemnation for the government crackdown.

While no single, simplistic analytical framework will determine the outcome of Egypt's revolution, the initial euphoria expressed as Mubarak exited the scene in February was subsumed by suddenly conflicting interests at remarkable speed. By late 2011, the revolution seemed, true to classical form, to be eating itself. Battles over a new form of constitution and government had begun almost immediately. Deadly clashes between marching Coptic Christians and the predominantly Muslim military during October appeared to mark the unravelling of the two religions' previous cooperation. By November, mass protests, running battles and shrines to the dead had again returned to Tahrir Square.

At the same time that our understanding of the Egyptian revolution is aided by accounts of former events, it is also entrapped by them. As this book has attempted to demonstrate, neither historical records nor individual memories of revolution are infallible. Gaining a real appreciation of what is at stake during the revolutions of our time necessitates dropping assumptions. Every uprising against entrenched power, violent or peaceful, led by slaves or gentlemen, is a philosophical revolution: a powerful new way for the participants and observers to remould their place in, and vision of, the world. Egypt, and the wider Arab Spring, are no different.

Across a broad sweep of time, revolutionaries have evolved popular movements into different forms according to their opponents and circumstances. The world has seen coups to re-impose ancient tradition. It has also seen revolutions which sought to erase all trace of former times and set the calendar back to 'Year Zero'. Charismatic leaders have aroused whole continents from political dormancy and instituted new bills of personal rights. Leaderless revolutions have attempted to destroy private property and render society perfectly equal. Slaves have revolted to escape confinement. Revolutionary nations have exerted control over slavery itself.

Global communism's failure at the end of the 1980s allowed capitalist cheerleaders to proclaim the 'End of History'; the great debates of ideology and civilisation apparently permanently settled. The myopia of such a view from an early-21st-century vantage point needs little amplification. History, somewhat inconveniently for the drafters of grand theories, does not end. Rather, it is in its permanent reinvention that history finds its only constant. The world's vision for the Arab people, the Middle East and democracy itself, now faces an exciting challenge.

This book's structure has followed a model of how revolutions are expected to progress from start to finish, a model whose application in full to real world events is limited. That limitation, however, should not subtract from the importance of understanding revolution, a political and social phenomenon which continues to emerge in various forms. If the outbreaks of 2011 can show anything with great certainty just yet, then it is that the relevance of popular participation in politics – people power – will do as much to shape the future of our world as the revolutions of the past have done the present.

Acknowledgements

To my parents, for calm, for tea and for even more inspiration than usual.

To Timothy Nairn, Rory McArdle, Amy Dickson, Cian Traynor, Darragh Walsh and Patrick & Lindi McGibney, who are offered special thanks.

To all other friends and family members who, over the past twelve months, have endured a barrage of obscure revolutionary facts and returned nothing but willing attention and constructive criticism.

To former professors, friends and library staff at University College Dublin, gratitude for hard work and priceless instruction.

To Olivia Bays and Alison Menzies at Elliott & Thompson, and to Ray Hamilton, for their support in bringing the project to life.

Finally, to my editor, Nick Sidwell, for his incalculable initiative and countless well-chosen words of help and encouragement.

Sources

INTRODUCTION

1. *Adbusters* #95: 'The Philosophy Issue', May/June 2011 (Adbusters Media Foundation, British Columbia, Canada).

DESPOTISM AND PERSECUTION

1. Gibbon, Edward, 1789. *The History of the Decline and Fall of the Roman Empire*, Volume X. Paris: Tournisen. p 71.

American Fall

1. Zinn, Howard, *A People's History of the United States*, Harper Perennial Classics (New York, 2005), pp 59–63.
2. *Common Sense*, London, 1792. Eighteenth Century Collections Online. Gale. University College Dublin. Accessed: 11/11/11, p 12.

Dancing About History

1. Daniel, Yvonne, *Dancing Wisdom: Embodied Knowledge in Haitian Vodou, Cuban Yoruba, and Bahian Candomblé*, University of Illinois Press (Chicago, 2005), p113.
2. Wilcken, Lois, 'The Sacred Music and Dance of Haitian Vodou from Temple to Stage and the Ethics of Representation', in *Latin American Perspectives*, Volume 32, No 1, Sage (Thousand Oaks, CA, 2005), p 193.
3. James, C.L.R., *The Black Jacobins: Toussaint L'Ouverture and the San Domingo Revolution*, 2nd Edition Revised, Vintage (New York, 1989), p 118.

Twin Peaks
1. Trotsky, L., *The Stalin School of Falsification*, 2nd Edition, Pioneer (New York, 1962), p 143.
2. The Brest in Belarus, rather than the one in Brittany, France. The resultant peace treaty is that of Brest-Litovsk, as the city was then known.
3. UN Security Council Resolution 1973 endorses 'all necessary means to protect civilians and civilian-populated areas'.

Rightly-guided
1. Moin, Baqer, *Khomeini: life of the Ayatollah*, I.B. Tauris (London, 1999), p 104.
2. Simpson, J., *Strange Places, Questionable People*, Pan (London, 1998).

Human Capital
1. Blustein, Paul, *And the money kept rolling in (and out): The World Bank, Wall Street, the IMF, and the Bankrupting of Argentina*, PublicAffairs (New York, 2005), p 12.
2. Public Broadcasting Service website. Interview with Joseph Stiglitz. http://to.pbs.org/sqT0ga Accessed: 09/08/11.

MARTYRS AND ICONS
1. Lippmann, W., *Public Opinion*, Filiquarian (Minneanapolis, 2007), p 219.

A Change in the Pipeline
1. 'Eurovision Joy Deflects Cares for a While', May 15th 2011. *New York Times*. [online] Available at: http://nyti.ms/svBqJ0 Accessed: 28/07/11.
2. Babayan, Kathryn, *Mystics, Monarchs, and Messiahs: the Cultural Landscape of Early Modern Iran*, Harvard University Press (Boston, 2002), p 269.

Another False Dmitri?
1. Julicher, Peter, *Renegades, Rebels and Rogues under the Tsars*, McFarland (Jefferson, 2003) p 98.

The Liberator's Liberator
1. Margolis, Mac, 'Hard-Left Heartthrob', *Daily Beast*, website http://bit.ly/vHUoR1 Accessed: 07/10/11.

2. Skidmore, T.E. & Smith, P.H., *Modern Latin America*, 6th Edition, Oxford University Press (New York, 2005) p 449.

Heaven on Earth
1. Spence, J.D., *God's Chinese Son: The Taiping Heavenly Kingdom of Hong Xiuquan*, W.W. Norton (New York, 1996).
2. Teng, S.Y., *The Taiping Rebellion and the Western Powers: A Comprehensive Survey*, Oxford University Press (London, 1971), p 77.
3. Huntington, Rania, 'Chaos, Memory, and Genre: Anecdotal Recollections of the Taiping Rebellion', *Chinese Literature: Essays, Articles, Reviews (CLEAR)*, Vol. 27 (Dec 2005), p 69.
4. See Reilly, Thomas H., *The Taiping Heavenly Kingdom: Rebellion and the Blasphemy of Empire*, University of Washington Press (Seattle, 2004), p 3 and Spence, J.D., *God's Chinese Son: The Taiping Heavenly Kingdom of Hong Xiuquan*, W.W. Norton (New York, 1996), p xxi.

History's Absolution
1. Guevara, Ernesto, *Guerrilla Warfare*, Monthly Review Press (New York, 1998), p 7.
2. Anderson, Jon Lee, *Che Guevara: A Revolutionary Life*, Bantam (London, 1997), p 305.

JUST VIOLENCE, RADICAL PEACE
1. Galeotti, Mark, *Gorbachev and his Revolution*, Macmillan (London, 1997), p 89.
2. Sewell, W.H., 'Historical Events as Transformations of Structures: Inventing Revolution at the Bastille', *Theory and Society*, Vol. 25, No. 6, December 1996, p 860.

Half the World
1. Al-Masudi, *Meadows of Gold and Mines of Gems*, trans. Sprenger, Aloys; John Murray (London, 1841), pp 324–5.

Hungry Philosophers
1. Wagner, Richard, *My Life – An Autobiography*, Wildside Press (Rockville, 2010), p 286.

Her Majesty's Witchdoctors
1. Transcipt from audio recording. Source: Brother Malcolm website. URL: http://bit.ly/tckSWi Accessed: 04/09/11.

2. Boehmer, Elleke, *Nelson Mandela*, Sterling (New York, 2008), p 138.
3. Arnold, David, *Gandhi*, Pearson (London, 2001), p 153.
4. Kyle, Keith, *The Politics of the Independence of Kenya*, Macmillan (London, 1999), p 45.
5. Ibid, p 53.
6. Ibid, p 61.
7. Webster, Wendy, 'There'll Always Be an England': Representations of Colonial Wars and Immigration, 1948–1968, *Journal of British Studies*, Vol. 40, No. 4, At Home in the Empire (Oct. 2001), p 557.
8. *Daily Express*, 26th January, 28th March, 5th January 1953, respectively. Source: http://www.ukpressonline.co.uk Accessed: 13/08/11.
9. Dyer, Richard, 'White', *Screen* (1988) 29(4): 44–65, p 49.
10. Berman, Bruce, 'Review: Mau Mau and the Politics of Knowledge: The Struggle Continues', *Canadian Journal of African Studies* Vol. 41, No. 3, 2007, p 538.

Velvet and Iron

1. Excerpt from Mikhail Gorbachev's speech to the 43rd United Nations General Assembly, December 7th 1988. *New York Times* online archive: http://nyti.ms/syq9FN Accessed: 13/10/11.
2. Garton Ash, Timothy, *Facts are Subversive: Political Writings from a Decade Without a Name*, Yale University Press (New Haven, 2010) p 61.
3. Transcription from video. Source: White House website. URL: http://1.usa.gov/ulVEH2 Accessed: 08/10/11.

THE HIDDEN HAND

Rebel City

1. Maradona, Diego, *El Diego*, Yellow Jersey Press (London, 2005), p 89.
2. Stothard, Peter, *On the Spartacus Road*, Harper Press (London, 2010), p 184.
3. Dickie, John, 'Stereotypes of the Italian South, 1860–1900', in *The New History of the Italian South: the Mezzigiorno Revisited*, eds. Robert Lumley and Jonathan Morris, University of Exeter Press (Exeter, 1997), p 122.

4. A Global Alliance Against Forced Labour: Global Report under the
    Follow-up to the ILO Declaration on Fundamental Principles and
    Rights at Work 2005, ILO Publications (Geneva, 2005), p 12.
5. See Bales, Kevin, *Disposable People: new slavery in the global
    economy*, University of California Press (Berkeley, 2004).

Summer in the City
1. Morrell, G., Scott, S., McNeish, D., & Webster, S., *The August
    Riots in England: Understanding the Involvement of Young People*,
    National Centre for Social Research (London, 2011), p 37.
2. Dyer, Christopher, *Standards of living in the later Middle Ages*,
    Cambridge University Press (Cambridge, 1989), p 159.
3. Froissart, Jean, *The Chronicles of Froissart*. Trans. Bourchier, J. &
    Berners, L., P.F. Collier & Son Company (New York, 1910), p 62.
4. Froissart, trans. Berners, ed. G.C. Macaulay, cf. Froissart,
    Chroniques, quoted in Dobson, R.B., *The Peasants' Revolt of 1381*,
    Macmillan (London, 1970), p 144.
5. Higden, *Polychronicon*, quoted in Dobson, R.B., *The Peasants'
    Revolt of 1381*, Macmillan (London, 1970), p 201.

A Guerrilla Tradition
1. Bannerman, Patrick, *Islam in Perspective: A Guide to Islamic
    Society, Politics and Law*, Routledge (London, 1988), p 150.

Sun and Steel
1. Seidensticker, Edward, 1971. 'Mishima Yukio', *The Hudson Review*,
    Vol. 24, No. 2, p 273.
2. Yourcenar, Marguerite, *Mishima: A Vision of the Void*, trans.
    Manguel, Alberto; Aidan Ellis (London, 1986), p 120.

Digital Renegades
1. McLuhan, Marshall, *Radio: The Tribal Drum, AV Communication
    Review*, Vol. 12, No. 2, Springer (New York, 1964), pp 133–45.
2. Ronfeldt, David, and Arquilla, John, *Networks and Netwars:
    The Future of Terror, Crime, and Militancy*, Rand Corporation
    (Arlington, VA, 2001), p 7.
3. Klein, Naomi, 'The Unknown Icon', foreword to *Ya basta!: ten
    years of the Zapatista uprising*, Marcos (Subcomandante.), ed. Žiga
    Vodovnik, AK Press (Edinburgh, 2004), p 20.

4.   Friedman, Milton, *Capitalism and Freedom*, University of Chicago Press (Chicago, 1962), p 13.

THE REVOLUTION EATS ITSELF

Not Just English; Not Only a Revolution
1.   http://www.guardian.co.uk/culture/2011/aug/28/scottish-independence-snp-iain-banks Accessed: 30/09/11.

Dying on Its Feet
1.   McLynn, Frank, *Villa and Zapata: A Biography of the Mexican Revolution*, Pimlico (London, 2001), p 29.

Zero Sums
1.   Hessel, Stéphane, *Time for Outrage!*, Quartet Books (London, 2011).
2.   Bolloten, Burnett, *The Spanish Civil War: revolution and counterrevolution*, University of North Carolina Press (Chapel Hill, 1991), p 10.
3.   Orwell, George, *Homage to Catalonia*, Penguin (London, 2000), p 5.
4.   Preston, Paul, *The Spanish Civil War: reaction, revolution and revenge*, Harper Perennial (London, 2006), p 7.

A Dutch Revolt
1.   Mackay, Charles, *Memoirs of Extraordinary Popular Delusions and the Madness of Crowds*, Routledge (London). Volumes 1–21856. p 89.
2.   Pilger, John, *The New Rulers of the World*, Verso (London: 2002) p 41.
3.   WWF Forest Conversion Programme Brochure: 'Oil palm, soy and tropical forests: a strategy for life', World Wide Fund for Nature (Gland: 2008).
4.   Toer, Pramoedya Ananta, *My Apologies, in the Name of Experience*, trans. Alex G. Bardsley, *Indonesia*, Vol. 61, Apr. 1996, p 5.

More Than One Viktor
1.   www.youtube.com/watch?v=S85onNzmd7s Accessed: 10/07/11.
2.   Garton Ash, Timothy, *Facts are Subversive: Political Writings from a Decade Without a Name*, Yale University Press (New Haven, 2010), p 29.
3.   *Wall Street Journal*, http://online.wsj.com/article/SB100014240531 1190346130457652467220915813.html Accessed: 10/11/11.

4. Menon, Rajan, Motyl, Alexander, 'Hope Fades for Ukraine', 2011. *Foreign Affairs*; Vol. 90 Issue 6, pp 137–48.

REMEMBERING THE FUTURE
1. Hannoum, A., *Violent Modernity: France in Algeria*, Harvard University Press (Boston, 2010), p 95.

A Star is Born
1. Faulkner, Neil, 'Hadrian and the Limits of Empire', published in *History Today*, August 2008.
2. Zerubavel, Yael, 'Bar Kokhba's Image in Modern Israeli Culture', in *The Bar Kokhba War Reconsidered: New Perspectives on the Second Jewish Revolt*, Ed. Schäfer, Peter, Paul Mohr Verlag (Tübingen, 2003), p 281.

Indomitable
1. Van Dam, Raymond, *Leadership and Community in Late Antique Gaul*, University of California Press (Berkeley, 1985), p 30.
2. Rubin, Zeev, *Mass Movements in Late Antiquity – Appearance and Realities. Leaders and Masses in the Roman World: Studies in Honor*, Eds. I Malkin & Z.W. Rubinsohn, Brill (New York, 1995), p 135.
3. Potter, David S., *The Roman Empire at Bay: AD180–395*, Routledge (New York, 2004), p 281.
4. Mommsen, Theodor, *A History of Rome under the Emperors*, Routledge (London, 1995), p 354.
5. Thompson, E.A., 'Peasant Revolts in Late Roman Gaul and Spain', *Past & Present*, No 2, 1952, p 292.
6. Van Dam, p 38.

Kidnapped!
1. Andress, David, *1789: The Revolutions That Shook the World*, Abacus (London, 2008), p 370.
2. Malia, Martin, *History's Locomotives: Revolutions in the Making of the Modern World*, Ed. Emmons, Terence; Yale University Press (New Haven, 2005), p 305.

Love the Future
1. Garton Ash, Timothy, *Facts are Subversive: Political Writings from a Decade Without a Name*, Yale University Press (New Haven, 2010), p 65.

Select Bibliography

If readers wish to understand more about the revolutions contained in this book, this select bibliography may be used as a guide. The titles collected here are not designed to be exhaustive and there are undoubtedly other fine publications not included. They do, however, represent the writing which I enjoyed and the learning which I found most enlightening during research – whether I have agreed with the author's conclusions or not. Some of these are classic works, now decades old. Wherever possible, I have provided the publisher and year of publication of the most recent edition.

American Fall: USA 1776

For a challenging 'bottom-up' view of the revolution, Howard Zinn's
  A People's History of the United States (Harper Perennial, 2005) is
  already a classic. Paul Johnson's *A History of the American People*
  (Phoenix, 2000) also offers a usefully succinct account.
For more on American folk memory of the past, and its development
  after the Revolution, read Michael Kammen's *Mystic Chords of Memory:
  The Transformation of Tradition in American Culture* (Vintage, 1993).
For the importance of American frontiers: *American Leviathan, Empire
  Nation and Revolutionary Frontier*, by Patrick Griffin (Hill and Wang,
  2007); and *Undaunted Courage* (Simon & Schuster, 1997), by Stephen
  Ambrose, on both the thrilling details and wider ramifications of the
  Lewis and Clark expedition.

Dancing About History: Haiti 1791

Médéric-Louis-Élie Moreau De Saint-Méry's description of mid-1790s
  Haiti, along with other original contemporaneous documents and
  comment, can be found in Laurent Dubois and John D. Garrigus'
  Slave Revolution in the Caribbean 1789–1804 (Bedford St. Martin's,
  Boston, 2006).

The most readable up-to-date account of the revolution is Laurent
Dubois' *Avengers of the New World: The Story of the Haitian Revolution*
(Harvard University Press, 2004).

Paul Farmer's *Uses of Haiti* (Common Courage, 1994) is a detailing of
more recent US policy towards Haiti. It does not make comfortable
reading.

UNESCO published a useful collection of Bolívar's writings on the
bicentenary of his birth, *Simón Bolívar: The Hope of the Universe*
(Paris, 1983).

Twin Peaks: Russia 1917

Martin Malia's *Soviet Tragedy* (Simon & Schuster, 1995) and Orlando
Figes' *A People's Tragedy* (Pimlico, 1997) are very readable accounts
of 1917. For a personalised log of the rural impacts of 1917 – as
well as most other important modern events in Russia – read Serge
Schmemann's *Echoes of Native Land: Two Centuries of a Russian
Village* (Abacus, 1998).

Steven G. Marks' provocative *How Russia Shaped the Modern World*
(Princeton University Press, 2004) opens with a fantastic account
of the transition from 19th-century anti-Tsarist terrorism, to the
earthquake of 1917 and how both ends of this spectrum have
influenced events elsewhere.

Richard Pipes' *Russia Under the Old Regime* (Penguin, 1995) compresses
several centuries of political, military and cultural development to
place the advent of the Soviet Union in its Russian context.

Frederick C. Corney, in *Telling October: Memory and the Making of the
Bolshevik Revolution* (Cornell University Press, 2004), shows how
Soviet historians and politicians made immediate use of the memories
of both revolutions in 1917 and of its 1905 precursor.

Robert Conquest and Sheila Fitzpatrick are authorities on the descent of
the optimistic 1920s into the darkness of the Stalinist Terror.

Rightly-guided: Iran 1979

Ryszard Kapuściński's *Shah of Shahs* (Vintage, 1982) is a brilliantly
idiosyncratic portrait of the Shah's Iran on the eve of revolution.

You can't fault John Simpson's uncanny ability to be in the right place
at the right time. His *Strange Places, Questionable People* (Pan, 1998)
documents a fascinating journalistic career and offers a short and
colourful account of the Iranian upheaval.

Baqer Moin's *Life of the Ayatollah* (Tauris, 1999) is one of many
biographies available of Ruhollah Khomeini.

Human Capital: Argentina 2001–02

Paul Blustein's outsider account of the crisis wears its heart on its sleeve about where blame lies: *And the money kept rolling in (and out): The World Bank, Wall Street, the IMF, and the Bankrupting of Argentina* (Public Affairs, 2005).

Economist Joseph Stiglitz's *Globalization and Its Discontents* (W.W. Norton, 2003) expands the criticism.

A Change in the Pipeline: Medieval Azerbaijan

Kathryn Babayan's *Mystics, Monarchs and Messiahs* (Harvard University Press, 2002) links the advent of millennial tendencies in ancient Persian religions to the revolutionary impulse within Islam.

Dilip Hiro's *Between Marx and Muhammad* (HarperCollins, 1995) traces the two most influential political forces on this important region.

Another False Dmitri?: The Pugachev Rebellion 1773–74

The great author and poet Alexander Pushkin wrote histories in later life. His first, *The History of Pugachev* (Phoenix, 2001), is a short and useful introduction to both the Russia of the rebellious Cossacks and the restlessness of Pushkin's early-19th-century period.

Nikolai Berdyaev's *The Russian Idea* (Greenwood Press, 1979) offers an idea of exactly what Russia's 'Third Rome' is supposed to represent.

The Liberator's Liberator: Gran Colombia 1820s

Pamela S. Murray's *For Glory and Bolívar* (University of Texas Press, 2008) is the most up-to-date and complete account of the life of Manuela Sáenz in English.

John Lynch's *Simón Bolívar* (Yale University Press, 2007) separates the man from the myth.

The *Penguin History of Latin America* (Penguin, 2009) by Edwin Williamson gives a colourful but succinct summary of the fates of all of Gran Colombia's constituent parts.

Heaven on Earth: Taiping Rebellion 1850–61

Jonathan D. Spence's *God's Chinese Son* (W.W. Norton, 1996) is a very readable account of the Taiping Heavenly Kingdom and the China from which it emerged.

History's Absolution: Cuba 1959

Jon Lee Anderson's *A Revolutionary Life* (Bantam, 1997) follows 'Che' Guevara from his early Argentine days, into the mountains of the Sierra Maestra, to government and beyond.

Hugh Thomas' *Cuba or The Pursuit of Freedom* (Da Capo, 1998) is a thorough survey of Cuban history before, during and after the late 1950s revolutionary period.

Half the World: Huang Chao and Tang China 874–88

S.A.M. Adshead's *T'ang China: The Rise of the East in World History* (Palgrave Macmillan, 2004) shows the Tang dynasty's global standing.

The original, 1841 English translation of Masudi's account of the Huang Chao rebellion is available online at the Internet Archive (www.archive.org/stream/historicalencycl00masrich#page/n5/mode/2up).

Hungry Philosophers: Europe 1848

Mike Rapport's *Year of Revolution* (Abacus, 2009) is the latest quality account of 1848.

A short and entertaining account of Wagner's life is given in *The Lives and Times of the Great Composers* (Icon, 2010) by Michael Steen.

Richard Wagner's boisterous self-penned version is available for free, online at Project Gutenberg (www.gutenberg.org).

A Pinch of Salt: India and Pakistan 1947

In *Gandhi* (Pearson, 2001), David Arnold profiles not just the man, but the aura he commanded.

Marshall J. Getz's *Subhas Chandra Bose* (McFarland, 2002) is a good, recent biography.

For an overview of the entire process, read Patrick French's *Liberty or Death: India's Journey to Independence and Division* (Penguin, 2011).

Her Majesty's Witchdoctors: The Mau Mau 1952–60

In *Mau Mau and Kenya* (Indiana University Press, 1993), W.O. Maloba, questions the desire of both conservative elites and socialists to adopt the legacy of the Mau Mau.

Caroline Elkins' *Imperial Reckoning* (Owl, 2005) recounts controversial oral testimony from those on both sides of the internment camps.

David Anderson's *History of the Hanged* (W.W. Norton, 2005) concentrates on the court records of the trials of Mau Mau subjects.

Odinga Odinga fought for Kenyan freedom, though not as a Mau Mau, and became an important political figure post-independence. His autobiography *Not Yet Uhuru* (Heinemann, 1968) charts the process.

Velvet and Iron: The Soviet Empire 1988–91

Read Timothy Garton Ash's *We the People* (Penguin, 1999), and his more recent *Facts are Subversive* (Yale University Press, 2010).

Eric Hobsbawm's *The Age of Extremes* (Vintage, 1996) is a fantastic read. It places the revolutions of 1989 into context at the close of a 'short 20th century'.

Rebel City: Spartacus' Revolt 73BC

Peter Stodthard mixes scholarly history and poetic travelogue in *On the Spartacus Road*, (Harper Press, 2010).

For more on the global slave industry, read Kevin Bales' *Disposable People* (University of California Press, 2004).

Summer in the City: The Revolt of 1381

Dan Jones' *Summer of Blood* (Harper Press, 2009) is a thoroughly readable introduction to the leading characters of the period.

A Guerrilla Tradition: The Arab Revolt 1916–18

Robert Fisk's *The Great War for Civilisation* (Harper Perennial, 2006) brings the wider ramifications of the Arab Revolt into the present day.

T.E. Lawrence's *Seven Pillars of Wisdom* is available ex-copyright at Project Gutenberg (www.gutenberg.com).

Sun and Steel: Japan 19th and 20th centuries

Marguerite Yourcenar succinctly analyses Mishima's life and work in *A Vision of the Void* (Aidan Ellis, 1986).

Read John W. Dower's *Embracing Defeat* (W.W. Norton, 1999) for the story of how Japan adjusted itself to life under American occupation.

Alex Kerr offers a pessimistic exposé of Japanese society in *Dogs and Demons: Tales from the Dark Side of Japan* (Hill and Wang, 2002).

Digital Renegades: The Zapatistas 1994–present

The writings of Subcomandante Marcos are collected in *Ya Basta!: ten years of the Zapatista uprising* (AK Press, 2004). This is only a sampling of the communiques available individually online.

Alex Khasnabish offers a recent, external view of the movement in *Rebellion from the Grassroots to the Global* (Zed Books, 2010).

Milton Friedman's classic *Capitalism and Freedom* (The University of Chicago Press, 1962) makes a convincing connection between free markets and democracy.

Not Just English; Not Only a Revolution: England and Scotland 1640–1707

Edward Vallance's *A Radical History of Britain* (Little Brown, 2009) covers a wide swathe of British radicalism, including John Lillburne of the 17th-century revolutionary era.

Any works or essays by Christopher Hill, John Morrill or Blair Worden will offer a challenging and sometimes conflicting perspective of the period.

Dying on Its Feet: Mexico 1910–17

Frank McLynn's *Villa and Zapata* (Pimlico, 2001) is a wonderfully readable account of the two main personalities of the period.

Zero Sums: Spanish Revolution 1936–38

Paul Preston's *The Spanish Civil War* (Harper Perennial, 2006) is an enjoyable account of the period, including the revolution.

George Orwell's *Homage to Catalonia* (Penguin Classics, 2000) is widely available.

Stéphane Hessel's *Indignez Vous!* (European Schoolbooks Limited, 2010) is published in English as *Time for Outrage!* (Quartet Books, 2011).

A Dutch Revolt: Indonesia 1945–49

Pramoedya's *Buru Quartet* is considered his masterpiece and published by Penguin. The component parts of the quartet are: *This Earth of Mankind* (Penguin, 1996), *Child of All Nations* (Penguin, 1997), *Footsteps* (Penguin, 1997) and *House of Glass* (Penguin, 1997).

Adrian Vickers *History of Modern Indonesia* (Cambridge University Press, 2006) uses the writings of Toer as backdrop to introducing the nation's story.

John Pilger's *The New Rulers of the World* (Verso, 2002) opens with an excoriating account of Western collusion with the genocidal Suharto regime.

John Martinkus' *A Dirty Little War* (Random House, 2001) covers Suharto's forces in East Timor prior to its independence.

Benedict Anderson's *Imagined Communities* (Verso, 2006) is not, strictly speaking, about the revolution. But the author is a south-east Asian specialist, a brilliant writer and Indonesia features prominently.

More Than One Viktor: Ukraine 2004

A collection called *Orange Revolution and its Aftermath* (Johns Hopkins University Press, 2010) edited by Paul J. D'Anieri is the most up-to-date collection of essays on the event.

Askold Krushelnycky's *An Orange Revolution* (Harvill Secker, 2006) is a personal reflection on the uprising before it took a repressive turn.

A Star is Born: Jewish Revolt of 132–136AD

The academic collection *The Bar Kokhba War Reconsidered: New Perspectives on the Second Jewish Revolt* (Tubingen, 2003) is edited by Peter Schäfer.

For both an account of the subject in general and the influence of organisations such as Betar specifically, read Walter Laqueur's *The History of Zionism* (Tauris Parke, 2003).

Indomitable: The Bagaudae 4th and 5th centuries

None other than Julius Caesar wrote an account of Gaul, as he fought the wars that would lead to its eventual romanisation: *The Gallic Wars* (Red and Black Publishers, 2008).

Greg Woolf charts the process thereafter in *Becoming Roman* (Cambridge University Press, 2000).

Popular Venom: The French Revolution 1789

William H. Sewell's *Logics of History* (University of Chicago Press, 2005) offers fascinating reflections on the meaning of the revolution.

Festivals and the French Revolution (Harvard University Press, 1991) by Mona Ozouf offers similar perspectives.

Kidnapped!: The Irish 1798 Rebellion

Thomas Pakenham's *The Year of Liberty* (Abacus, 2000) goes into detail on the rebellion. *Ireland 1798–1998* (Wiley-Blackwell, 2010) by Alvin Jackson covers its influence in the following centuries. Diarmaid Ferriter's entertaining *The Transformation of Ireland (1900–2000)* takes up the story.

Love the Future: China's 20th century

Edgar Snow was an American lecturer and journalist, resident in China until his death in 1972. In *The Long Revolution* (Random House, 1972) he relates personal encounters with Mao and other major Chinese leaders.

Rae Yang's *Spider Eaters* (University of California Press, 1998) is a powerful personal memoir of late 1950s China and the Cultural Revolution.

Sidney Shapiro translated Shi Nai'an and Luo Guanzhong's bandit classic *Outlaws of the Marsh* (Foreign Languages Press, 1980).

Index